Photoshop® Elements by Example

MARK CLARKSON

McGraw-Hill/Osborne

New York   Chicago   San Francisco
Lisbon   London   Madrid   Mexico City
Milan   New Delhi   San Juan
Seoul   Singapore   Sydney   Toronto

McGraw-Hill/Osborne
2100 Powell Street, 10th Floor
Emeryville, California 94608
U.S.A.

To arrange bulk purchase discounts for sales promotions, premiums, or fund-raisers, please contact **McGraw-Hill**/Osborne at the above address. For information on translations or book distributors outside the U.S.A., please see the International Contact Information page immediately following the index of this book.

Photoshop® Elements by Example

1234567890 WCT WCT 0198765

ISBN 0-07-225857-8

Vice President & Group Publisher	Philip Ruppel
Vice President & Publisher	Jeffrey Krames
Acquisitions Editor	Margie McAneny
Project Editor	Jody McKenzie
Acquisitions Coordinator	Agatha Kim
Technical Editor	Kathy Eyster
Copy Editor	Lunaea Weatherstone
Proofreader	Stefany Otis
Indexer	Valerie Perry
Composition	Jimmie Young / Tolman Creek Design
Cover Design	James C. Korne
Creative Director	Scott Jackson

This book was composed with Adobe InDesign™.

About the Author

Mark Clarkson has been using and writing about Photoshop since 1993, when that program first appeared for the Windows operating system. He is the author of three books about Photoshop and Photoshop Elements, and a co-author or contributing author to three more. His other books cover Macromedia Flash, cartooning, Artificial Life, Robotics, and C and C++ programming. Mark is also the author of countless articles on everything from nanotechnology to online gaming.

A self-described dilettante, he writes, designs, cartoons, and animates from his secret office, buried beneath his home in Wichita, Kansas. Visit him on the Web at www.markclarkson.com.

About the Technical Editor

Kathy Eyster is a photography and digital imaging instructor who works with 35mm and digital cameras and concentrates on landscape and macro photography. Before turning to photography, Kathy had a 15-year career as a technical writer for university computing centers and writing teacher for high schools and colleges. Kathy's teaching and computing experiences come together in digital imaging. With her mastery of Photoshop and digital fine printing, Kathy excels at simplifying complex digital photography equipment and processes. In addition to teaching, Kathy is a member of the Adobe beta team, a technical editor of digital photography books, and a contributing writer for *Camera Arts* magazine.

To Mom. Thanks for the bananas.

Acknowledgments

Thanks to Jeff Berg, Teresa Lunt, Ned Benjamin, Kier Darby, Tom Szurkowski, Anson Vogt, Man1c M0g, and Bas Hijmans for their contributions.

CONTENTS

SECTION II | Sketching and Painting

SECTION III | Aging and Glamorizing Photos

SECTION IV | Pretty Posters

SECTION V | Fun with 3-D

SECTION VI | The Dark Side

SECTION VII | Potpourri

Introduction

Tools, Techniques, and Conventions Used in this Book

Welcome to *Photoshop Elements by Example*. This book comprises 31 very different projects, from creating digital graffiti to swapping people's heads around. You needn't do them all or do them in sequence. Open the book up to any page; try the projects in any order. I'll take you through the process of creating them, step by step. Each project contains a number of different techniques, all applied toward creating a single cool image.

Some of the projects create images from scratch; others include one or more JPEG images. The images necessary for following along with the projects in the book can be downloaded free of charge from the book's Web site, www.elements-by-example.com, or from the publisher's Web site, http://shop.osborne.com/cgi-bin/osborne/0072258578.html.

In this book you will do the following:

- Make basic photo corrections
- Create realistic planets and nebula
- Turn day into night
- Turn photos into paintings
- And much more

How to Do It

Since you can partake of the projects in any order, any given project may be the first one to direct you to select a layer or change the foreground color. Yet, if every project included an explanation of how to accomplish these basic tasks, there'd scarcely be room for anything else. Instead, I'll try, in this introduction, to cover the basic tasks that appear over and over throughout the book.

Figure 1 shows the Elements Standard Edit workspace on a Windows XP computer, where all the projects in this book will take place.

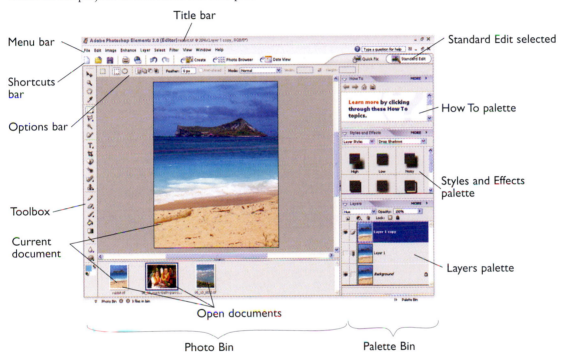

Figure 1: The Standard Edit workspace in Windows XP

From the Menu, Choose …

Many of Elements' tools and commands are accessible through its menus. In this book, I'll direct you through the nested menus like this: From the menu, choose Edit | Preferences | Display & Cursors. Here's how that translates: on the menu bar, click the word Edit to open the Edit menu, as shown in Figure 2. Next, click the word Preferences to open the Preferences submenu, as shown in Figure 3. Finally, click on the words Display & Cursors, as shown in Figure 4, to open the Display & Cursors Preferences dialog.

Menu commands will sometimes be written in a shorter form, such as: Open the Display & Cursors Preferences dialog (Edit | Preferences | Display & Cursors).

Figure 2: Open the edit menu …

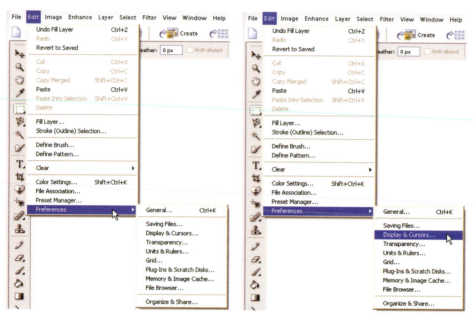

Figure 3: … then the Preferences submenu …

Figure 4: … then the Display and Cursors dialog

Tool Preferences

Let's use a menu command now. To make sure that what you see on your screen as you work corresponds to the screenshots in this book, choose Edit | Preferences | Display & Cursors from the menu, as detailed above. If you're working on a Macintosh, choose Photoshop Elements | Preferences | Display & Cursors. In the Display & Cursors dialog, select Brush Size for the Painting Cursors, and Standard for Other Cursors, as shown in Figure 5. Click OK.

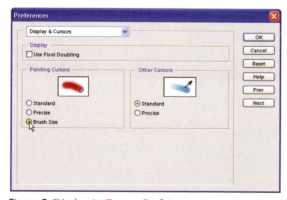

Figure 5: Display & Cursors Preferences

In the Options Bar

I'll often direct you to change some settings in the Options bar. The Options bar appears above the work area, just beneath the Shortcuts bar. Each tool has its own set of options available. The Move tool only has two options, while the Text tool has more than a dozen.

Brush Size

The most common changes you'll make to tool options are brush settings: size, shape, and hardness. Many of Elements' tools are brush-based: the Brush tool, of course, but also the Sponge tool, the Smudge tool, the Eraser tool, the Selection Brush tool, and the Clone Stamp tool, to name a few. The basic brush settings on all of these tools are the same.

The text may call for, say, a hard, round, 19-pixel brush (Figure 6), or a soft, round, 21-pixel brush (Figure 7). Almost every brush setting recommended in the book is available from the preset drop-down lists.

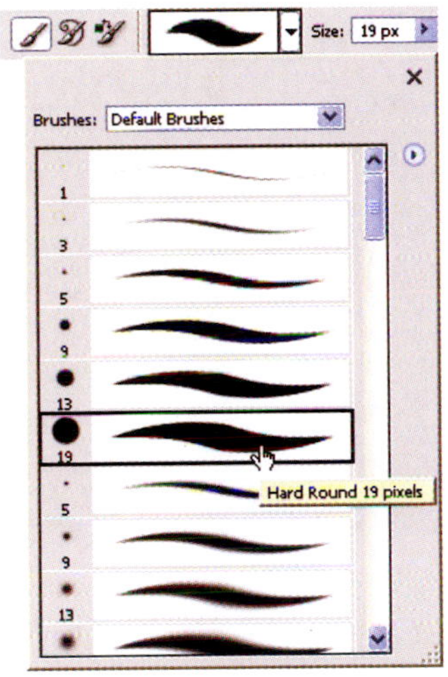

Figure 6: A hard round brush

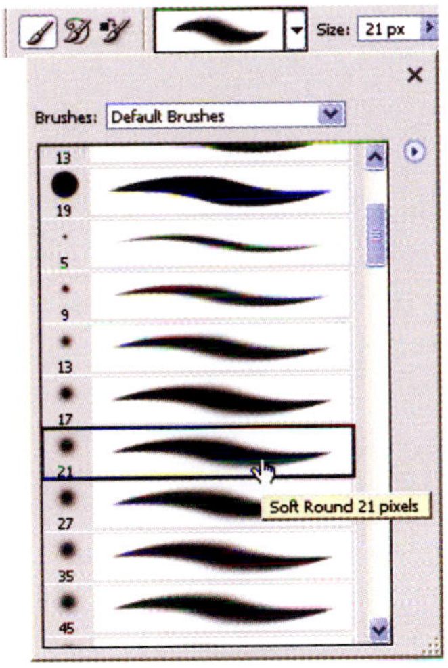

Figure 7: A soft round brush

Select the Tool from the Toolbox

Elements brushes and other tools are available from the Toolbox palette. By default, the Toolbox palette is docked along the left edge of the workspace. At any given time, it shows 22 different tools: the Move tool, the Zoom tool, and so forth. If you hover the cursor over any of the tools, without clicking, a tool tip appears with that tool's name and keyboard shortcut, as shown in Figure 8.

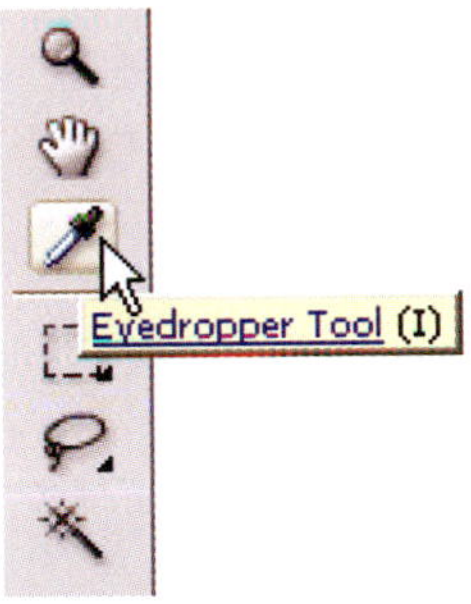

The Toolbox actually holds 44 tools; half of them are hidden. Look carefully and you'll see that roughly half of the tools in the Toolbox have a small, black triangle in the bottom-right corner, like the one in Figure 9. When you see this, it means that there are additional, related tools available "beneath" that button. To access them, click and hold on the button until a fly-out menu appears. In Figure 9, the fly-out reveals the three Lasso tools: the Lasso tool, the Magnetic Lasso tool, and the Polygonal Lasso tool. Click on any of these to select that Lasso tool. Figure 10 shows all the tools available via the ten fly-out menus.

Figure 8: Tool tip

Figure 9: The Lasso tool flyout

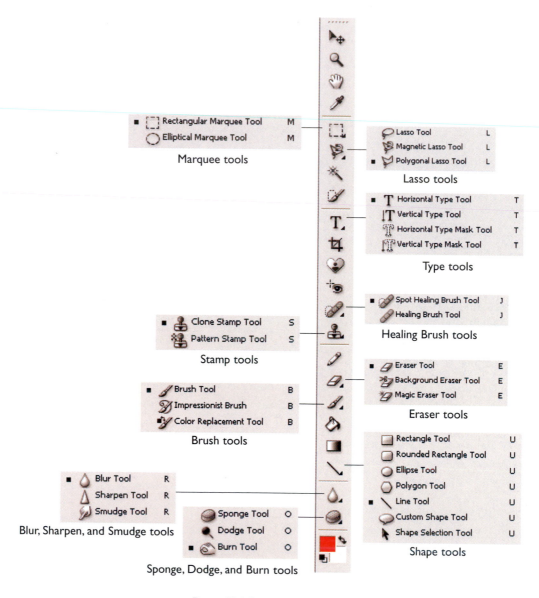

Rectangular Marquee Tool — M
Elliptical Marquee Tool — M
Marquee tools

Lasso Tool — L
Magnetic Lasso Tool — L
Polygonal Lasso Tool — L
Lasso tools

Horizontal Type Tool — T
Vertical Type Tool — T
Horizontal Type Mask Tool — T
Vertical Type Mask Tool — T
Type tools

Spot Healing Brush Tool — J
Healing Brush Tool — J
Healing Brush tools

Clone Stamp Tool — S
Pattern Stamp Tool — S
Stamp tools

Eraser Tool — E
Background Eraser Tool — E
Magic Eraser Tool — E
Eraser tools

Brush Tool — B
Impressionist Brush — B
Color Replacement Tool — B
Brush tools

Rectangle Tool — U
Rounded Rectangle Tool — U
Ellipse Tool — U
Polygon Tool — U
Line Tool — U
Custom Shape Tool — U
Shape Selection Tool — U
Shape tools

Blur Tool — R
Sharpen Tool — R
Smudge Tool — R
Blur, Sharpen, and Smudge tools

Sponge Tool — O
Dodge Tool — O
Burn Tool — O
Sponge, Dodge, and Burn tools

Figure 10: The Toolbox annotated

Now, if the text calls for you to select the Polygonal Lasso tool, you'll know where to look for it, even if it's hiding under the Magnetic Lasso tool.

In the Layers Palette

The Layers palette is where you manipulate the layers in your document. Documents in Elements can contain almost any number of layers, stacked on top of each other. Layers contain images, shapes, text, colors, and so forth.

The Layers palette appears in the Palette Bin on the right side of the workspace. If it's not visible, you can make the palette visible by choosing Window | Layers from the menu. The Layers palette is shown in Figure 11.

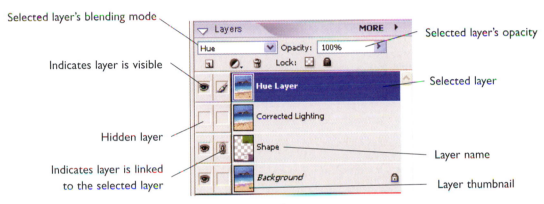

Selected layer's blending mode

Indicates layer is visible

Hidden layer

Indicates layer is linked to the selected layer

Selected layer's opacity

Selected layer

Layer name

Layer thumbnail

Figure 11: Layers palette

To select a layer in the Layers palette, simply click on its thumbnail or name.

A layer can be obscured, either partially or completely, by layers placed on top of it. Figure 12 shows a document with two layers, a Background layer containing a photo of an island, and another layer, named Joe, which holds a photo of a sleeping boy. Notice that the Layers palette shows a thumbnail of each layer's contents.

The photo of the boy is smaller than the photo of the island, so part of that layer is empty. The island shows through in this empty space and is hidden elsewhere. This is the same thing you'd see if you stacked one real photograph atop another.

Figure 12: Two layers in Normal mode

In Elements, layers can also interact with each other, using a variety of blending modes. As the name implies, these modes control the way layers blend together. For example, Screen mode lightens the underlying layers, as shown in Figure 13. The lighter the screen layer, the more it lightens the layers beneath it.

In Darken mode, on the other hand, only parts of the image that are darker than the underlying layers appear, as shown in Figure 14. Anywhere the Darken layer is actually lighter than the underlying layers, there's no effect at all.

To change a layer's blending mode, make certain that the correct layer is selected, then select a new blending mode from the drop-down list, as shown in Figure 15.

Figure 13: The top layer in Screen mode

Figure 14: The top layer in Darken mode

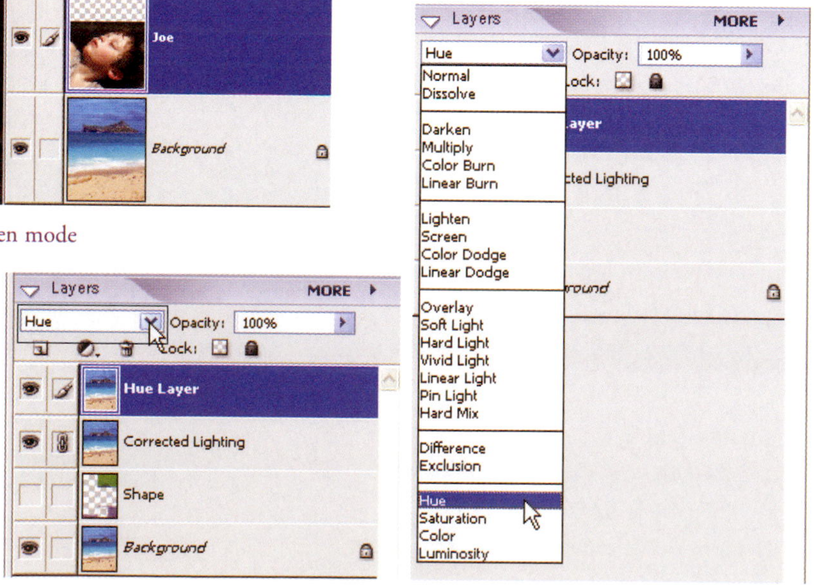

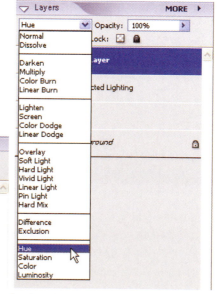

Figure 15: The Layers pallete Blending Modes drop-down list

You can also change the way layers blend together by reducing the opacity of one or more layers, as shown in Figure 16. Either use the slider to reduce a layer's opacity, or simply type in a new opacity value, from 0 to 100.

To rename a layer, you need to double-click on its name in the Layers palette, and then type in the new name, as shown in Figure 17.

In the Styles and Effects Palette

The Styles and Effects palette, like the Layers palette, appears in the Palette Bin on the right side of the workspace. If this palette is not visible, you can make it visible by choosing Window | Styles and Effects from the menu. The Styles and Effects palette is shown in Figure 18. To apply a layer style or effect, simply click on its icon.

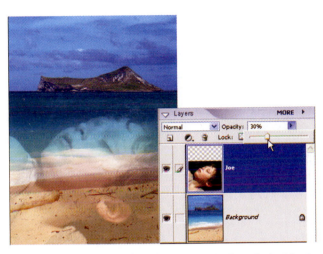

Figure 16: Even in Normal mode, the boy blends with the island, thanks to his reduced opacity.

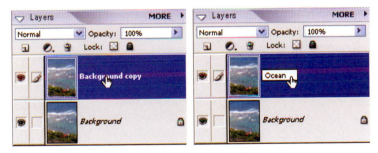

Figure 17: Double-click a layer's name to rename it.

Figure 18: Click here to apply a soft edge drop shadow.

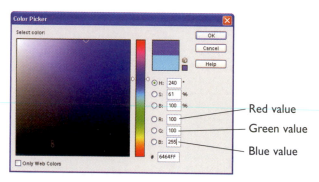

Figure 19: Selecting a shade of blue (100,100,255) from the Color Picker

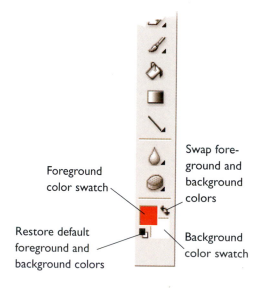

Figure 20: The foreground and background colors in the Toolbox

Set the Color to 0,0,0

The text will often direct you to set a color (the foreground color, text color, and so forth) using the Color Picker dialog. There are a lot of ways to specify colors in Elements, but in this book all colors are specified in terms of their red, green, and blue (RGB) components. The color shown in Figure 19, a deep blue, would be specified in the text as 100,100,255. You can type those values directly into the R, G, and B boxes, as shown.

Set the Foreground and Background Colors

The text will often direct you to set, reset, or swap Elements' foreground and background colors. The controls for Elements' foreground and background colors are found at the bottom of the Toolbox palette, as shown in Figure 20. The two large squares show the current foreground color (above and left) and background color (below and right).

To change the foreground color, click on the Foreground Color swatch at the bottom of the Toolbox to bring up the Color Picker dialog. In the Color Picker dialog, you can specify the color by entering its red, green, and blue components, as described above. You can also click anywhere on the open document, as shown in Figure 21, to sample a new foreground color from it.

You set the background color the same way, beginning with clicking on the Background Color swatch at the bottom of the Toolbox.

To reset the foreground and background colors to their defaults (black and white), click on the small black and white boxes just beneath the Foreground Color swatch.

To swap the current colors, so that foreground becomes background and vice versa, click on the two-headed arrow just above the Background Color swatch.

Zoom, Zoom!

You'll often need to zoom in or out as you work. As with almost everything in Elements, there are many ways to zoom in and out on your work. Here's one: Select the Zoom tool from the Toolbox palette. Select the Zoom In button in the Options bar, as shown in Figure 22, and click on an image to zoom in on it. Select the Zoom Out button in the Options bar and click on an image to zoom out.

Figure 21: When in the Color Picker, you can sample colors from any open document.

Figure 22: Zoom options

With Zoom In selected, you can also zoom in on a particular area by clicking and dragging to select it with the Zoom tool, as shown in Figure 23. When you release the mouse button, Elements zooms to fill the work area with the selected area, as shown in Figure 24.

Figure 23: Click and drag with the Zoom tool to zoom in on that selected area.

Figure 24: The selected area fills the screen.

Ready, Steady, Go!

And that, my friends, is all you need to know to complete any project in this book, so pick one that appeals to you and get started.

If you have any questions, comments, problems, or praise, you can visit me at www.elements-by-example.com.

Photo Correction Essentials: Levels, Straightening, and Cropping

In This Project You Will:

☐ Use Levels to correct badly lit photographs

☐ Use Shadows/Highlights to lighten photos

☐ Use the Move tool to rotate pictures and correct perspective

Some photographs are, admittedly, beyond repair, but Photoshop Elements can salvage all but the very worst of them. Elements includes many fine automated tools, such as Smart Fix and Auto Contrast, but some photos can fool these tools for one reason or another. Let's take a look at a couple of examples.

Japanese Temple

Open the file temple.jpg (Figure 1-1), a digital photograph of the roof of a Buddhist temple, and save it as new-temple.psd. Believe it or not, there are some very cool architectural details hiding in there. Normally, the first step would be to rotate and crop the photo, if necessary. But in this case, the photo is so dark that we need to correct it a bit before we can see what we're doing.

Figure 1-1: A very dark temple

Elements' Auto Smart Fix feature (Enhance | Auto Smart Fix) will make the photo look much better, as shown in Figure 1-2, but you can do even better than that. Trust me.

Much of this photo is lost in shadow, and Elements 3.0 has a new tool that's great for retrieving detail from the shadows: Lighten Shadows. From the menu, choose Enhance | Adjust Lighting | Shadows/Highlights. For most photos, lightening the shadows by 25% to 50% will suffice, but this one is so dark, it calls for maximal help. Slide the Lighten Shadows slider to 100%, as shown in Figure 1-3, and click OK.

Figure 1-2: Auto Smart Fix makes things better.

Figure 1-3: Lighten the shadows.

Rotate and Crop

Finally, we can see well enough to rotate and crop the image. Rotate first. You can't rotate the Background layer; you must first convert it to a standard layer. From the menu, choose Layer | New | Layer from Background. Click OK to create the layer.

Now select the Move tool. Zoom out far enough to see the entire canvas, then click and drag outside of one of the corner handles to rotate the layer, as shown in Figure 1-4. Rotate it counterclockwise until the rotation angle in the Options bar reads about –4°, as shown, and then press ENTER (RETURN on the Macintosh) to accept the rotation. You can see why you want to rotate before you crop: rotating the image leaves areas at the corners where the background shows through.

Select the Crop tool from the Toolbox and click and drag on the canvas to define your crop, as shown in Figure 1-5. Press ENTER to crop. You crop before doing any color and lighting correction so you don't waste time correcting areas only to crop them off later.

Tweak the Light

Let's fix the lighting now. From the menu, choose Enhance | Lighting | Levels. In the Levels dialog, grab the white point slider beneath the histogram and drag it to the left, as shown in Figure 1-6. This brightens the highlights. The farther left you go, the more of the photo will be forced to pure white and the brighter the highlights will become. The farther you drag it, the more detail will disappear in the very brightest parts of the photo. I moved it left until the corresponding input level read 210. Much farther, and the highlights on the roof begin to disappear.

Rotation angle — Rotate cursor

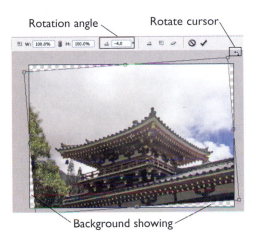

Background showing

Figure 1-4: Rotate the photo.

Figure 1-5: Crop the temple.

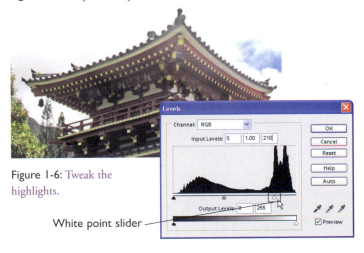

Figure 1-6: Tweak the highlights.

White point slider

Still in the Levels dialog, grab the black point slider and drag it to the right, as shown in Figure 1-7. This darkens the shadows. The farther right you go, the more of the photo will be forced to pure black, and the darker the shadows will become. The farther you drag it, the more detail will disappear in the very darkest parts of the photo. I moved it right until the corresponding input level read 48. Much farther, and the important details in the shadows begin to disappear.

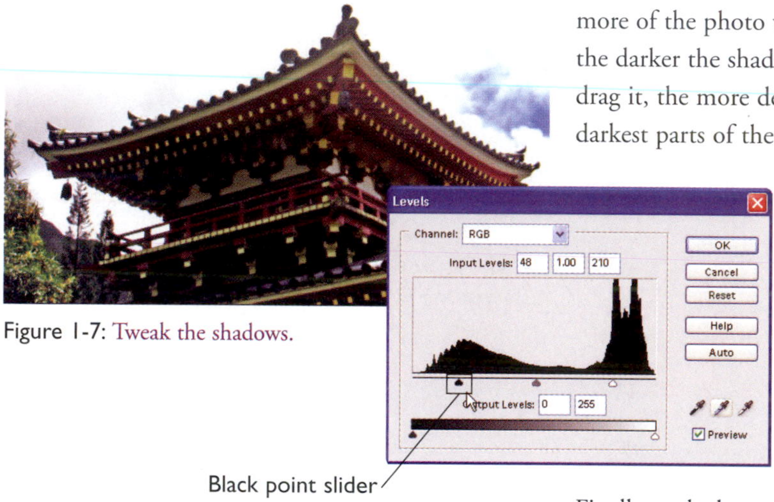

The closer the white point and black point sliders are to each other, the greater the contrast in the photo.

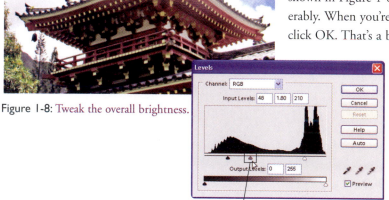

Figure 1-7: Tweak the shadows.

Black point slider

Finally, grab the gray point slider. This one can go either way. Drag it left, and Elements "stretches" the highlights, brightening the image overall. Drag it right, and Elements stretches the shadows, darkening the image overall. I moved the slider left to 1.80, as shown in Figure 1-8, brightening the image considerably. When you're happy with the adjustments, click OK. That's a big improvement.

Save your work and close the image.

Figure 1-8: Tweak the overall brightness.

Gray point slider

The Buddha

Take a look at the photo in Figure 1-9. It's the Golden Buddha from inside the same temple. As the statue was large and high up in the air, with people standing in front of it, I couldn't get the straight-on shot I wanted. I settled for this angle, knowing I could fix it, digitally, later on.

If you look at Figure 1-10, you can see many elements in the photo that tell your eye what the camera's perspective is. Horizontal lines converge to the right of the photo, showing that I was to the left of the statue, and the vertical lines converge towards the top of the photo, showing that I was looking up.

To follow along with my corrections, open the file buddha.jpg and save it as buddha.psd. The original Background layer of a document is locked; before you can move it around and alter its perspective, you must convert it into a standard layer. From the menu, choose Layer | New | Layer from Background. Click OK to create the layer.

Select the Move tool from the Toolbox and handles appear around the outside of the photo. If you can't see them, zoom out until you can, as shown in Figure 1-11.

Figure 1-9: The Golden Buddha

Vertical sight lines

Horizontal sight lines

Figure 1-10: Telltale lines give away the perspective.

Figure 1-11: Zoom out to work.

Figure 1-12: Stretch the top-right corner up.

I began by correcting the right-to-left perspective. With the Move tool selected, hold down the CTRL key (the CMD key on the Macintosh) and SHIFT key and click on the top-right corner handle. Drag upwards a bit, as shown in Figure 1-12, until the blue beam appears relatively straight. Holding down the CTRL/CMD key allows you to move one corner handle without affecting the position of the others. Holding down the SHIFT key constrains your movements to straight lines.

Hold down the CTRL/CMD and SHIFT keys and click and drag downward on the bottom-right handle, as shown in Figure 1-13, until the blue handrail at the bottom of the photo is more or less level. Press ENTER to accept the transformation.

Vertical Lines

Figure 1-13: Stretch the bottom-right corner down.

Next, we'll do the same thing to straighten out the vertical lines. The horizontal lines (the handrail and the roof beam) were near enough to the edges of the photograph to adjust by eye, but for the vertical lines let's call in a little help. From the menu, choose Edit | Preferences | Grid (on the Macintosh, go to Photoshop Elements | Preferences | Grid). In the Grid dialog, set the Color to Light Red, and specify a gridline every 5 percent, with one subdivision, as shown in Figure 1-14. Click OK. Turn on the grid (View | Grid).

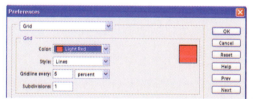

Figure 1-14: Change your grid preferences.

Select the Move tool, hold down the CTRL/CMD and SHIFT keys, and click on the upper-left corner handle. Drag the handle to the left until the wooden column on the left of the statue is more or less vertical, as shown in Figure 1-15.

Figure 1-15: Adjust the top-left corner.

Repeat the process with the upper-right corner handle, straightening the right column. You might have to go back and forth between the two corners a few times before you get both columns standing up straight, as shown in Figure 1-16. When you're happy, press ENTER to accept the transformation.

Figure 1-16: Adjust the top-right corner.

The last two steps left Buddha looking a bit squashed. Look at the circle behind his head and you'll see that it's wider than it is tall. Turn off the grid (View | Grid); we'll use a different reference for the next step.

Select the Ellipse tool from the Toolbox. In the Options bar, set its color to bright green (R=0, G=255, B=0), then hold down the SHIFT key and click and drag to create a circle roughly the size of the circle behind the Buddha's head, as shown in Figure 1-17. In the Layers palette, reduce the new shape layer's opacity to 20% so you can see the statue behind it, as shown in Figure 1-18. Use the Move tool to move the circle into position over the Buddha's head. SHIFT-click and drag on the corner handles to size it up or down until it matches the width of the circle, as shown in Figure 1-19. Press ENTER when you are satisfied with the changes.

Figure 1-17: A green circle shape

Figure 1-18: Reduce its opacity.

Figure 1-19: Resize it to fit, width-wise.

Figure 1-20: Stretch the photo up to match the circle.

In the Layers palette, select the original photograph layer. Select the Move tool and click and drag on the top center handle to stretch the statue upwards until its height matches the green guide circle as well as its width, as shown in Figure 1-20. If you can't see the handles, zoom out until you can. When you're happy with the look, press ENTER to accept the transformation. You may need to reselect the shape layer and reposition the green guide circle to keep it in place over the statue's head. When you're done, select the green circle shape layer in the Layers palette and choose Layer | Delete Layer to get rid of it.

Crop It

I want the Buddha to be the centerpiece of the shot, but there's a lot of distraction in the original photo, including the heads of a couple of nameless tourists. It's time to crop them out. Select the Crop tool from the Toolbox. Click and drag to create a crop that retains all (or most) of the Buddha statue while eliminating most of the background, as shown in Figure 1-21. When you're happy with the composition, press ENTER to crop the photo.

Figure 1-21: Crop to emphasize the statue.

Improve Contrast with Levels

The lighting of the photo looks a little bit flat. Elements has a lot of automated tools to help you tweak the lighting and contrast of a photo, but they rarely do as good a job as you can yourself, with a judicious application of Elements' Levels command. Bring it up now by choosing Enhance | Adjust Lighting | Levels.

Begin with the highlights. I moved the white point slider left until the corresponding input level read 225, as shown in Figure 1-22. Much farther, and the highlights on the chest and face begin to disappear.

Still in the Levels dialog, grab the black point slider and drag it to the right, as shown in Figure 1-23. I moved it right until the corresponding input level read 35.

Finally, grab the gray point slider. I moved the slider left to 1.15, as shown in Figure 1-24, brightening the image a bit. When you're happy with the adjustments, click OK. Save your work and close the photo.

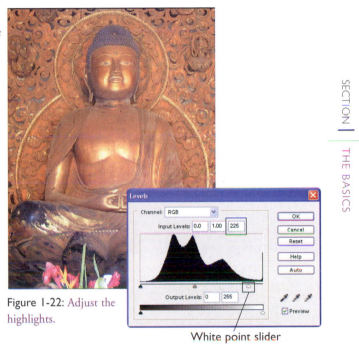

Figure 1-22: Adjust the highlights.

White point slider

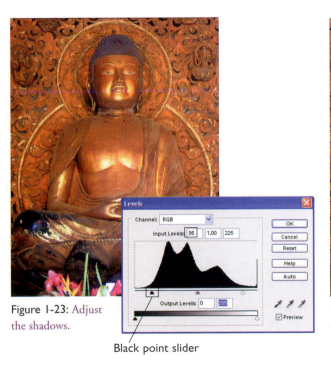

Figure 1-23: Adjust the shadows.

Black point slider

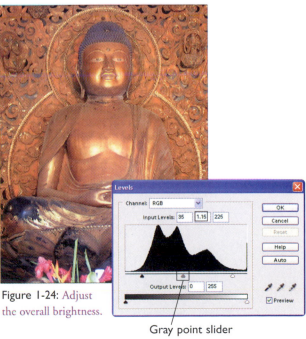

Figure 1-24: Adjust the overall brightness.

Gray point slider

The Rule of Thirds: Recompose a Photo

2

In This Project You Will:

- ☐ Create and use a template to guide in cropping photos

- ☐ Use layer modes to make multiple layers visible at the same time

- ☐ Crop an image to the contents of a layer

Sometimes it's fairly obvious how to crop a photo to obtain a more pleasing composition. Other times, you can tell it's not quite right, but you're not sure how to fix it. That's when it's time for the rule of thirds.

Figure 2-1: Beth in Hawaii

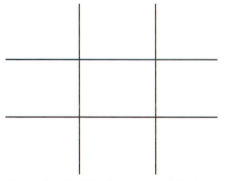

Figure 2-2: Dividing by the rule of thirds

Look at this picture of my lovely wife, Beth, in Figure 2-1. She's looking happy because she's on vacation, but it's a little hard to notice that at first. There's so much other stuff in the shot—tables, trees, chairs, water—that the eye has a hard time knowing where to go.

The composition isn't quite right; the photo needs to be cropped.

The Rule of Thirds

You probably encountered the rule of thirds back in grade school. It goes something like this: divide a rectangle evenly into thirds, both horizontally and vertically, as shown in Figure 2-2. For a pleasing composition, place the center of interest along one of the lines or even better, at one of the four intersections. Place strong divisions, such as the horizon, along one of the lines. In Figure 2-3, the single white flower among the school of black carp is at the lower-right intersection. And in Figure 2-4, the horizon runs along the lower guide.

Figure 2-3: Fish and flowers follow the rule of thirds.

Figure 2-4: A landscape cropped in accordance with the rule of thirds

Note

Keep the rule of thirds in mind when you are shooting your photos in the first place, and you'll find yourself needing to perform less corrective surgery on them in the computer.

Let's take a look at Beth again, with a rule of thirds grid laid over her in Figure 2-5. The initial composition's not horrible. Her body is near the bottom-right intersection. But we can do better than that.

The crop in Figure 2-6 is a little better. Beth's face is at one of the intersections and her body runs down the right vertical line between the two right intersections. A good deal of junk has been trimmed out.

Figure 2-7 shows the crop I finally went with. By switching to a portrait aspect ratio, where the image is taller than it is wide, I can get close to Beth, the actual subject of the photo. Her eyes are at the top-right intersection. Her upper body runs between the two right intersections. She describes a rough diagonal running between the top-right and lower-left intersections. There are a few elements surrounding her—the table and chairs, the pond behind her with blossoms floating in it, the tropical vegetation in the background—to help place the photo, but I wanted to emphasize the portrait aspects of the photo. That is, I chose to see it as a photo of my wife, rather than a photo of a garden with my wife in it.

Figure 2-5: Laying a grid over the photo

Figure 2-6: A first attempt at a crop

Note

People look first at other people's eyes. When placing a face within a composition, center an intersection point between the eyes, or on one eye.

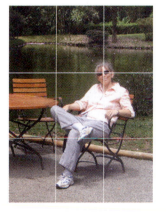

Figure 2-7: My final crop of the photo

Figure 2-8: A crop too far

I could have gone even further, as shown in Figure 2-8. There's nothing wrong with this composition, but it cuts out too much of the background for my taste. It also leaves me with too small a final image, pixel-wise; you can only crop an image so far before you run out of adequate resolution.

When you're using the rule of thirds, remember that it's only a suggestion and needn't be slavishly followed. Don't wreck a composition that looks good to you just to get an eye line exactly at the intersection. And sometimes the rule of thirds seems to lead to surprisingly bad-looking compositions.

Create a Template

How do you crop an image so that a particular line or element ends up just where you want it? Unfortunately, Photoshop Elements provides no easy way to judge exactly where elements will be after a crop. But you can make a simple tool that'll help a great deal: a template.

Create a new document (File | New | Blank File). Name the document thirds-template and make it 800 pixels wide by 600 pixels tall with a white background.

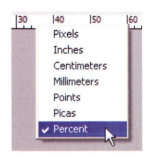

Figure 2-9: Set the rulers to Percent.

Select the Line tool from the Toolbox. In the Options bar, set the tool's color to black and its weight to 4 pixels.

Make sure rulers are visible (View | Rulers). Right-click on either ruler (CONTROL-click on a Macintosh) and choose Percent from the pop-up menu, as shown in Figure 2-9. Select the Zoom tool from the Toolbox and zoom in to 300% so that you can see the individual percentages on the ruler bar. (The zoom amount is displayed in the title bar at the very top of the Elements workspace.)

Press the space bar to temporarily select the Hand tool. Click and drag on the canvas to slide your image around until you can see 33% on the ruler at the left and can also see the left edge of the canvas.

Move the cursor slightly beyond the leftmost part of the canvas at 33%. Click to begin your line, as shown in Figure 2-10. Hold down the SHIFT key to constrain the line to horizontal and drag to the right to draw a line across the entire canvas, as shown in Figure 2-11. Don't worry if the lines go outside of the canvas.

Scroll down and repeat the process at 67%, creating another horizontal black line across the entire canvas. Repeat the process at 33% and 67% from top to bottom. When you're finished, choose View | Fit on Screen to see the entire template. You should wind up with something like Figure 2-12. Note that some of the lines extend beyond the canvas but that's just fine; they'll get trimmed off when you save the file.

There are five layers in the document now, one for the white background and one for each line, but you'll be saving it as a simple bitmap file. Choose File | Save. Save the file as thirds-template.jpg in a folder you'll be able to find later. When the JPEG Options dialog appears, drag the slider all the way to the right until the Quality setting reads 12, as shown in Figure 2-13. Click OK to save the file. Close the thirds-template document (File | Close) without saving.

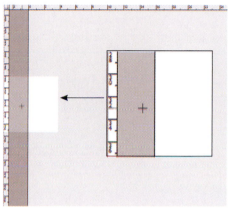

Figure 2-10: Begin a horizontal line at 33%.

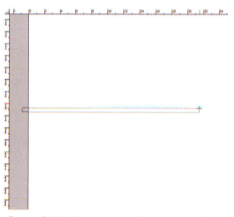

Figure 2-11: Complete the first horizontal line.

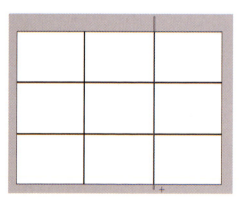

Figure 2-12: The finished rule of thirds template

Figure 2-13: Set JPEG Quality option to Maximum.

The Black Swan

Now let's use the template. Open the file black-swan.jpg (Figure 2-14), or any of your own photos that may be in need of a crop.

Open the thirds-template.jpg file you created in the previous steps. Copy the template by choosing Select | All, then choosing Edit | Copy to copy the contents to the clipboard.

Return to the swan photo. Choose Edit | Paste to paste the template to a new layer above the photo, as shown in Figure 2-15.

In the Layers palette, click the layer containing the template to select it. Select Overlay from the Blending Modes drop-down list, as shown in Figure 2-16.

With the template in Overlay mode, the photograph shows through, but you can clearly see the template and the template lines as well, as shown in Figure 2-17.

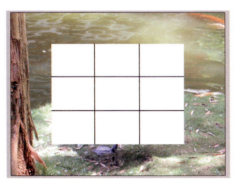

Figure 2-14: A black swan

Figure 2-15: The thirds
template

> **Note**
>
> The template has a 4×3 aspect ratio, the same as most computer monitors. Always hold down the SHIFT key when resizing it to keep this aspect ratio.

Figure 2-16: Change the template's blending mode to Overlay.

Figure 2-17: The swan showing through the template

Choose the Marquee tool. Then select Image | Transform | Free Transform to enter Free Transform mode. You can

- Click and drag within the template to reposition it on the canvas.
- Click and drag on one of the corner handles while holding down the SHIFT key to resize the template.
- Click and drag outside of the template, while holding down the SHIFT key, to rotate the template.

Position, resize, and rotate the template until it frames a composition you like. When you're happy, CTRL-click (CMD-click on the Macintosh) on the thumbnail of the thirds template in the Layers palette,

Figure 2-18: CTRL-click or CMD-click on the thumbnail.

as shown in Figure 2-18. This selects the area covered by the template and leaves any area outside of the template unselected.

Select Image | Crop to crop the photo to fit the template. Choose Select | Deselect to turn off the selection outline. In the Layers palette, click the eye icon on the template layer to hide that layer and see the final results. What did you come up with? Here's my favorite crop, shown in Figure 2-19.

Figure 2-19: My new crop of the swan photo

Sometimes the rule of thirds just doesn't fit—you want to put the horizon way down low to emphasize the big sky or way up high to emphasize the vastness of the ocean. Even so, your template comes in handy when cropping (see Figure 2-20). It gives you a preview of which elements will be cropped off, and which ones will remain (and where) afterwards.

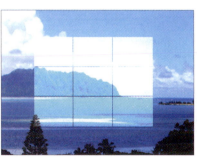

Figure 2-20: The rule of thirds suggests one possible crop of this landscape photo.

Despeckling: Remove Blemishes and "Speckles"

Our Angel

In This Project You Will:

☐ Use the Dust & Scratches tool to remove blemishes

☐ Use layer blending modes to remove speckles

☐ Use the Cookie Cutter to frame a photo

No matter how many megapixels and automatic shooting modes your digital camera sports, some photos just come out looking … bad. Some photos are just too speckled, too "noisy," to be saved. Or are they?

A Badly Speckled Photo

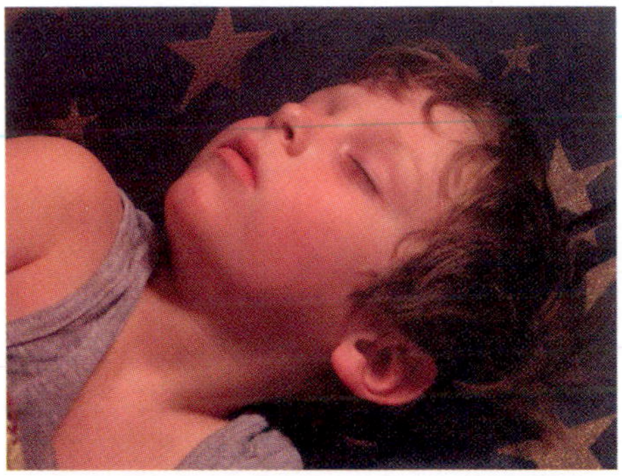

Begin by opening the file sleeping-boy.jpg (Figure 3-1). This photo was taken in a dark room without a flash. (It would be cruel to shoot off a xenon flash in the face of a sleeping boy.) It's noisy and dark, but it can be salvaged.

Photoshop Elements offers automatic correction tools, such as Smart Fix, but with a little effort you can almost always produce a better end result. Figure 3-2 is an example. This is Elements' attempt to Smart Fix the photo. Not bad—in fact, it's pretty good—but we can do better. Let's see how.

Save the document as boy.psd.

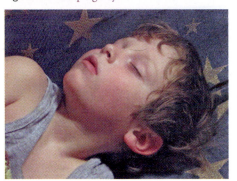

Figure 3-1: Sleeping boy

Figure 3-2: Auto-correct with Smart Fix

Auto Levels

For starters, this photo is too dark and the colors are off: it's way too red. This calls for one of Elements' automatic correction tools which we *will* use: Auto Levels. From the menu, choose Enhance | Auto Levels. The results, shown in Figure 3-3, are a marked improvement in terms of both lighting and color cast. Still, if you zoom in to about 200%, as shown in Figure 3-4, you'll see one big problem shared by many badly lit photos: colored noise. The boy's cheek is speckled with bits of blue, purple, yellow, and green that don't belong there.

Fortunately, there's a time-honored way of dealing with this problem.

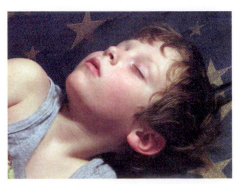

Figure 3-3: Auto Levels corrects the lighting.

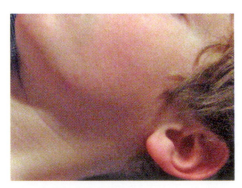

Figure 3-4: Colored speckles

Blur Your Way to Better Skin

From the menu, choose Layer | New | Layer via Copy to copy the photograph to a new layer. From the menu, choose Filter | Blur | Gaussian Blur. In the Gaussian Blur dialog, set the Radius to 4.0 pixels, and click OK. The results, as shown in Figure 3-5, are seemingly too blurry to be of any use, but they're not.

In the Layers palette, change the top blurred layer's blending mode to Color. If we zoom in, we see that the speckles remain, but the erroneous colors have disappeared, as shown in Figure 3-6. This method works because most of the pixels are more or less the correct color. When you blur the image, the little bits of purple and yellow disappear into the sea of flesh tones. And we're only using the colors from the blurred image to paint the underlying, unblurred image.

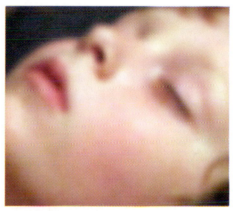

Figure 3-5: Gaussian blurred

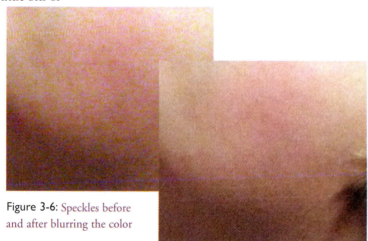

Figure 3-6: Speckles before and after blurring the color

From the menu, choose Layer | Flatten Image to merge the layers together.

No More Speckles

Time to tackle those spots and speckles themselves. From the menu, choose Layer | New | Layer via Copy twice, to make two copies of the Background layer. In the Layers palette, name the middle layer Medium, and the top layer Heavy, as shown in Figure 3-7. Hide the top, Heavy layer by clicking its eye icon as shown.

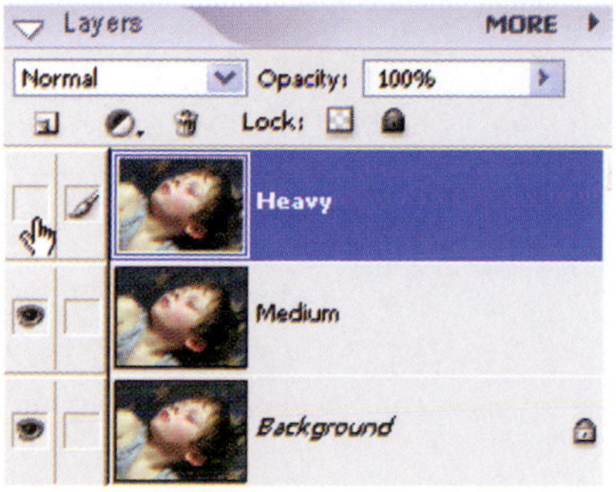

Figure 3-7: You should have three layers.

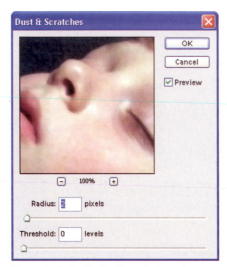

Figure 3-8: Apply the Dust & Scratches filter.

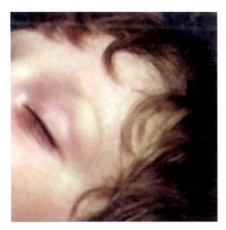

Figure 3-9: Detail is missing.

Figure 3-11: Select the layer content.

Now select the Medium layer. From the menu, choose Filter | Noise | Dust & Scratches. In the Dust & Scratches dialog, set the Radius to 2 pixels, and the Threshold to 0 levels, as shown in Figure 3-8. Click OK.

Unfortunately, the Dust & Scratches filter can't distinguish very well between, say, a scratch in a scanned photo and a strand of hair in that same photo. So, while the filter has reduced the speckling, it's also blurred out all the detail in the hair and eyelashes, as shown in Figure 3-9. To restore that detail, select the Eraser tool from the Toolbox. In the Options bar, select a soft, round, 35-pixel brush and set its opacity to 50%. Erase over the hair to allow the detail from the underlying layer to show through, as shown in Figure 3-10. Switch to a smaller brush and restore detail to the eyelashes, and other smaller areas.

When you're done, reduce the Medium layer's opacity to 70% to improve the blend. Then select Layer | Merge Down from the menu to combine the Medium layer with the Background.

Now would be a good time to save your work so far.

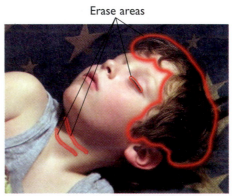

Figure 3-10: Erase in these areas.

In the Layers palette, click on the Heavy layer to restore the layer's visibility, as shown in Figure 3-11.

From the menu, choose Filter | Noise | Dust & Scratches again. This time, set the filter's Radius to 6 and the Threshold to 4. Click OK.

Again, select the Eraser tool and set the opacity to 50%. As before, use soft round brushes to erase any areas where the filter has obliterated needed detail: the hair, the eyelashes, and so forth. When you're finished, reduce the Heavy layer's opacity to 50%, then choose Layer | Merge Down from the menu.

Add Some Hue

The boy's skin tone is still a bit blotchy, owing to the less than optimal lighting conditions when the photo was taken. To fix this, let's overlay the whole image with a nice skin tone to even things out a bit. To get an appropriate color, we'll sample the color from the boy's face.

We want the average skin tone, but any single sample of the face might be a bit darker, or lighter, or redder than average. So let's create an average skin tone.

Select the Elliptical Marquee tool from the Toolbox and use it to select an area of skin from the cheek, as shown in Figure 3-12. Don't grab any hair, lips, or nostrils, just skin. From the menu, choose Layer | New | Layer via Copy to copy the cheek to a new layer of its own. The selection disappeared when the new layer was created with a copy of the selected area. To reselect it, CTRL-click (CMD-click on the Macintosh) on the new layer's thumbnail in the Layers palette. Choose Filter | Blur | Average from the menu to blur the sample into the average skin tone from the boy's cheek.

In the Layers palette, rename the new layer Skin Tone. Use the Eyedropper tool to sample the color, as shown in Figure 3-13, and then remove the selection (Select | Deselect).

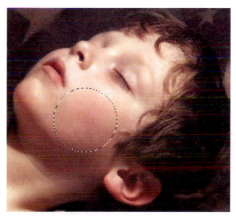

Figure 3-12: Select a circle of cheek.

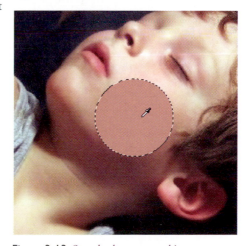

Figure 3-13: Sample the average skin tone.

Make certain that the Skin Tone layer is selected in the Layers palette, and choose Edit | Fill Layer from the menu. In the Fill Layer dialog, choose Foreground Color from Contents. Make sure the Mode is Normal and Opacity is 100%, then click OK to fill the entire layer with the sampled skin tone.

Change the Skin Tone layer's blending mode to Hue, and reduce its opacity to 50%. This pulls the remaining green and yellow tones out of the boy's skin. Note that this also dulls the blue background, but that's okay, as we don't really care about that, anyway.

Save your work so far.

Photo Filter

Figure 3-14: Apply a photo filter.

That's looking better and better, but the lighting is still a little cold. One last step and we'll call it done. From the menu, choose Layer | New Adjustment Layer | Photo Filter and click OK. In the Photo Filter dialog, choose Warming Filter(85), set the Density to 25%, and make sure Preserve Luminosity is checked, as shown in Figure 3-14. Click OK. This filter warms the lighting of the photo a bit, adding a soft orange light overall, as shown in Figure 3-15.

Flatten the image (Layer | Flatten Image), and save your work. You can call it good at this point, if you want to.

Frame Your Photo

The photo is looking pretty good, but it could do with a good crop. Elements' Cookie Cutter tool will do just the trick, but first let's rotate the photo into a slightly better orientation.

Figure 3-15: The photo looks a lot nicer than before.

Copy the Background layer to a new layer (Layer | New | Layer via Copy). In the Layers palette, select the new layer and choose Image | Rotate | Free Rotate Layer from the menu. In the Options bar, set the Rotate value to 10.0°, as shown in Figure 3-16. Press ENTER (RETURN on a Macintosh) to accept the rotation.

In the Layers palette, select the Background layer, then choose Edit | Fill Layer from the menu. Choose White for the Contents and click OK to fill the Background layer with white.

Select the Background copy layer in the Layers palette, then select the Cookie Cutter tool from the Toolbox. In the Options bar, open the Shape Picker and then click the small triangle in the upper-right corner, as shown in Figure 3-17, to open the Shape Library pop-up list. Select Crop Shapes from the pop-up.

Select Crop Shape 6 (a ragged oval) from the Shape Picker. Click and drag on the canvas to create the shape, as shown in Figure 3-18. Click and drag on the handles to fine-tune the shape and position of the crop. When you're satisfied, press ENTER to apply the Cookie Cutter.

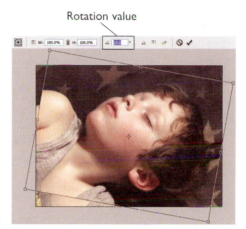

Rotation value

Figure 3-16: Rotate the boy a bit.

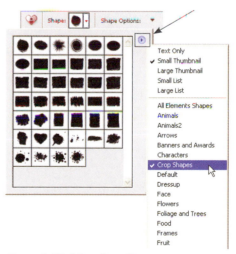

Figure 3-17: Select Crop Shapes.

Figure 3-18: Click and drag to start the Cookie Cutter.

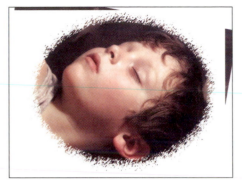

Figure 3-19: Moving the layer reveals extra bits.

You may want to use the Move tool to reposition the cropped photo in the canvas. If any extra bits pop into view, as in Figure 3-19, use the Eraser tool set at 100% opacity to get rid of them.

Congratulations! That looks great. Flatten the image (Layer | Flatten Image), then save your work. You're done! (Of course, if you want to add a caption, I won't stop you.)

Thanks to my buddy Jeff Berg (www.pixelplay.org/jeff) for his help with this project.

In Technicolor:
Hand-Tint a Photo

In This Project
You Will:

☐ Blur to obscure unwanted background elements

☐ Create a faux layer mask

☐ Use blending modes to hand-tint photos

My father used to hand-tint photographs and I've always loved that effect, that combination of photography and painting. It's one of my favorite digital photography techniques.

Get Rid of the Extra Junk

Start by opening the file rhythm.jpg (Figure 4-1) or your own favorite old-timey photo. Save the document as hand-tint.psd.

This is a photograph of my dad, singing in a band back in 1958. The original photo was in horrible shape, so I've already subjected it to some serious despeckling (à la Project 3).

The background of the photo is ratty looking, and none of the detail in there is worth preserving, in my opinion, so I'm not going to bother. The subject of this photo is my dad; the rest can go.

From the menu, choose Layer | New | Layer via Copy to copy the original Background to a new layer. In the Layers palette, rename the new layer to BG. From the menu, choose Filter | Blur | Gaussian Blur. In the Gaussian Blur dialog, enter a Radius of 20 pixels and click OK. The blurry results are shown in Figure 4-2.

Figure 4-1: The Rhythm Ramblers

Figure 4-2: That's very blurry.

Figure 4-3: Making things much darker

Now, darken the layer by choosing Enhance | Adjust Lighting | Brightness/Contrast. Reduce the Brightness all the way to −100, and the contrast to −70, as shown in Figure 4-3, and click OK.

Make a Mask

Of course, we don't ultimately want that dark blurry background in front of my dad; we want it to appear behind him. To create the effect, we'll create a mask layer to hide the parts of the background that obscure Dad.

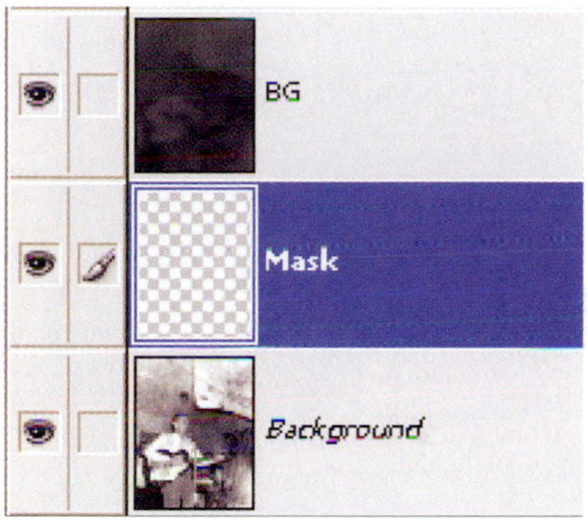

Figure 4-4: The Mask layer goes between the other two.

In the Layers palette, select the Background layer, then choose Layer | New | Layer from the menu. Name the new layer Mask, and click OK. This creates a new blank layer between the Background and BG layers, as shown in Figure 4-4. Select the topmost BG layer, then choose Layer | Group with Previous from the menu. This groups the BG layer with the new Mask layer beneath it, as shown in Figure 4-5. This also causes the dark, blurred background to disappear, revealing the original photo again. With the two layers grouped, pixels in the top layer only show where pixels in the lower layer are filled. Since the lower layer, Mask, is empty, nothing shows through from above.

Select the Mask layer again in the Layers palette. Select the Brush tool from the Toolbox. In the Options bar, choose a soft, round, 100-pixel brush. Set the Foreground Color to white (255,255,255) and begin painting at the top of the photo. As the brush fills pixels in the Mask layer, the BG layer begins to appear, as shown in Figure 4-6. Notice that the white contents of the Mask layer itself don't appear.

Figure 4-5: The BG layer is grouped with the Mask layer.

Figure 4-6: Paint the background back in.

Figure 4-7: The blurred background in place

You paint in the Mask layer to reveal the blurred background, and erase in the Mask layer to hide the blurred background. Continue painting until the blurred background appears everywhere it should, as shown in Figure 4-7. Switch to progressively smaller brushes as you work closer to the foreground singer. If necessary, switch to the Eraser tool and erase any errant bits of the Mask layer. To see the Mask layer itself, hide the blurred BG layer by turning off its eye icon in the Layers palette, as shown in Figure 4-8.

The advantage of this method over simply erasing a Dad-shaped hole in the top layer is that you can easily go back with the Eraser and Brush tools, as often as you'd like, to add to or subtract from the mask until you're happy with it.

When you're happy, reduce the Mask layer's opacity to about 75%, as shown in Figure 4-9, to restore some of the background and to ease the blend around the mask.

Figure 4-8: Revealing the Mask layer

Figure 4-9: Reduced opacity improves the blend.

Create a Spotlight

Dad deserves a spotlight, don't you think? Let's add one. In the Layers palette, select the topmost layer, BG, then choose Layer | New | Layer from the menu. Name the new layer Spotlight. Make sure Group with Previous Layer is selected, then click OK.

Select the Brush tool from the Toolbox. In the Options bar, choose a soft, round, 200-pixel brush. Set the Foreground color to white (255,255,255) and paint a big ol' blob around my dad, as shown in Figure 4-10. When you're done, reduce the Spotlight layer's opacity down to 25–40%.

Flatten the image (Layer | Flatten Image).

Give the entire image a slight yellowed cast by choosing Enhance | Adjust Color | Adjust Hue/Saturation from the menu. Select Colorize, then set the Hue to 25, the Saturation to 10, and the Lightness to 0. Click OK to apply the color cast.

Save your work.

Figure 4-10: Painting a spotlight

Let's Get Painting

Time to add some color. We're going to color each part of the photo on its own layer. From the menu, choose Layer | New | Layer. Name the new layer Flesh, set its Mode to Color, and click OK to create it.

Select the Brush tool from the Toolbox. In the Options bar, choose a soft, round, 13-pixel brush. Set the Foreground Color to R=255, G=180, B=140 and paint over the face and hands, as shown

Figure 4-11: Painting in the flesh tones

in Figure 4-11. If you get a little sloppy, use the Eraser tool to clean things up. Don't worry about being too precise; the results are supposed to look hand-tinted, after all. When you're happy, reduce the Flesh layer's opacity to about 55% for a subtler, more believable look, as shown in Figure 4-12.

Create a new layer (Layer | New | Layer) named Guitar, in Color mode. Use the Brush tool to paint over the guitar with bright red (255,25,0), then reduce the Guitar layer's opacity to 20%.

Repeat the process for the shoulder epaulettes and pants, creating new Color mode layers and reducing their opacity as detailed in Figure 4-13. Note that the colors in this figure are shown as opaque for clarity only. Your actual image will look more like Figure 4-14.

Figure 4-12: A subtler effect

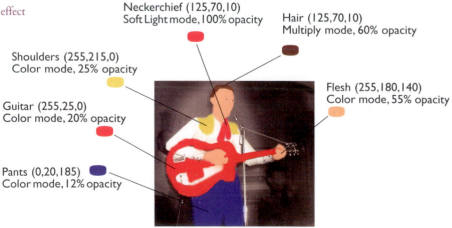

Neckerchief (125,70,10)
Soft Light mode, 100% opacity

Hair (125,70,10)
Multiply mode, 60% opacity

Shoulders (255,215,0)
Color mode, 25% opacity

Flesh (255,180,140)
Color mode, 55% opacity

Guitar (255,25,0)
Color mode, 20% opacity

Pants (0,20,185)
Color mode, 12% opacity

Figure 4-13: Colors to paint with

Figure 4-14: Our work so far

Color mode doesn't affect pure black or white, only shades of gray

Create a new Neckerchief layer in Soft Light mode at 100% opacity.

Create a new Hair layer in Multiply mode at 60% opacity.

Zoom in and look around for any areas of color that are too sloppy for you, then use the Brush and Eraser tools to clean them up.

When you're satisfied, flatten the image (Layer | Flatten Image).

Finally, use the Crop tool to crop the final image, placing more emphasis on the foreground figure, as shown in Figure 4-15.

Save your work.

Figure 4-15: Making the final crop

Cleaning House: Remove Unwanted Elements

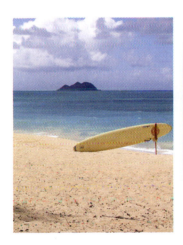

I f you're like me, you often find otherwise flawless photos diminished by distracting bits of trash in the background, or your vacation photos are frequently cluttered up with total strangers. In the pre-digital age, you just had to live with that, but no more. Photoshop Elements will remove those unwanted distractions from your photos.

In This Project You Will:

- ☐ Use the Spot Healing Brush to remove unwanted elements

- ☐ Use the Clone Stamp tool to remove unwanted elements

- ☐ Use layers to remove unwanted elements

Healing a Beach Mat

Open the file surfboard.jpg (Figure 5-1) and save the document as surfboard.psd.

Let's begin by getting rid of the beach mat at the right edge of the photo, below the surfboard. Elements' Spot Healing Brush tool does a great job of removing spots and blemishes. It will also remove larger items, such as beach mats, provided they're relatively isolated against a simple background such as sand. So, while it wouldn't work very well for removing a single person from a crowd, it works just fine for removing a single person from the middle of a field or a mat from a sandy beach.

Zoom in to 200% so you can see what you're doing. Select the Spot Healing Brush tool from the Toolbox palette. In the Options bar, select a soft, round, 27-pixel brush.

Click on the mat and, without releasing the mouse button, drag to select the entire beach mat, as shown in Figure 5-2. When the whole thing's selected, release the mouse button to "heal" the beach, eliminating the mat, as shown in Figure 5-3. If you have any strange spots remaining, apply the Spot Healing Brush tool a second time to get rid of them.

Figure 5-1: A typical vacation photo

Figure 5-2: Select the mat with the Spot Healing Brush.

Figure 5-3: The beach has been "healed."

Goodbye, Girl

The next task is to remove the girl running across the sand. The Spot Healing Brush tool does a worse job if we try to use it to remove the running girl to the left of the surfboard, as shown in Figure 5-4. The tool has a lot more colors and shades to deal with. It makes

Figure 5-4: The Spot Healing Brush fails.

a pretty good guess, but the results clearly show that something artificial has happened here. That's not what we want, so it's time to switch to the Clone Stamp tool.

Select the Clone Stamp tool from the Toolbox palette. In the Options bar, select a soft, round, 27-pixel brush and be sure Aligned is checked. The Clone Stamp tool copies parts of an image from one place to another. When using the Clone Stamp, you need to be careful about where you are copying from. If you sample the darker water far above the girl, for example, the results are extremely nasty looking, as shown in Figure 5-5. Not convincing at all.

Figure 5-5: The sampled water doesn't match.

Paint here   Sample from here

Figure 5-6: Clone over her head.

Figure 5-7: Replace her top half with water.

Figure 5-9: Cloning can leave artificial patterns.

We want to sample from water that looks more or less the same as the water behind the girl would look if we could see it. ALT-click (OPTION-click on the Macintosh) to the right of the girl's head, as shown in Figure 5-6, to sample the water from there. Release the ALT or OPTION key, and then paint out the girl's head with the Clone Stamp tool.

Continue downward to replace the top half of the girl with water, as shown in Figure 5-7.

Now ALT-click or OPTION-click to pick up a new sample from the sand on the beach. Sample from the left of the girl, rather than the right; the surfboard is on the right and we don't want to copy that. Release the ALT or OPTION key and paint out the bottom half of the girl, as shown in Figure 5-8. In the Options bar, set the tool to a hard, 9-pixel brush, better suited to the delicate work of erasing the leg and foot close to the surfboard. Be careful not to cut into the surfboard itself.

Figure 5-8: Replace her bottom half with sand.

Use short strokes, and ALT-click or OPTION-click several times as you paint, to sample from different areas of the photo. If you don't change the area you're sampling from, you'll wind up with visible patterns, like the one shown in Figure 5-9.

You'll probably be left with some messiness where the sand meets the sea, but we'll fix that next.

ALT-click or OPTION-click on a piece of unaltered shoreline—where the beach ends and the sea begins—as shown in Figure 5-10 to sample the beach. Release the ALT or OPTION key and, using several short strokes, carefully trace in a new shoreline, as shown in Figure 5-11.

Paint here   Sample from here

Figure 5-10: Sample from intact beach.

Figure 5-11: Carefully paint in a new shoreline.

Who's That Hiding?

Use the same technique to erase the head and legs of the second child, mostly hidden behind the surfboard, as shown in Figure 5-12.

Figure 5-12: Erase the person behind the surfboard.

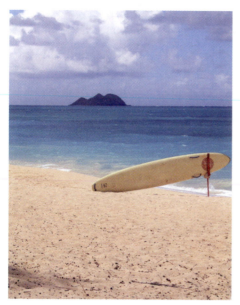

Figure 5-13: It's as if they were never there!

Lastly, look for any area where you may have left telltale patterns. Use a soft brush and the Clone Stamp tool to replace the patterned elements with other pixels sampled from elsewhere. Use Edit | Undo to reverse any cloning steps that you don't like. The final results, shown in Figure 5-13, should bear no obvious traces of your pixel surgery.

Save your work and close the picture.

Bye-Bye Love

Of course, sand and surf are about the easiest backgrounds imaginable to replace: one bit of sand looks much like another. Let's bump the complexity up a bit with the photo shown in Figure 5-14. Our assignment: to remove the woman (my wife) and the car from the photo. Start by opening up the file, highway.jpg, shown in Figure 5-15, and save it as highway.psd.

Figure 5-14: A roadside photo

Figure 5-15: A crop is a good way to begin.

If you're observant, you noticed that I made a big change before we even start. I've cropped off quite a bit of the original photo shown in Figure 5-14. This isn't simply because I'm lazy; it's also to make a point. Don't waste a lot of time removing or correcting elements you don't actually need in your final composition. Why spend the extra time carefully removing my wife from the guardrail, if I don't actually need the guardrail in the finished image?

Even the cropped version leaves my wife's head and shoulders to be removed. Let's get started removing her. (Sorry, honey.)

The straight lines of the highway should run right through the space she's currently occupying. Zoom in to about 300%. Select the Clone Stamp tool from the Toolbox. In the Options bar, choose a hard, round, 17-pixel brush.

Hold down the ALT or OPTION key and make sure that the horizontal bar of the crosshair cursor is immediately below the white line, as shown in Figure 5-16. Click on the white lane divider stripe to begin sampling. Then release the ALT or OPTION key.

Move the cursor to the white divider line immediately to the left of her arm. Hold down the ALT or OPTION key again, but *do not click*. Position the crosshair cursor so that it is in exactly the same position relative to the white divider line as it was when you sampled, as shown in Figure 5-17. When it's in position, release the ALT or OPTION key (Figure 5-18) then, *without moving the cursor*, begin to paint. This guarantees that the white divider line will appear in the proper position; it won't be too high or too low.

Figure 5-16: Carefully line up the crosshair.

Figure 5-17: Match the crosshair's position.

Figure 5-18: Replace my wife with highway.

Continue cloning, using the bushes to cover her head, and extending the highway,
wall, fence, and curbing. Be careful to line up strong horizontal or vertical lines
using the crosshairs, as you did with the divider stripe, as shown in Figure 5-19.
You'll need to resample often and use many short strokes to line up sections where
obvious lines meet.

Figure 5-19: Continue cloning over my wife.

I decided that I wanted to keep the highway sign in the final image. Use the same
process to duplicate the right sign post to replace the missing left post, as shown in
Figure 5-20. Your image should resemble Figure 5-21. Then save the file.

Figure 5-20: Clone a second sign post.

Figure 5-21: Your work so far

Car-go

Let's try a third technique to get rid of the car. Select the Rectangular Marquee tool from the Toolbox and use it to select an area of car-free highway from behind the car, as shown in Figure 5-22. Make the selection larger than the car. From the menu, choose Layer | New | Layer via Copy to copy the selected area to a new layer.

Next, select the Move tool from the Toolbox and slide the contents of the new layer to the right, to cover the car, as shown in Figure 5-23. Click and drag on the bottom handle to resize the layer slightly for a better fit.

Figure 5-22: Select some car-free highway.

Figure 5-23: Cover the car.

Figure 5-24: Hide the new layer.

In the Layers palette, hide the new layer by clicking on its eye icon, as shown in Figure 5-24. Select the Polygonal Lasso tool and click multiple times to select the car, but very little else, as shown in Figure 5-25. From the menu, choose Select | Inverse. Now everything is selected *except* for the car. In the Layers palette, click on Layer 1, and then press DELETE to remove the selected background elements around the car. By deleting all but the minimum necessary to hide the car, you minimize the problems of blending the "patch" into the rest of the image.

Remove the selection (Select | Deselect), then choose Layer | Flatten Image to eliminate the new layer.

Finally, return to the Clone Stamp tool. Use a small, soft brush to paint over any obvious edges where the copied section of the wall meets the original photo.

Save your work.

Figure 5-25: Select the car.

A Perfect World:
Spruce Up the Sky
(or Other Backgrounds)

In This Project
You Will:

☐ Create random clouds

☐ Change layer opacity to improve blending

☐ Blend the sky from one photo with the foreground of another

An otherwise good outdoor photograph is often diminished by a washed-out sky. With Photoshop Elements, you're not limited to the sky your camera recorded, or even to the sky that nature provided.

Figure 6-1: This sky is almost gone.

Punch Up a Washed-Out Sky

Figure 6-1 shows a typical photo with a washed out sky. Let's look at one quick and easy way to punch it up a bit. If you want to follow along, open the file corrected-temple.jpg now and save it as temple.psd.

Notice that there is one spot of blue sky on the right edge of the photo. Select the Eyedropper tool from the Toolbox and sample this blue as the new Foreground Color. Set the Background Color to white (255,255,255).

Let's add some clouds on a new layer. Create a new layer by choosing Layer | New | Layer from the menu. Name the new layer Clouds, and click OK to create it. From the menu choose Filter | Render | Clouds. This will fill the new Clouds layer with randomly generated clouds, varying between the blue color you sampled from the sky and white, as shown in Figure 6-2.

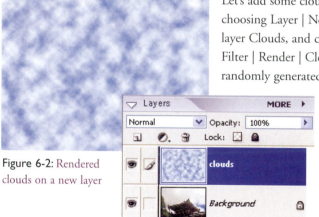

Figure 6-2: Rendered clouds on a new layer

In the Layers palette, set the Clouds layer's mode to Darken. This layer now shows up only where its contents are darker than the underlying photograph, as shown in Figure 6-3. While the clouds are quite visible in the sky—which was mostly white—most of the temple itself is unaffected. Use the Eraser tool with a soft, round, 65-pixel brush to erase any of the clouds that are visible over the temple. Finally, reduce the Clouds layer's opacity to about 40–45% to blend the randomly generated clouds more believably into the sky, as shown in Figure 6-4.

Figure 6-3: Rendered clouds add detail to the sky.

Figure 6-4: Reduce the clouds' opacity for a more realistic blend.

Flatten the image by choosing Layer | Flatten Image from the menu. Save the document, then close it.

Add a New Sky

Figure 6-5 shows another outdoor shot suffering from a white, washed-out sky. This photograph can benefit from the same quick-and-easy application of the Clouds filter, as shown in Figure 6-6.

To give artificial clouds more apparent depth, select the Move tool and CTRL-click (CMD-click on the Macintosh) and drag on the various corners of the Clouds layer to distort the clouds' perspective to better fit the scene, as shown in Figure 6-7. Zoom out to see the handles on the Move tool. When you like the effect, press ENTER (RETURN on a Macintosh) to accept the change.

But let's try something different with this photograph; let's replace the existing sky with a more dramatic sky stolen from another photograph. Open the files mountain.jpg and fluffy-clouds.jpg. With the fluffy-clouds.jpg document active, select the entire photo by choosing Select | All from the menu, and then copy the photograph to the clipboard by choosing Edit | Copy. Switch to the mountain.jpg document and paste the clouds into a new layer (Edit | Paste). In the Layers palette, rename the new layer Clouds, and then hide it by clicking on its eye icon, as shown in Figure 6-8.

Figure 6-5: Another white, washed-out sky

Figure 6-6: The sky full of random clouds

Figure 6-7: Distort the clouds' perspective.

Figure 6-8: Hide the Clouds layer.

Figure 6-9: Select all of the sky.

Select the Background layer in the Layers palette. Select the
Magic Wand tool from the Toolbox. In the Options bar,
set the tool's tolerance to 32, and select Anti-Aliased and
Contiguous. Leave Use All Layers unchecked. Now click on
the white sky to select it. If any areas of the sky aren't selected,
hold down the SHIFT key and click on them with the Magic
Wand tool to add them to the selection, as shown in Figure
6-9.

The old sky is selected; now copy it to a new layer above the
background by choosing Layer | New | Layer via Copy. In
the Layers palette, rename the new layer Mask. It should be
between the Background layer and the Clouds layer, as shown
in Figure 6-10.

Figure 6-10: The new Mask layer in place

Select the Clouds layer in the Layers palette, then choose
Layer | Group with Previous from the menu. The Clouds
layer is now "grouped" with the Mask layer beneath it, as
shown in Figure 6-11. This means that the clouds only show
where the Mask layer is filled. Since the Mask layer contains a
copy of the photo's original sky, the Clouds layer only shows
up in the sky, as shown in Figure 6-12. Handy, huh?

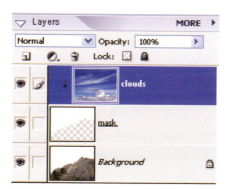

Figure 6-11: The Clouds layer grouped
with the Mask layer

Figure 6-12: New clouds over the mountain

The sky looks too dark for this photo; the sky is a little too deep. Reduce the effect somewhat by reducing the opacity of the Mask layer (not the Clouds layer) to somewhere between 25% and 75%, as shown in Figure 6-13.

Here's a quick trick that might not occur to you: flip the clouds, right for left. Select the Clouds layer in the Layers palette, then choose Image | Rotate | Flip Layer Horizontal from the menu. To my eye at least, this version of the sky, shown in Figure 6-14, is much more pleasing.

Figure 6-13: Reduce the sky's opacity.

Drop in a Sunset

Experiment with dropping in different skies. Figure 6-15 shows a photo I took of a sunset, sunset.jpg. Open this file and choose Select | All, then Edit | Copy. Switch to the mountain.jpg image. In the Layers palette, select the Clouds layer and delete it (Layer | Delete Layer). Paste in the sunset sky (Edit | Paste) and group it with the mask (Layer | Group with Previous).

Figure 6-14: Swap the clouds, right for left.

Click on the Mask layer and change its opacity back to 100% to see the full intensity of the sunset colors, as shown in Figure 6-16. Select the new Clouds layer and use the Move tool to reposition the sunset so more of the orange sky is visible.

Figure 6-15: A sunset

Figure 6-16: Sunset over the mountain

The results don't look quite right, though. If you're looking into a sunset, the foreground objects would be silhouetted against the bright sky, not brightly lit as they are here. To make the image more believable, I selected the Background layer and used the Levels command (Enhance | Adjust Lighting | Levels). In the Levels dialog, I dragged the gray point slider to the right, until the Input levels read 0, 0.50, 255, as shown in Figure 6-17, then clicked OK. This stretches the shadows and makes the photo much darker overall, more in keeping with the sunset sky.

When you like what you see, flatten the image (Layer | Flatten Image), and save the document under a new name.

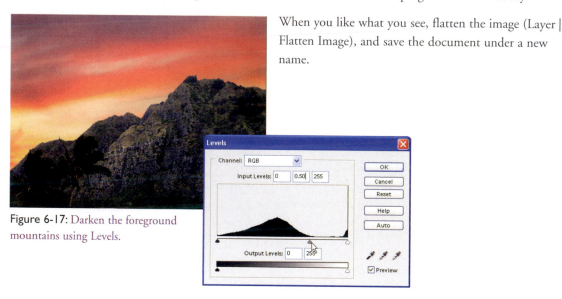

Figure 6-17: Darken the foreground mountains using Levels.

Faux Pencil Drawing: Create a Quick Pencil Sketch

In This Project You Will:

☐ Use Blurs and Blending modes to create a faux pencil effect

☐ Use Blending modes to colorize an image

☐ Create a textured paper effect

☐ Remove red eye using the Red Eye Removal tool

Did you know that you can use Photoshop Elements to turn any photo into a pencil sketch? Of course you did. Although Elements provides many filters to give a photo a hand-drawn look, my favorite method uses layer blending modes. Follow along, won't you?

Invert Me

Figure 7-1: The original photo

Open the file pam.jpg (Figure 7-1) or your own photo. Save the document as pencil-sketch.psd. This photograph has a bad case of red eye, but that doesn't matter in a pencil sketch. Don't worry about it for now.

Begin by copying the original photo. From the menu, choose Layer | New | Layer via Copy. In the Layers palette, rename the new layer to Drawing. From the menu, choose Enhance | Adjust Color | Remove Color. This converts the photo from color to black and white.

Copy the Drawing layer (Layer | New | Layer via Copy) and rename the new layer Inverted.

In the Layers palette, select the Inverted layer. Change its blending mode to Color Dodge. From the menu, choose Filter | Adjustments | Invert, to invert the colors on the layer, black for white. At this stage, the image completely (or almost completely) disappears. Never fear, it'll be back in a moment.

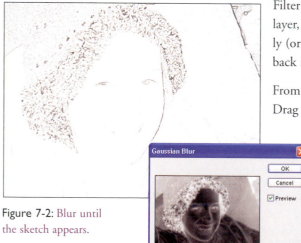

Figure 7-2: Blur until the sketch appears.

From the menu, choose Filter | Blur | Gaussian Blur. Drag the Radius slider slowly to the right, and watch as the "sketch" begins to appear (Figure 7-2). The more you blur the Inverted layer, the wider and softer the lines become, as shown in Figure 7-3. If you blur things too far, the pencil sketch look is lost altogether. I think that 10 pixels of blur looks best on this photo, but it all depends on your personal taste. When you like what you see, click OK to apply the blur.

Make sure the Inverted layer is selected in the Layers palette, and choose Layer | Merge Down to combine it with the Drawing layer beneath it.

Figure 7-3: Sketches created with a blur of 3 pixels, 7 pixels, 10 pixels, and 20 pixels

Burn and Dodge

That's 90 percent of the technique, right there. You can save your work and call it done, but I usually take it a step or two further, selectively darkening some of the lines and shading.

From the Toolbox, choose the Burn tool. In the Options bar, select a soft, round, 27-pixel brush. Set the tool's Range to Shadows, and its Exposure to 30%, as shown in Figure 7-4.

With the Burn tool, paint over any lines which you feel should be darker, as shown in Figure 7-5. Use multiple strokes to darken the lines gradually. Which lines?

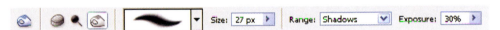

Figure 7-4: Burn options

How dark? That's entirely a matter of taste. I decided that the lines of the face were the most important, so I spent most of my darkening efforts there, as shown in Figure 7-6, but you may feel differently.

Conversely, you can use the Dodge tool to lighten any areas you think are too dark already. I feel that the shadows in the hat are too strong, overshadowing the

Figure 7-5: Use the Burn tool to darken some lines.

Figure 7-6: After burning, the outlines are more distinct.

Figure 7-7: Lighten the hat.

Background areas

Figure 7-8: After erase

face. To mute them somewhat, change to the Dodge tool. In the Options bar, select a soft, round, 65-pixel brush. Again, set the Range to Shadows and the Exposure to 30%. Using multiple strokes, paint over the dark parts of the hat, where it surrounds the face, to lighten it, as shown in Figure 7-7. When you're satisfied, save your work.

Lose the Background

The background in this picture isn't adding much to the composition; in fact, it's distracting. Let's delete it or, rather, paint over it.

Set the Foreground color to white (255,255,255), and then select the Brush tool from the Toolbox. In the Options bar, select a soft, round, 65-pixel brush. Carefully paint over the background elements as shown in Figure 7-8. Be careful not to erase into the foreground elements. If necessary, reduce the size of your brush to work in close to the edges.

Save your work.

You could have deleted the background before turning the photo into a pencil sketch, but it's easier now when everything's in black and white.

Add Texture

Whether this next step helps or hurts your drawing is entirely a matter of taste. Try it out and, if you don't like it, undo it.

To better emulate a real-world sketch, let's add a realistic texture to the digital "paper" the sketch is on.

In the Layers palette, select the Drawing layer. From the menu, choose Filter | Texture | Texturizer. In the Texturizer dialog, choose Canvas from the Texture drop-down list. Set the Scaling to 200%, and the Relief all the way down to 1, as shown in Figure 7-9. (This very small Relief value makes the texture very subtle.) Choose Top from the Light drop-down box. Click OK to apply the texture.

Hate it? Choose Edit | Undo Texturizer from the menu.

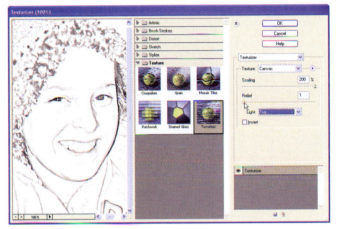

Figure 7-9: Use the Texturizer to create a canvas.

Colored Pencils

Sometimes, you'll want to put some color back into your pencil sketch—there are colored pencils, after all. It's not a problem. In fact, that's why we've kept the original photo around all this time, in the background. In the Layers palette, select the Background layer now. From the menu, choose Layer | New | Layer via Copy to copy the photo to a new layer.

In the Layers palette, click on the Background copy layer, drag it to the top of the stack, and release, as shown in Figure 7-10. Rename the new layer Color.

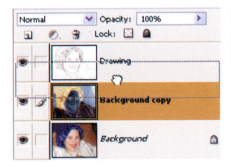 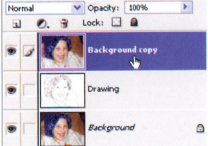

Figure 7-10: Drag the middle layer to the top.

We're going to use this layer for its color, and that means that it's finally time to fix that red eye. Zoom in on the eyes. Select the Red Eye Removal tool from the Toolbox. In the Options bar set both Pupil Size and Darken Amount to 50%. Click on the red pupils to fix them, as shown in Figure 7-11. Be patient; sometimes it takes Elements a moment to make the correction. Zoom back out to see the effect.

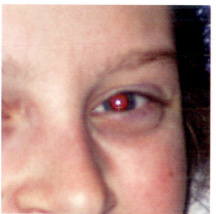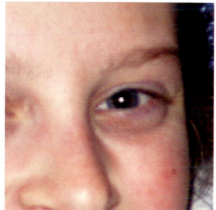

Figure 7-11: The Red Eye Removal tool does its thing.

Figure 7-12: The colored pencil look

In the Layers palette, set the new Color layer's blend mode to Color. Now the colors from the new layer replace the colors—well, shades of gray—on the layer beneath it, as shown in Figure 7-12.

This reintroduces unwanted color into the background we so carefully painted out in a previous step. Select the Eraser tool from the Toolbox and, in the Options bar, select a soft, round, 65-pixel brush. Make sure the Color layer is still selected in the Layers palette and erase the background to remove its color from the final image. Don't worry about being too precise—it's a sketch after all.

If the color effect seems too strong, try reducing the Color layer's opacity. When you're happy, flatten the image (Layer | Flatten Image) and save your work.

This technique isn't limited to portraits of people; it works on a variety of subjects, as shown in Figures 7-13 and 7-14.

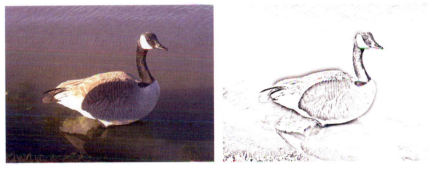

Figure 7-13: The same technique applied to some wildlife

Figure 7-14: The same technique applied to an ornate door

Candy Shop: Paint with Filters, Distortion, and Color Replacement

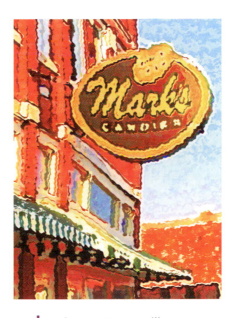

In This Project You Will:

☐ Use Replace Color to replace individual colors

☐ Use Twirl and Ripple filters to simulate brush strokes

☐ Use the Dry Brush filter to simulate brush strokes

☐ Saturate individual colors

In this project you'll create an Impressionist painting based on a photo. Don't worry if you can't draw a straight line or haven't figured out the Brush tool yet; the painting in this project is created by filters, distortions, and color replacement.

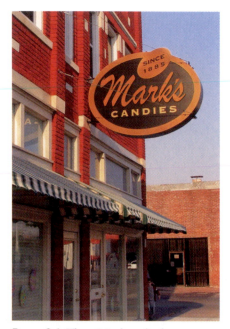

Figure 8-1: The original candy shop

Selective Saturation

Start by opening the file candy-shop.jpg (Figure 8-1), or your
own photo, in Photoshop Elements. Save the document as
candy-shop.psd.

The first thing we're going to do is to brighten up the colors.
From the menu, choose Enhance | Adjust Color | Adjust Hue/
Saturation. Although Adjust Hue/Saturation is usually used to
change the image as a whole, it also lets you adjust individual
colors and ranges of colors. You can, for example, make the
blues brighter without affecting the reds. Let's do that now.
Choose Blues from the Edit drop-down list, as shown in Figure
8-2. Drag the Saturation slider to the right to about +70. *Don't
click OK.* Choose Cyans from the Edit drop-down list, and
drag the Saturation slider to about +16, as shown in Figure 8-3.
Finally, choose Yellows and drag the Saturation slider to about
+45, as shown in Figure 8-4. Click OK.

Increasing the saturation of the blues and cyans really deepens
the sky. Saturating the yellows brightens up the sign considerably. The red brick was fine the way it was, in my opinion, so I
left the reds alone.

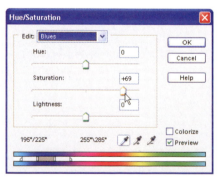

Figure 8-2: Saturate the blues.

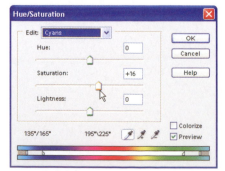

Figure 8-3: Saturate the cyans.

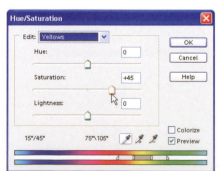

Figure 8-4: Saturate the yellows.

Brush and Distort

Elements has plenty of painterly filters to choose from. Let's use one now. From the menu, choose Filter | Artistic | Dry Brush. If necessary, click on the minus button beneath the preview so you can see the entire image in the window. In the Dry Brush dialog, set Brush Size to 9, Brush Detail to 1, and Texture to 3, as shown in Figure 8-5. Click OK. Figure 8-6 shows the results.

From the menu, choose Filter | Distort | Ripple. In the Ripple dialog, set the Amount to 60% and the size to Large, as shown in Figure 8-7. Click OK. The Ripple filter twists and turns the lines in the image, making it seem more impressionistic and less like a straight-up photograph, as shown in Figure 8-8.

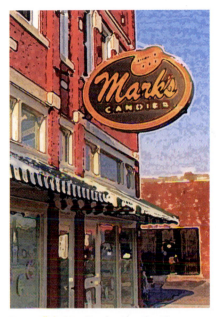

Figure 8-6: Dry Brush gives the photo a hand-painted look.

Figure 8-5: Apply the Dry Brush filter.

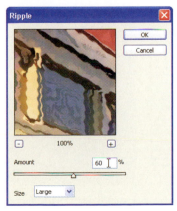

Figure 8-7: The Ripple filter

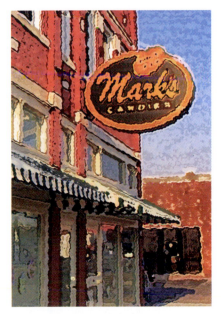

Figure 8-8: The rippled photo

Select color here or here

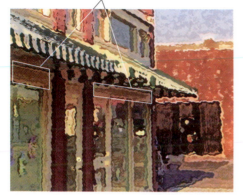

Figure 8-9: Click here to select the icky green.

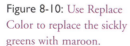

Figure 8-10: Use Replace Color to replace the sickly greens with maroon.

Replace Color

Looking at the picture so far, I've decided that I'm not happy with the washed-out green tones. Time to replace them. From the menu, choose Enhance | Adjust Color | Replace Color. Click in the brown in the awning above the shop windows, as shown in Figure 8-9. Similar green tones throughout the image show up as white in the Replace Color preview, as shown in Figure 8-10. In the Replace Color dialog, set the Fuzziness to 50, the Hue to –40, and the Saturation to +40. The washed-out greens become deep maroons. Click OK.

You can repeat this process to alter any of the colors in the image to suit your tastes. Use SHIFT-click to select multiple colors to replace.

I like bright colors in my faux paintings, and these aren't bright enough to suit me. From the menu, choose Enhance | Adjust Color | Adjust Hue/Saturation. Drag the Saturation slider right to +50. The results are shown Figure 8-11.

Save your work.

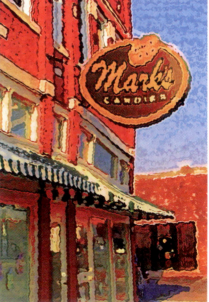

Figure 8-11: More deeply saturated colors

The main lines in the image are still pretty straight—too straight for my idea of an impressionist painting. To bend them a bit, choose Filter | Distort | Twirl from the menu. In the Twirl dialog, set the Angle to 12 degrees as shown in Figure 8-12, and click OK. This gives the long vertical lines a nice bend, as shown in Figure 8-13.

That's looking pretty good. Save your work. You can call it quits right here, if you want to.

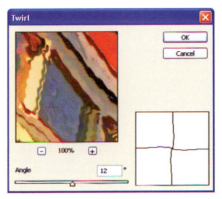

Figure 8-12: The Twirl filter

Final Levels and Crop

The results so far are just too dark for my tastes. I want a lighter, airier effect … something like a watercolor. To get it, I first go to the Levels dialog (Enhance | Adjust Lighting | Levels). Set the Input Levels to 0, 0.80, and 190, as shown in Figure 8-14. This brightens the image up overall. Now, set the Output Levels, at the bottom of the dialog, to 45 and 255. This gets rid of all the pure black and near black in the image. The darkest tones are now only 80% as dark as they were before. (Pure black is hard to come by in a watercolor, after all). Click OK.

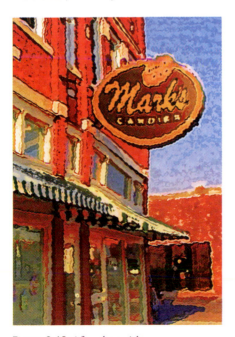

Figure 8-13: After the twirl

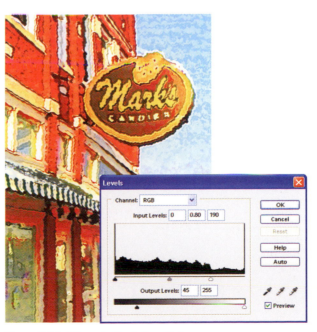

Figure 8-14: Adjust the levels for a lighter, brighter look.

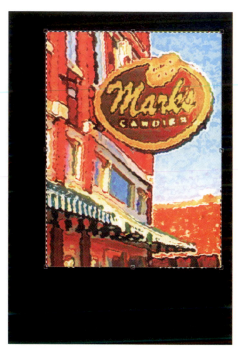

Figure 8-15: A final crop

Finally, I used the Crop tool to crop the image, as shown in Figure 8-15, to 700×950, to place more emphasis on the sign itself.

Save your work. You're done.

This project was inspired by some fine tutorials by Teresa Lunt (www.teresalunt.com). Thanks, Teresa!

Van Gogh Night Scene: Work with Filters

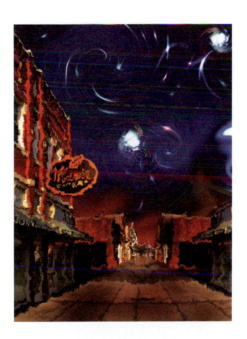

9

In This Project You Will:

☐ Use the Liquify filter to twirl the background

☐ Use the Smudge tool to simulate brush strokes

☐ Combine multiple photos into a single "painting"

☐ Duplicate and re-use elements

Like the previous project, this project emulates painting with a variety of filters, as well as some twirling, smudging, and burning. I've tried to capture a little something of the wild style of Vincent Van Gogh.

Figure 9-1: Starry-night.jpg

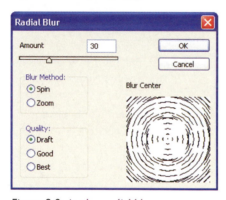

Figure 9-2: Apply a radial blur.

Get Started with Radial Blurs

Start by opening the nighttime sky photo starry-night.jpg (Figure 9-1). Save the document as starry-night.psd. Copy the Background layer to two new layers by choosing Layer | New | Layer via Copy from the menu, two times.

Let's get to swirling things. In the Layers palette, select the top-most of the three layers, and then choose Filter | Blur | Radial Blur from the menu. In the Radial Blur dialog, set the Amount to 30, Method to Spin, and Quality to Draft, as shown in Figure 9-2, and click OK. Set the layer to Lighten mode, allowing it to blend with the layer beneath, as shown in Figure 9-3.

Next, select the middle of the three layers in the Layers palette, and again choose Filter | Blur | Radial Blur. This time set the Method to Zoom. Leave the other settings and click OK. Set this layer's mode to Lighten, as well. The results are shown in Figure 9-4.

Combine the three layers by choosing Layer | Flatten Image from the menu.

To make the sky look more painterly and impressionistic, choose Enhance | Adjust Color | Adjust Hue/Saturation. Increase the Saturation to +75, as shown in Figure 9-5, and click OK.

Figure 9-3: Blending the layers together

Figure 9-4: Both blurs show through.

Increase the sky's contrast by choosing Enhance | Adjust Lighting | Levels. Find the three triangular sliders—black, gray, and white—as shown in Figure 9-6. Drag the black slider to the left, until the first input level

Figure 9-5: Crank up the color.

reads 15, as shown. This darkens the darkest shadows. Next, drag the gray slider left to 1.20 to brighten the image overall. Finally, drag the white slider to the left to 200 to brighten the very brightest areas. Click OK.

Smudge the Stars

Select the Smudge brush from the Toolbox. In the Options palette, select a soft, round, 27-pixel brush. Set the tool's Mode to Lighten and its Strength to 30%.

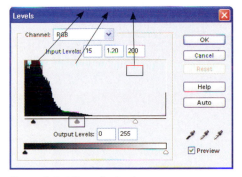

Figure 9-6: Adjust the levels.

Zoom in on a part of the sky. Click on a star and drag out, from the center, multiple times as shown in Figure 9-7, to create big, bright stars. Make them pointy, or swirly, or blobby—whatever appeals to you.

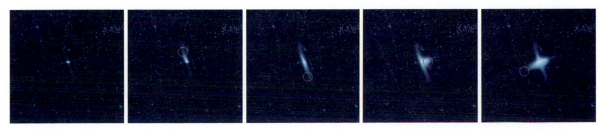

Figure 9-7: Blurring a star

Twirl clockwise

Twirl
counterclockwise

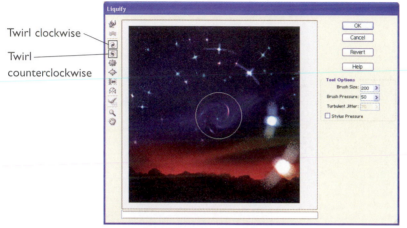

Figure 9-8: Twirling the sky

When you're happy with your smudged stars, choose Distort | Liquify from the menu. Select the Clockwise Twirl tool and set the brush size to 200 pixels, as shown in Figure 9-8. Click and drag on the image to produce rippling distortions. Click and hold for a few seconds to twirl a circular area into a spiral.

Alternate between the Clockwise Twirl and Counterclockwise Twirl tools to twist different areas of the sky in different directions. When you're satisfied, click OK to apply the filter. My results are shown in Figure 9-9.

Foreground Buildings

Time to put some buildings in front of that sky. Open the file downtown.jpg. Select the entire image (Select | All) and copy it to the clipboard (Edit | Copy). Close the downtown.jpg document and return to the starry-night document. Paste the downtown photo on a new layer (Edit | Paste).

Figure 9-9: Impressionistic stars

Make sure Snap to Grid is enabled (View | Snap to Grid). Select the Move tool from the Toolbox. Hold down the SHIFT key and slide the photo to the left until it snaps up against the left edge of the canvas, as shown in Figure 9-10. In the Layers palette, rename the new layer Buildings.

Figure 9-10: Add the foreground photo.

Let's erase that blue sky. Select the Magic Eraser tool
from the Toolbox. In the Options bar, set the tool's
Tolerance to 32. Select Anti-aliased and Contiguous.
Make sure Use All Layers is not selected. Click repeatedly
within the sky to delete large chunks of it, as shown in
Figure 9-11.

Select the Polygonal Lasso tool from the Toolbox and
use it to select the lamppost at the right of the photo, as
shown in Figure 9-12. Press DELETE to delete it. Remove
the selection by choosing Select | Deselect.

Copy the Buildings layer (Layer | New | Layer via Copy).
From the menu, choose Image | Rotate | Flip Layer
Horizontal (*not* Flip Horizontal) to flip the new layer
over. Use the Move tool to position the new layer as
shown in Figure 9-13.

Use the Polygonal Lasso tool to select the top of the
building on the right, as shown in Figure 9-14, and delete
it. Remove the selection (Select | Deselect).

Figure 9-11: Magically erasing the sky

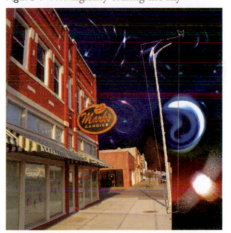

Figure 9-12: Remove the lamppost.

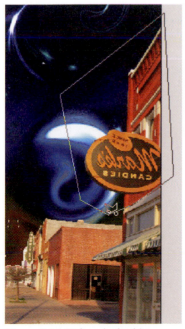

Figure 9-14: Delete the building top.

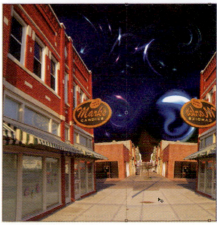

Figure 9-13: Copy the buildings.

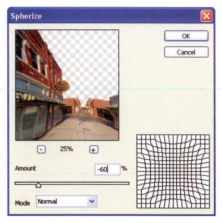

Figure 9-15: Spherize

Figure 9-16: Spatter strokes applied

Figure 9-17 Increased contrast

Combine the two building layers by choosing Layer | Merge Down from the menu.

Next, choose Select | All, followed by Image | Crop. Use Select | Deselect to remove the outline. This doesn't seem to do anything, but in fact, it trims off all the extra parts of the building that remain hidden outside of the canvas.

Now to make the daytime photograph look like a nighttime painting. Begin by distorting things with the Spherize Filter (Filter | Distort | Spherize). In the Spherize dialog, set the Amount to about –60%, as shown in Figure 9-15.

To emulate the look of brush strokes, select Filter | Brush Strokes | Spatter. In the Spatter dialog, set the Spray Radius to 22, and the Smoothness to 15. Click OK, and you should see something like Figure 9-16.

The buildings still don't match our sky. To fix them, choose Enhance | Adjust Lighting | Levels. Set the input levels to 30, 0.60, 220, and click OK. This darkens the shadows and midtones, while brightening the brightest parts of the image, as shown in Figure 9-17.

Select the Burn tool and, in the Options bar, choose a soft, round, 35-pixel brush. Set the tool's Range to Midtones and its Exposure to 30%. Use the brush to darken the bright orange buildings near the center of the image, as shown in Figure 9-18, and any other areas that are too bright to suit you.

Figure 9-18: Burn the buildings, before and after

Move the Stars

You may want to reposition the background sky at this point, to display it for better effect between the buildings. In the Layers palette, select the Background layer and duplicate it (Layer | New | Layer via Copy). Use the Move tool to reposition the new Background copy layer into a more pleasing position between the buildings to better show off your favorite swirls.

Flatten the image by choosing (Layer | Flatten Image).

Time to crop the image a bit. Let's use the Canvas Size command to do it. From the menu, choose Image | Resize | Canvas Size. In the Canvas Size dialog, be sure Relative is unchecked and select Pixels from the units drop-down list. Enter a width of 600 pixels and a height of 800 pixels. Select the right-center anchor point, as shown in Figure 9-19. This tells Elements to keep the right side of the picture and trim off the left. Click OK. Elements warns you that you're about to clip off some of your image. Click Proceed to crop the image, as shown in Figure 9-20.

This would be a good time to save your work.

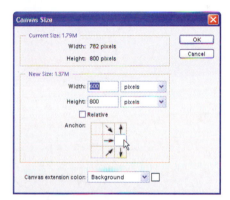

Figure 9-19: Crop using Canvas Size.

Figure 9-20: The picture so far

Finish Up

Return to the Liquify filter (Filter | Distort | Liquify). Use a 90-pixel brush with the Clockwise Twirl tool to twist the store sign into an unrecognizable shape, as shown in Figure 9-21. Click OK to apply the filter.

Now, select the Dodge tool. In the Options bar, select a soft, round, 65-pixel brush. Set the tool's Range to Midtones and its Exposure to 30%. Paint on the sign with the Dodge tool to brighten it up, as shown in Figure 9-22.

Use the Burn tool to clean up any areas that are still too light.

Save your work.

Figure 9-21: Twirl the sign.

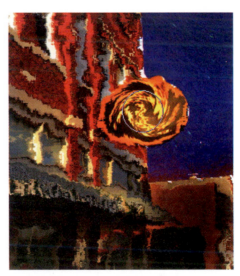

Figure 9-22: Dodge the sign.

Painting Lilacs: Create a Painting from Your Photo

10

In This Project You Will:

☐ Use the Smudge tool to emulate a paintbrush

☐ Use Replace Color to replace background colors

☐ Apply a texture to an image

With Photoshop Elements, you can turn any photo, even a blurry one, into a unique digital painting. Rather than resorting to filters and distortions, as did the previous project, here you'll be responsible for painting in every single brush stroke by hand. Don't worry; it's easier than it sounds.

Start with a Snapshot

I started with the rather blah and mostly out of focus picture of a lilac bush shown in Figure 10-1. (For this project, it doesn't matter if your starting photograph is a little blurry.) I found a small, acceptably interesting area near the top, as shown in Figure 10-2, and cropped the rest out. I resized the resulting, cropped photo back up to 1024×768.

Figure 10-1: A lilac bush

> **Note**
>
> Whenever possible, shoot at the highest resolution and quality settings your camera has. I took the photo which forms the basis for this project at 2592×1944, the maximum resolution for my camera. That allowed me to crop it pretty severely and still end up with a useable image.

Your Friend, the Smudge Tool

This project is done almost entirely with a single tool: the Smudge tool.

Open the photo lilacs.jpg and save it as lilacs.psd. Use the Zoom tool to zoom in on the petal in the upper right of the photo, as shown in Figures 10-3 and 10-4.

Figure 10-2: My initial crop

Figure 10-3: Zoom in on this petal.

Figure 10-4: Zoomed in and ready to work

Grab the Smudge tool from the Toolbox. In the Options bar, choose a soft, round, 35-pixel brush. Set the tool's Strength to 30%.

Click and drag along the top edge of the petal, as shown in Figure 10-5. The pixels smear to follow your brush stroke, as though you were dragging your finger through wet paint. Repeat the process along the bottom edge of the petal. You might have to make multiple strokes; the effect of Smudge tool fades as you drag.

Click and drag within the petal, as shown in Figure 10-6, to paint over those pixels. There is no one right way to do this. There are an infinite number of perfectly acceptable ways to smudge the same small area. Figure 10-7 shows two of them. It's up to you and your own style and tastes.

Figure 10-5: How to smudge

Figure 10-6: Paint the petal with the Smudge tool.

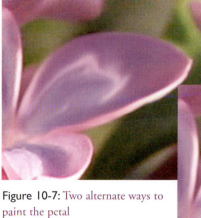

Figure 10-7: Two alternate ways to paint the petal

Figure 10-8: If you stroke this way multiple times, the effect becomes more pronounced.

I hate to admit it, but that's basically the whole technique. Still, there are a few things to keep in mind.

First, smudging drags colors from the beginning of the stroke toward the end of the stroke. So if you start your stroke in a dark area and pull into a light area, you'll pull darkness into the light. If you pull the other way, you'll pull light into the darkness.

Next, repeating the same stroke over the same area multiple times will drag progressively more "paint" along the area covered by those strokes, as shown in Figures 10-8 and 10-9.

Move closer to the center . . .   closer . . .   and closer.

Figure 10-9: Multiple strokes: one stroke, five strokes, eight strokes

That, my friends, is about all there is to it. Lather, rinse, repeat. You're painting with pixels. I think of this method as a cross between tracing and paint by numbers. Go over every single pixel in the photo, smudging it in whatever way seems best to you. In places where a 35-pixel brush seems too large (or too small) for the job at hand, change its size in the Options bar.

Don't forget to save your work from time to time.

This method is simple but it can take you a while. That's okay. There's no rush. You're painting. Relax and enjoy the process. You can't get this project wrong. Your colors come from the pixels in the photograph, so you know you're going to get them right.

Now, admittedly, you can achieve painterly effects with some of Elements' filters with a lot less time and effort. But I like doing it this way. It's personal. No two people will achieve the same results from the same photo. When I'm done, I feel like I've actually created a painting.

Figure 10-10 shows the way the painting progressed when I did it, but yours may look very different.

Figure 10-10: The progression of my painting

New Background Colors

If there's one thing that's bothering me about the painting so far, it's all those blobs of green in the background (actually, blurry leaves). There's nothing wrong with the color green, especially in a painting of flowers. But in this case, I feel that it contrasts too strongly with the lilac color, which should be the focus of the picture. Let's change it.

From the menu choose Enhance | Adjust Color | Replace Color. In the Replace Color dialog, click on a green leaf to sample some of the background green, as shown in Figure 10-11. Set the Fuzziness to 150 to select a wide range of greens and yellows. Drag Hue to −50 to push the selected colors further into the red. Drag the Saturation slider left to −50, and drag the Lightness slider right to 30. Don't click OK yet.

Setting Saturation to −50 washes out the selected colors. This makes the foreground colors stand out all the more strongly. That's one way to go.

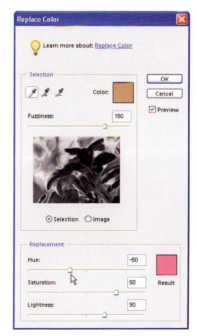

Figure 10-11: Replace the background colors.

Now, drag the Saturation slider to the right, to +50. This has the opposite effect, making the background colors bolder and brighter. For me, this works too. The background greens have been transformed to complement the foreground lilacs, rather than fighting with them.

So … minus 50 or plus 50? It's your choice. Choose whichever works best for you, and click OK. My results are shown in Figure 10-12.

Figure 10-12: After color replacement

If the previous steps have created any funky lines where the background meets the foreground, pick your Smudge tool again and paint them out. Save your work.

Painting on a Canvas

You can call it done at this point, but if you'd like to make it look just a bit more like a traditional painting, you can add a nice canvas texture.

Figure 10-13: Using Texturizer

From the menu choose Filter | Texture | Texturizer. Choose Canvas from the Texture drop-down list at the right side of the Texturizer dialog. Set the Scaling to 100%, the Relief to 2, and the Light to Top Left, as shown in Figure 10-13. The higher the Relief setting, the more conspicuous the canvas texture will be. You can preview the results at the left side of the Texturizer dialog and try adding in more or less relief, and moving the light around.

When you're satisfied, click OK to apply the texture.

That's it; you're done. Save your work.

To give you an alternate take on this project, Figure 10-14 shows another painting, which I made from a different section of the original photograph.

Figure 10-14: An alternate painting

Can You Sepia Me? Use Layer Effects to Age a Photo

11

In This Project You Will:

☐ Use blending modes to add blemishes

☐ Create scratches and splotches with the Brush tool

☐ Incorporate multiple scanned elements into a composition

Photoshop Elements is a great tool for making bad photos look good, but it's even more fun to make good photos look bad. I love adding tears and scratches and blotches and blemishes, making a new photo look old.

Mount It with a Border

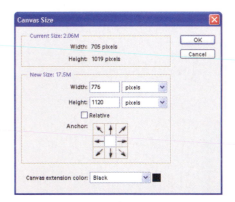

Figure 11-1: Increase the canvas size.

Begin by opening the photo hiker.jpg or one of your own photos. Copy the Background to a new layer by choosing Layer | New | Layer via Copy from the menu. In the Layers palette, rename the new layer to Photograph.

Next, create a border around the photograph by resizing the canvas. From the menu choose Image | Resize | Canvas Size. Select Pixels from the units drop-down list, and size the canvas to 776 pixels wide by 1120 pixels tall, as shown in Figure 11-1. Set the Canvas Extension Color to Black, then click OK to create a black border.

Save the document as sepiatone.psd.

In the Layers palette, select the Background layer. Fill the Background with black, by choosing Edit | Fill Layer. Set the Contents to Black and click OK.

Now your photograph is mounted above a black background, as shown in Figure 11-2. We're going to be tearing off some edges later on, and the black will show through.

Figure 11-2: A black border

Adjust Levels

The original photo is a little flat. Let's bump up the contrast. Select the Photograph layer. From the menu choose Enhance | Adjust Lighting | Levels. Set the input levels to 15, 1.00, 215, as shown in Figure 11-3. This makes the dark tones darker and the light tones lighter, increasing the overall contrast, as shown in Figure 11-4. Click OK.

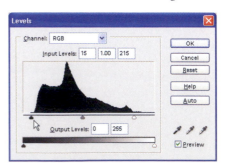

Figure 11-3: Levels

Make It Sepia

The first thing that tells us that this isn't really an old-time photograph is the color. Time to get rid of that. From the menu choose Layer | New Adjustment Layer | Hue/Saturation. Check Colorize, then drag the Hue slider to the left, to about 35. Set Saturation to 50, and Lightness to 0, as shown in Figure 11-5, and click OK. This removes all the colors from the photo and replaces them with a light brown, as shown in Figure 11-6.

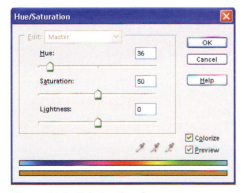

Figure 11-5: Colorize the photo.

You could have adjusted the photo's hue and saturation directly, rather than creating an adjustment layer. Heck, Elements even provides a Sepia tone layer style. But an adjustment layer lets you slip additional elements in later on, and they'll all take on the same hue automatically.

Save your work. If you want, you can quit here, but you'll be missing the really fun parts.

Figure 11-4: An improved photo

Figure 11-6: Now it's sepia toned.

Figure 11-7: A torn edge

Tear It Up

Next, let's age the photo by adding a torn edge to it. I scanned in the edge of an old, crumpled photo, seen in Figure 11-7. Open that scan (torn-edge.jpg), or scan in your own ratty edge.

Choose Select | All, then Edit | Copy to copy the scan to the clipboard. Close the torn-edge.jpg document and return to your sepiatone.psd document. In the Layers palette, select the Photograph layer, then choose Edit | Paste to paste the torn edge onto a new layer above the Photograph layer.

Choose the Magic Eraser tool from the Toolbox. In the Options bar, set the Tolerance to 24, and check Anti-aliased and Contiguous. When you click with the Magic Eraser tool, Elements deletes all pixels of similar color surrounding your click. Click on the large white area to delete it. Click the areas to the left of the torn edge to delete them, as shown in Figure 11-8. If necessary, select the Eraser tool and use a small, hard brush to erase any remaining bits and pieces. You should wind up with something like Figure 11-9.

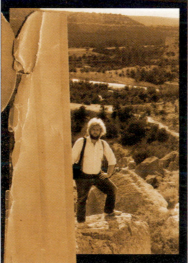

Figure 11-8: Delete the background with the Magic Eraser tool.

From the menu choose Enhance | Adjust Color | Remove Color to remove any color from your torn edge. In the Layers palette, rename the new layer to Torn Edge and set its blending mode to Overlay. Overlay mode increases the contrast of the underlying photo layer. It should look like Figure 11-10.

From the menu choose Layer | New | Layer via Copy to duplicate the Torn Edge layer. In the Layers palette, set the new, Torn Edge copy layer to Multiply mode and reduce its opacity to about 60%. Multiply uses the new Torn Edge copy layer to darken the underlying layers. Your document now consists of five layers, as shown in Figure 11-11.

Now is a good time to save your work.

Figure 11-10: Set the torn edge to Overlay mode.

Figure 11-9: The trimmed, torn edge

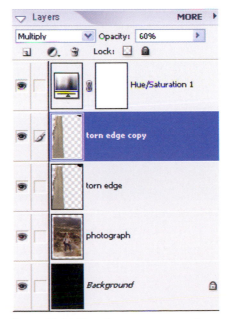

Figure 11-11: Your document now consists of five layers.

Create a Border

You've probably noticed that the photograph still extends beyond the torn edges, which somewhat ruins the effect. Time to fix that. In the Layers palette, select the topmost layer—the Hue/Saturation adjustment layer. From the menu choose Layer | New | Layer. Name the new layer Black Border and click OK. Fill the new Black Border layer with black by choosing Edit | Fill Layer and selecting Black for the Contents. Click OK. This turns everything black, but not to worry.

Now to reveal the photo beneath. We'll start with the area under the torn edge. In the Layers palette, CTRL-click (CMD-click on the Macintosh) on the Torn Edge layer's thumbnail. This selects all the filled pixels in the Torn Edge layer, as shown in Figure 11-12, while leaving the Black Border layer active. Press DELETE to delete the selected pixels and reveal the ravaged portions of the photo beneath, as shown in Figure 11-13.

Figure 11-12: Initial selection

Figure 11-13: The initial selection deleted

From the menu choose View | Fit on Screen, so that you can see around the edges.

In the Layers palette, with the Black Border layer still selected, CTRL-click or CMD-click on the Photograph layer's thumbnail to select that layer's contents.

Select the Rectangular Marquee tool from the Toolbox. ALT-click or OPTION-click beyond the upper-left corner of the canvas and drag to deselect everything left of the tattered edge, as shown in Figure 11-14. Holding the ALT key causes the tool to subtract from the current selection, rather than beginning a new selection.

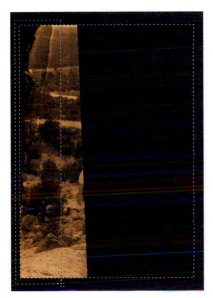

Figure 11-14: Select the area over the photo.

Press DELETE to remove the remaining selected pixels, then choose Select | Deselect.

From the Toolbox, select the Magic Wand tool. In the Options bar, set the Tolerance to 2, and check Anti-aliased, Contiguous, and Use All Layers. Click within the black border somewhere to select it. From the menu choose Edit | Fill Selection and select Black as the Contents. Click OK, then choose Select | Deselect from the menu. The image looks the same as it did before, but now the Black Border layer is a complete black border. Before, there was a missing chunk, although you couldn't see it, as shown in Figure 11-15.

Figure 11-15: The Black Border layer before and after the fill

Notice in the Layers palette that the black border is the topmost layer. This way, it will hide any elements on underlying layers that go beyond the edge of the photo.

Save your work.

Let's fade the photograph around the edges. In the Layers palette, select the top-most torn edge layer, Torn Edge copy. Create a new layer above this by choosing Layer | New | Layer. Name the new layer Border Glow and click OK.

CTRL-click or CMD-click on the Photograph layer's thumbnail to select its contents, but do not select the Photograph layer.

Convert the selection to a border by choosing Select | Modify | Border. In the Border Selection dialog, enter a value of 20 pixels and click OK. Fill the selection with white by choosing Edit | Fill Selection and choosing White from the Contents drop-down list. Click OK.

Remove the selection (Select | Deselect). In the Layers palette, reduce the Border Glow layer's opacity to 50%.

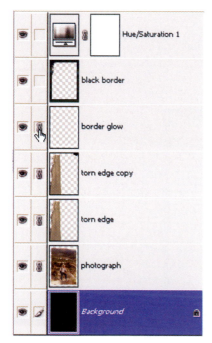

Figure 11-16: Link layers together.

You're getting a goodly number of layers. Let's combine a few of them now. In the Layers palette, select the Background layer. Link the Background layer to the Photograph, Torn Edge, Torn Edge copy, and Border Glow layers by turning on the chain link icon in each layer, as shown in Figure 11-16. Leave the Hue/Saturation adjustment layer and the Black Border layer unlinked.

From the menu choose Layer | Merge Linked. The five linked layers are combined into a new Background layer which looks exactly the same. (Merged layers always inherit the name of the bottommost layer.)

Add Blotches and Scratches

In the Layers palette, select the Background layer, then choose Layer | New | Layer. Name the new layer Clouds, set to Screen mode, and click OK. Fill the new Clouds layer with black by choosing Edit | Fill Layer and choosing Black from the Contents drop-down list. Then click OK.

Set the Foreground color to brown (165,95,20) and the Background color to black (0,0,0). From the menu choose Filter | Render | Difference Clouds. Repeat the Difference Clouds filter a second time. These dark brown clouds lighten the underlying image slightly at random.

From the menu, choose Layer | Merge Down to merge the Clouds layer with the Background.

Finally, an old photo needs a scratch or two. In the Layers palette, select the Background layer, then create a new layer above it (Layer | New | Layer). Name the new layer Scratches, set it in Screen mode, and click OK. Fill the Scratches layer with black (Edit | Fill Layer, Contents: Use Black).

To draw the scratches, select the Brush tool from the Toolbox. In the Options bar, select a hard, round, 1-pixel brush. Set the Foreground Color to white, and use a series of rapid strokes to draw long and short scratches across the photo. Scratches often come in groups, so make numbers of scratches that all go the same direction, in the same general area. Imagine turning the photo face down on a rough surface and dragging it. Don't scribble back and forth or in circles or you'll get unrealistic results.

When you're done, reduce the Scratches layer's opacity to 20–30% in the Layers palette, then merge it into the background (Layer | Merge Down).

Flatten the image (Layer | Flatten Image) and save your work.

With the Background layer still selected, create a new layer (Layer | New | Layer). Name it Blemishes and set it in Overlay mode. Select the Brush tool and choose a soft, round, 45-pixel brush. Set the tool's opacity to 30% in the Options bar.

Set the Foreground color to black (0,0,0) and paint over some lighter parts of the photo, as shown in Figure 11-17.

Figure 11-17: Paint with black over light areas.

Change the Foreground color to dark orange (255,175,0) and paint over a few dark areas, as shown in Figure 11-18. When you're done, reduce the Blemishes layer's opacity to 40–50%.

Flatten the image and save your work.

I used a hard, round, 13-pixel brush at 100% opacity and black to paint out the topmost edge of the photo on the Black Border layer, making it seem even more torn.

Figure 11-18: Paint with orange over dark areas.

Fast Photo Retouching: Turn a Snapshot into a Portrait

In This Project You Will:

- ☐ Crop a photo via copy-and-paste

- ☐ Combine blend modes to create a glowing complexion

- ☐ Use the Spot Healing Brush to remove facial blemishes

With Photoshop Elements, it's surprisingly easy to turn a mundane snapshot into a "glamour photo." In fact, you can obtain surprisingly good results from decidedly mediocre snapshots. (It's even easier if you start with a decent photo.)

Getting Started

Figure 12-1: A snapshot of Kerry

Start by opening the file kerry-original.jpg (Figure 12-1) or your own potential glamour photo. As promised, this is a pretty mediocre snapshop.

The first step would usually be to rotate and crop the photo, but this time I'm taking a different tack. Let's say I know that I want to end up with a portrait, 625 pixels wide by 750 pixels tall. Rather than crop the original photo to those dimensions, let's create a new file of the appropriate size, and then copy and paste the original photo into it. Choose Select | Select All to select the entire photo, and copy the photo to the clipboard (Edit | Copy).

From the menu choose File | New | Blank File. Set width to 625 pixels and height to 750 pixels. Make sure Color Mode is set to RGB Color, and click OK to create the new file. Save the document as glamour.psd.

Now choose Edit | Paste to add the photo as a new layer in the Glamour document. Don't worry that part of it is "off screen." In the Layers palette, name the new layer Face.

The basic color balance and lighting is acceptable—on the face, at least, which is all we're concerned about in this project.

Rotate

Time to rotate Kerry into a more or less vertical orientation. Elements' automatic Straighten Image command is unlikely to give you good results in a case like this; there aren't enough clues for the software to work with. You'll have to do it manually.

Turn on the grid (View | Grid), so you can better see what you're doing. Select the Move tool from the Toolbox. Handles appear at the sides and corners of the photo. Click just outside of one of the corner handles and rotate the image counterclockwise until the face is more or less vertical. You can see the exact amount in the Rotation Angle box that appears in the Options bar as soon as you begin to rotate the image. I rotated it about –9.5 degrees, as shown in

Figure 12-2. You can also just type –9.5 directly in the Rotation Angle box. When you have the correct angle, press ENTER (RETURN on a Macintosh) to accept the change. Then hide the grid (View | Grid).

Click and drag on the photo to move it to the left, as shown in Figure 12-3. Kerry's left eye should be more or less centered, horizontally.

I often prefer this method—creating a new file and copying and pasting a photo into it—to just cropping the original photo. I find it easier to see just what the final composition will look like.

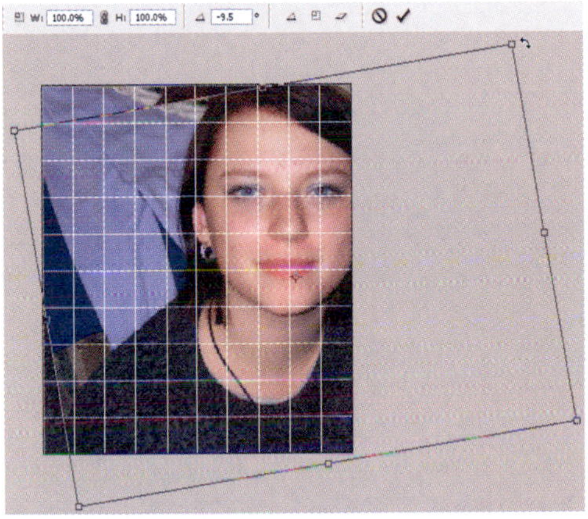

Hair Extensions

You'll notice that the top of Kerry's head is chopped off in this photo. We'll have to do something about that.

First, click the eye icon for the Background layer in the Layers palette, hiding it, as shown in Figure 12-4. Select the Polygonal Lasso tool from the Toolbox. I found some hair on the left side of her head with some nice shiny bits in it that seem to be going more or less the right direction. With the Polygonal Lasso tool, click multiple times to select a good-sized chunk of this hair, as shown in Figure 12-5. Select Layer | New | Layer via Copy to copy the selected hair to a new layer.

Figure 12-2: Rotate to vertical.

Figure 12-3: Move to a better position.

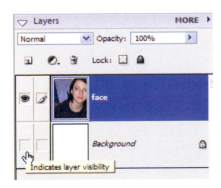

Figure 12-4: Hide the background layer.

Figure 12-5: Select some hair.

Figure 12-6: Position the hair.

Figure 12-7: Erase extra hair for a better fit.

Choose the Move tool from the Toolbox. Move the hair extension up toward the missing chunk of Kerry's head, as shown in Figure 12-6. Click and drag outside of one of the corner handles and rotate it slightly to better fit the curve of her head. Press ENTER when you have the piece in position.

Grab the Eraser tool from the Toolbox. In the Options bar, choose a soft, round, 13-pixel brush. Reduce the brush's opacity to 35%. Now erase around the outside of the head to match the outline that would be there if the photographer had actually captured the entire head. Erase around the forehead to let the original hairline show through. Erase anywhere the new extension doesn't quite fit in with the existing hair, as shown in Figure 12-7, leaving just enough to fill in the curve of the head.

Repeat the process with a chunk of hair from the other side of Kerry's head, as shown in Figure 12-8. Be sure to return to the Face layer to copy the pixels of hair. When you're satisfied with the results, click on the Face layer and select Layer | Merge Visible. Then save your work.

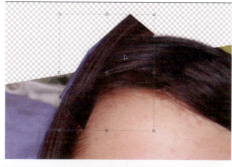

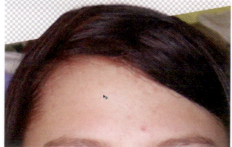

Figure 12-8: Select more hair, position it, and erase a bit for a smooth blend.

Select the Eraser tool
from the Toolbox. In
the Options bar, select
a hard, round, 19-pixel
brush and set the opac-
ity to 100%. Use the
Eraser to carefully erase
around the outside
of Kerry, as shown
in Figure 12-9. Then
increase the brush size
to 100 pixels and erase
the rest of the back-
ground (Figure 12-10).

Figure 12-9: Erase a line around Kerry.

Figure 12-10: Erase the rest of the background.

Blur, Blur, Blur Those Blemishes Away

Click the Face layer in the Layers palette to select it. From the menu, choose Layer
| New | Layer via Copy. Name the new layer Blur, and click OK. In the Layers pal-
ette, lock the new layer's transparent pixels, as shown in Figure 12-11. Blur the new
layer by choosing Filter | Blur | Gaussian Blur and applying a setting of 4.5 pixels,
as shown in Figure 12-12.

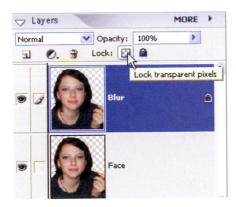

Figure 12-11: Lock transparent pixels.

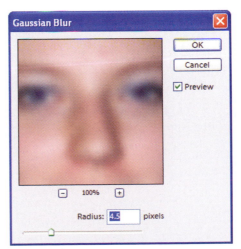

Figure 12-12: Gaussian Blur

Figure 12-13: Slightly blurry

Locking the layer before the blur keeps the filter from blurring beyond the outline of Kerry's head. Unlock the layer's transparent pixels again.

The results are shown in Figure 12-13. I know, that looks terrible! But most of the facial blemishes and such have been erased in one easy go. The skin tone has been smoothed out. In fact, most of the human face looks okay if it's really blurry. There's not a lot of detail—at least not a lot of detail that we really want—in most areas. But some areas, such as the eyes, nose, mouth, ears, and hair, *need* detail. Let's restore it.

Select the Eraser tool from the Toolbox. Choose a soft, round, 13-pixel brush. In the Options bar, set the tool's opacity down to 30%.

Carefully erase around the eyes, nose, mouth, ears and hair. You'll need to use several strokes to completely erase an area, but this gives you the ability to partially erase areas and more seamlessly blend blurred and non-blurred areas. Repeatedly turn the blur layer's visibility on and off (by clicking its eye icon in the Layers palette) to check the results. If you go too far, choose Edit | Undo Eraser a few times and try again.

For softer details like laugh lines, wrinkles, and dimples, set the Eraser to about 20% opacity. Erase around these areas until they show enough detail to suit you but not too much in the way of blemishes.

Keep turning the new layer's visibility on and off. Is anything important disappearing, such as part of an eye or a dimple? Erase that part of the blurred image.

When you're happy with the face, increase the Eraser's opacity to 100% and erase the blurred layer over Kerry's hand and sweater.

When you're finished, choose Layer | Merge Down from the menu to merge the two face layers together.

Zoom way in and examine the places where the blurred and non-blurred areas meet. If the transition is too obvious, select the Blur tool, and reduce its Strength to 20% in the Options bar. Paint with a soft, round brush to smooth out the transitions.

No More Zits

There are still a few blemishes visible, but they are a snap to fix using Elements' Spot Healing Brush tool. Select the Zoom tool and zoom in to 300% or so. Find the blemish below Kerry's lip, shown in Figure 12-14. Select the Spot Healing Brush, and choose a hard, round, 13-pixel brush in the Options bar. Brush around the blemish, as shown in Figure 12-15 and, voila! The zit is gone. Repeat the process for any other blemishes that catch your eye.

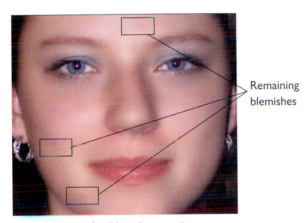

Figure 12-14: A few blemishes remain.

Remaining blemishes

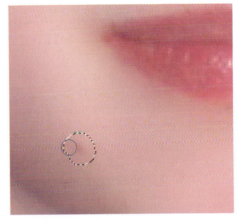

Figure 12-15: Painting over a blemish with the Spot Healing Brush

A Glowing Complexion

In the Layers palette, select the Face layer. Now choose Layer | New | Layer via Copy from the menu to duplicate the Face layer. Name the new layer Soft Light and set its Blending Mode to Soft Light. Placing an image on top of itself in Soft Light mode, as we've done here, makes the light parts lighter and the dark parts darker. It also creates a nice, glowing effect, as you can see in Figure 12-16.

If the effect is too strong and the face begins to look too plastic, reduce the Soft Light layer's opacity. Trust your eye—there's no science to it.

Figure 12-16: Soft light lends a lovely glow.

Figure 12-17: Restore the hair's highlights.

Soft Light mode tends to darken shadows, rendering the hair, already dark, as almost black. Select the Eraser tool and use a soft, round, 65-pixel brush to erase the hair from the Soft Light layer, returning some shine to it, as shown in Figure 12-17. When you're done, choose Layer | Merge Down from the menu to merge the two face layers.

Black Out the Background

In the Layers palette, select the Background layer. From the menu, choose Edit | Fill Layer. Set the Contents to black and click OK. That's looking pretty good. Time to save your work.

You may need to clean up around the edges, particularly around the hair, to eliminate parts of the original background that you haven't completely erased, as shown in Figure 12-18. Use the Eraser tool with a soft, round, 35-pixel brush on the Face layer to perform any necessary cleanup.

You can stop right there if you want—Kerry's looking pretty good. But if you'd like to take it further, follow me to the next project.

Remaining fringe

Figure 12-18: Erase any "fringe" of remaining background color around the head.

Glamour Photo: From Simple Portrait to Glamour Shot

13

In This Project You Will:

☐ Use Blend modes to add color to a photo

☐ Create a new layer from a selection

☐ Use the Dodge tool to remove shadows

☐ Use the Smudge tool to replace missing hair

This project builds on the previous project, making our family friend Kerry look even more glamorous. If you haven't completed that project yet, this might be a good time to do so. We'll wait right here.

Open Your Work thus Far

Start by opening the file glamour.psd, which you created in Project 12, or opening the file kerry-made-up.jpg. Save the document as glamour2.psd.

If the file has multiple layers, flatten it now by choosing Layer | Flatten Image from the menu.

Eyelashes

Let's start by making the eyelashes longer and fuller. Select the Smudge tool from the Toolbox. In the Options bar, select a hard, round, 1-pixel brush. Set the Strength to 50% and the Mode to Darken.

Zoom way, way in, as shown in Figure 13-1 and find an eyelash. Now drag outward following the line of the lash, as shown in Figure 13-2. Drag multiple times to get the length and thickness you want, and then repeat the process on the other lashes. Zoom back out from time to time to check your work in the context of the entire portrait. Don't go nuts—unless you want to! Figure 13-3 shows the before and after of the process.

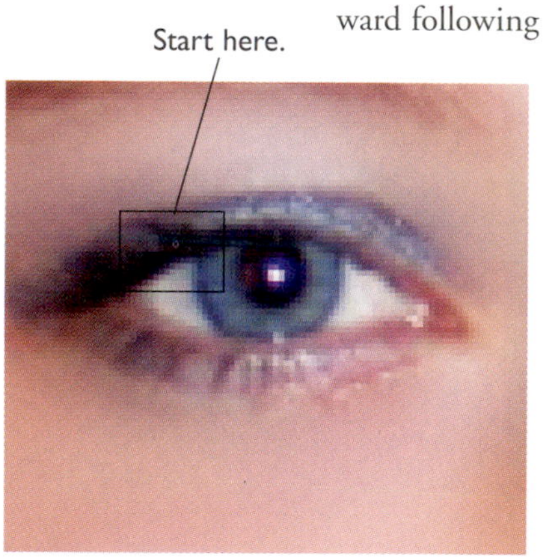

Start here.

Figure 13-1: Start the stroke here.

Drag this way.

Figure 13-2: Drag to here.

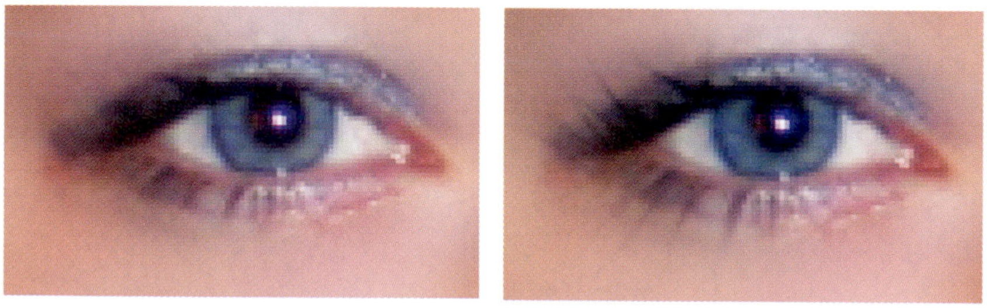

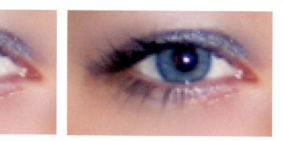

Figure 13-3: Eyelashes: before and after

Whitening Teeth

Kerry's teeth aren't showing in this photo, but if you're working on a photo with a visible smile, you'll often want to whiten the teeth. Open the file ember.jpg if you want to follow along with this part.

To whiten the teeth, select the Dodge tool. In the Options bar, set the Exposure to 10% and the Range to Midtones. Use a soft, round brush a little smaller than the individual teeth. Go over the teeth several times to gradually brighten them, as shown in Figure 13-4. Don't go too far—it'll look like they glow in the dark.

Now use the Sponge tool set to Desaturate and Flow at 50% to pull any yellow color out of the teeth, as shown in Figure 13-5. But not the gums and lips! The teeth will look brighter with shades of gray than with shades of yellow, even if you don't dodge them. Even subtle whitening makes a big difference, as shown in Figure 13-6.

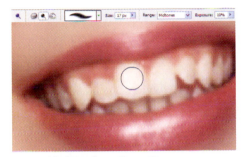

Figure 13-4: Brighten the teeth.

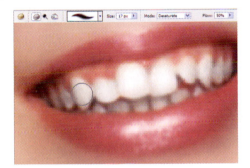

Figure 13-5: Sponge away any yellow.

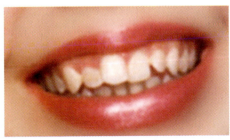 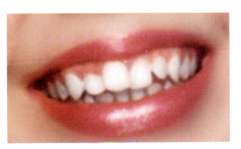

Figure 13-6: Teeth: before and after

Lips

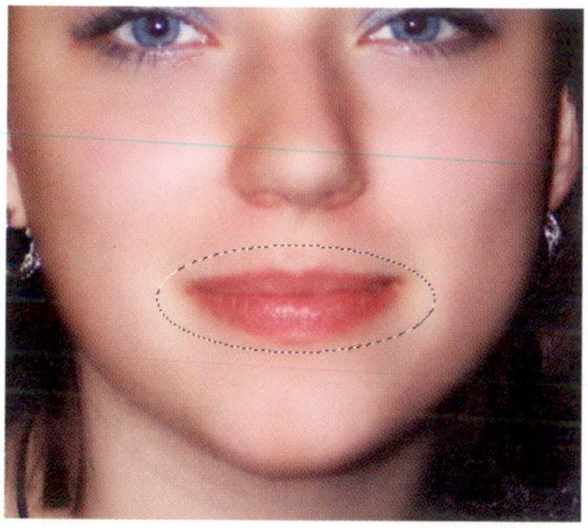

If you have taken the opportunity to practice whitening teeth, return now to the glamour2 document. Select the Elliptical Marquee tool from the Toolbox and click and drag to select the mouth, as shown in Figure 13-7. Don't worry if you get some of the surrounding face. From the menu, choose Layer | New | Layer via Copy to copy the selected mouth to its own layer. Name the new layer Lips. From the menu, choose Enhance | Adjust Color | Adjust Hue/Saturation. Turn the saturation up and try out different hues, as shown in Figure 13-8. This also colors the area surrounding the mouth, but we'll erase that in the next step.

When you're happy, click OK. (Remember, with an adjustment layer, you can go back and tweak it again later.)

In the Layers palette, click on the Lips layer. Select the Eraser tool and use a soft, 13-pixel brush to erase anywhere the new color bleeds into the skin or teeth, as shown in Figure 13-9. Adjust the opacity of the adjustment layer to lessen the effect and aid the blend. When you're satisfied, save your work.

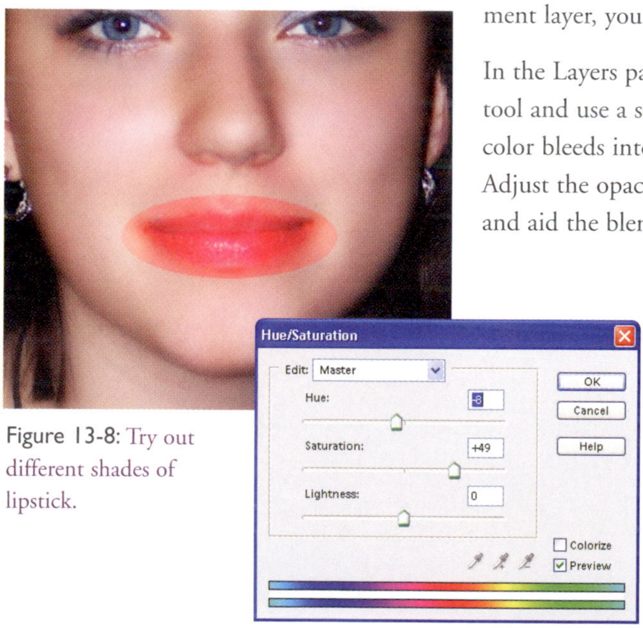

Figure 13-7: Select the lips.

Figure 13-8: Try out different shades of lipstick.

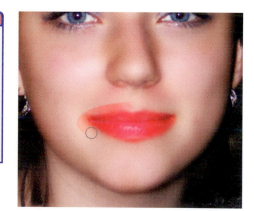

Figure 13-9: Erase the extra color.

Eyelids

There are many ways to selectively add color to parts of an image. Let's use a different one to bump up Kerry's eye shadow.

Select the Background layer. Choose Layer | New | Layer from the menu. Name the new layer Eye Shadow, set it to Color mode, and click OK.

Figure 13-10: Paint in some eye shadow.

Set the Foreground color to a nice blue (don't worry too much about the color right now). Select the Brush tool from the Toolbox. In the Options bar, select a soft, round, 13-pixel brush. Set the opacity down to 10%, and click on the Airbrush button. Zoom in on the eyes, and use the Brush tool to paint in eye shadow, as shown in Figure 13-10. Use multiple strokes to build up the color and blend it into the rest of the face. Move over to the other eye and repeat the process. Remember: the eyes should match each other. That's more important than having the color right at this point.

With the eye shadow in place, choose Enhance | Adjust Color | Adjust Hue/Saturation to bring up the Hue/Saturation dialog. Drag the Hue slider back and forth to try out different colors of eye shadow. Try turning the Saturation and Lightness up and down, too. When you're happy, click OK.

If the effect is too severe, reduce the opacity of the Eye Shadow layer to suit. Then save your work.

In case you're wondering, yes, you could use this technique for lips, as well. You can also use this technique to enhance or change the color of eyes, as shown in Figure 13-11.

Figure 13-11: Even change eye color.

Create New Hair

Sometimes it's almost impossible to cut out a background behind a person's hair without creating unnaturally flat areas—places that look obviously cut out. With Kerry's dark hair against a black background, this problem is minimized, but with other photos this can be a big problem.

It's easier to see what I mean on a photo with dark hair against a light background, such as the photo of Ember in Figure 13-12, but this technique will work on Kerry's photo, too. To create new hair, use the Smudge tool with a 1-pixel brush, in Darken mode, at 75% Strength. Swirl it around the edges of the hair to create new strands of hair and soften the bad transition. Try some more strokes with a 2-pixel brush at 45% opacity. (If the hair is darker than the background, set the Smudge tool to Lighten, rather than Darken, mode.)

Figure 13-12: Create new hair.

When you're happy with your hairdo, choose Layer | Flatten Image from the menu.

Fixing the Lighting with Levels

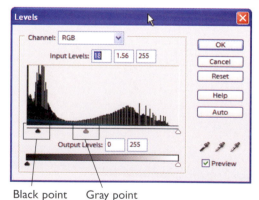

Black point slider   Gray point slider

Figure 13-13: Adjust levels to lighten the face.

Kerry's face has gotten a little dark in places, a result of the Soft Light layer applied earlier. To fix it, choose Enhance | Enhance Lighting | Levels from the menu. Drag the gray point slider to the left to lighten up her face a bit, as shown in Figure 13-13. I wound up with a gray point of 1.56. Next, drag the black point slider to the right to about 18. This darkens the shadows a bit and increases the contrast. Click OK.

You should have something resembling Figure 13-14.

New Neckline

Kerry's T-shirt/sweater combo doesn't bespeak glamour. Let's lose it.

Set the Foreground color to black (0,0,0). Select the Brush tool, and in the Options bar select a soft, round, 9-pixel brush at 100% opacity. Follow along the lines of the black necklace cord on the left to create the beginnings of a neckline, as shown in Figure 13-15. Do the same along the edge of the gray T-shirt and dark sweater on the right. When the neckline's complete, use a larger brush to paint over the rest of the sweater and Kerry's hand.

Save your work. This photo's looking great (Figure 13-16).

Figure 13-14: The story so far

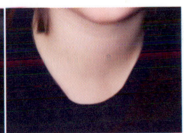

Figure 13-15: Use the brush to paint in a new neckline.

You can stop here if you want.

Figure 13-16: Looking good!

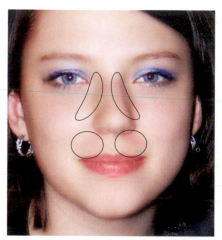

Figure 13-17: Areas to dodge

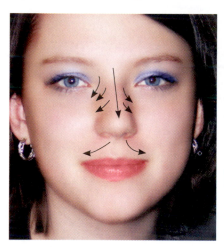

Figure 13-18: Direction to dodge

Shadows and Twinkles

There are some faint shadows in Kerry's face (Figure 13-17). To remove them, select the Dodge tool with a soft, round, 45-pixel brush. Set the Range to Midtones and reduce the Exposure to 20%. Stroke over shadows repeatedly to gradually lighten them. Make your strokes follow the line of the shadow you are erasing, as shown in Figure 13-18. Figure 13-19 shows my results.

Figure 13-19: No more shadows

Hair Dye

Finally, let's dye Kerry's hair, using the same method you used to apply the eye shadow. Create a new layer (Layer | New | Layer). Name it Hair Color, and set it to Color mode. Click OK.

Set the Foreground color to a bright red. Use the Brush tool, with a soft, round, 45-pixel brush to paint over the hair in the new layer, as shown in Figure 13-20.

That hair's way too red, so turn down the effect by lowering the layer opacity down to 20–60%, depending on how prominently tinted you want Kerry's hair to be. You can also adjust the color by selecting the Hair Color layer in the Layers palette and choosing Enhance | Adjust Color | Adjust Hue/Saturation. Drag the Hue slider back and forth to try out different hair colors.

Flatten your layers (Layer | Flatten Image) and save your work. You're done! Gaze at Figure 13-21 to see how far you've come.

Figure 13-20: That hair's too red!

Figure 13-21: Before and after

Cover Girl: Create a Magazine Cover

14

In This Project You Will:

☐ Place text over a photo

☐ Browse through your installed fonts

☐ Combine fonts and colors in a single block of text

O ne fun way to use any favorite photo is to feature it on the cover of your favorite magazine, real or imagined. This project uses the "glamour photo" created in the previous two projects, but I'll provide a photo for you to work with if you've skipped ahead.

Getting Started

Begin by creating a new document, 625 pixels wide by 750
pixels tall. Make sure that Color Mode is set to RGB color
and click OK. From the menu, choose Edit | Fill Layer. In
the Fill Layer dialog, choose Black for the contents and click
OK to fill the Background layer with black. Save the new
document as magazine.psd.

Open the image you created in Project 13, or you can use
the file kerry-glamour.jpg or an image of your own that
you'd like to see on the cover of a magazine. Select the image
(Select | All) and copy it to the clipboard (Edit | Copy).
Return to the magazine.psd document (Window | magazine.
psd) and paste the photo onto a new layer (Edit | Paste).

Select the Move tool and slide the photo around into a pleasing position, as shown in Figure 14-1. If necessary, resize it
by SHIFT-clicking and dragging on the corner handles with
the Move tool. (Holding down the SHIFT key keeps the
original proportions while resizing.)

Figure 14-1: Position your photo on
the cover.

Create the Title Text

Time to add the type. Select the Type tool. In the Options bar, set the font size
to 48 and the color to white. Click on the canvas, type **Kerry** (don't worry about
the font just yet), and press CTRL-ENTER (CMD-RETURN on a Macintosh) to finish
entering text. With the Type tool still selected, click within the font family box
in the Options bar, as shown in Figure 14-2. Use your keyboard's arrow keys, or
your mouse wheel, to scroll through your installed fonts until you come to one
that strikes your fancy. Next, set the font size so that the title more or less fills
the image from side to side; I chose a 148 point Bermuda Solid. Finally, in the
Options bar, set the text's color to 225,255,185, a bright yellow-green.

Use the Move tool to position the title text near the top of the frame, more or less centered. You can also click and drag on any of the side or corner handles to resize the text, as shown in Figure 14-3.

Next, let's put a contrasting red border around the title text. Elements offers a bundle of layer effects, but none of them creates the effect I want. No problem, we'll create it ourselves.

Start by simplifying the Kerry text layer (Layer | Simplify). This converts it from vector text to pixels. Now, in the Layers palette, CTRL-click (CMD-click on a Macintosh) on the layer's thumbnail to select its contents, as shown in Figure 14-4. From the menu, choose Edit | Stroke (Outline) Selection. In the Stroke dialog, set the Width to 2 px, the Color to red (255,0,0), and the Location to Outside, as shown in Figure 14-5. Click OK to stroke a 2 pixel red line around the outside of the selected text (Figure 14-6). Remove the selection (Select | Deselect).

Font family   Font size

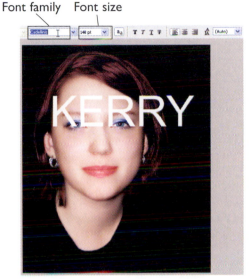

Figure 14-2: Type some title text.

Figure 14-3: Position the title.

Figure 14-4: Select the layer contents.

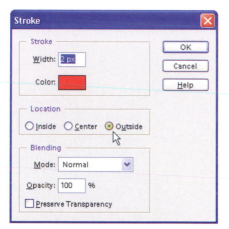

Figure 14-5: Set up a 2 pixel outline.

Figure 14-6: The outline stroke in place

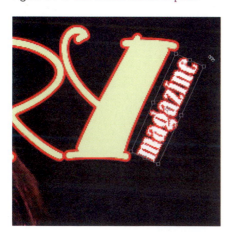

Figure 14-7: Rotate "magazine" into position.

Select the Type tool again and click on the canvas to start a new line of text. Type **magazine**, and press CTRL-ENTER or CMD-RETURN. In the Options bar, set the text's color to white (255,255,255) and choose a smaller font. I used 30 point Bernhard Bold Condensed. Again, simplify the layer (Layer | Simplify). CTRL-click or CMD-click on the layer thumbnail to select its contents, and then place a 1 pixel red stroke (255,0,0) around it (Edit | Stroke (Outline) Selection).

Remove the selection (Select | Deselect) and use the Move tool to position the new text at the end of the magazine title. Click and drag outside of the corner handles to rotate and resize (if necessary) the text, as shown in Figure 14-7. Press ENTER (RETURN on a Macintosh) to accept the transformation.

Merge the two text layers by choosing Layer | Merge Down.

Use the same method to add a date and headline, as shown in Figure 14-8, but don't outline this new text.

14 point Billboard

30 point Bernhard Bold Condensed

Figure 14-8: A date and headline in place

Mix It Up

Although it may not be obvious at first, you needn't use the same size of text throughout a type layer; you can mix it up. Let's do that now. SHIFT-click on the canvas to start a new type layer, but don't start typing just yet. Pick an 18 point font—I'm using Billboard, the same font family as I used for the date. In the Options bar, select Right Align Text, as shown in Figure 14-9. Finally, type in five short lines of text, pressing ENTER at the end of every line. Don't press CTRL-ENTER or CMD-RETURN yet.

When you're done typing, click and drag to select the bottom three lines of text, as shown in Figure 14-10. With that text selected, change the font size in the Options bar to 14 point. I inserted a carriage return between the large and small text, as well. Press CTRL-ENTER or CMD-RETURN to finish off this type layer.

Right align text

Figure 14-9: Type some right aligned text.

Figure 14-10: Changing the size on some of the text

You can change more than the size within a block of text; you can change the font family and color as well. SHIFT-click with the Type tool elsewhere on the canvas to start another type layer. Then set the Type tool's font size up to about 30 point. Enter six or seven short lines of text, as shown in Figure 14-11. Use all capitals to give a few of the lines special emphasis.

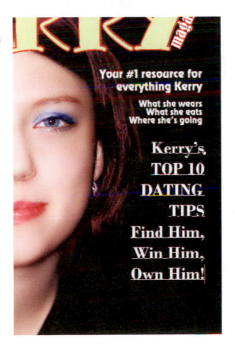

Figure 14-11: Add more text.

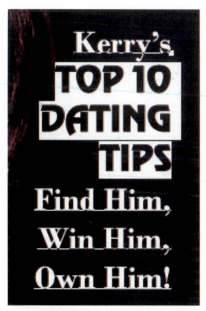

Figure 14-12: Change the font family.

Select the all-caps lines and, in the Options bar, change the font family. I chose the Billboard font again, as shown in Figure 14-12.

Now select the bottom lines of text. Again, change the font family in the Options bar. I went with Calligraph421 BT. Reduce the font size to 24 point, as shown in Figure 14-13. Finally, select a single word—I chose the word "Own" on the bottom line—and, in the Options bar, change its color to red or orange, as shown in Figure 14-14. Press CTRL-ENTER or CMD-RETURN to finish your text on this layer.

Add some more blocks of text here and there. Switch from Right Align Text to Left Align Text when you're placing text on the left side of the canvas. Mix up the sizes, fonts, and colors, but don't feel compelled to use every font you own. My results are shown in Figure 14-15. Things look a bit sloppy, but we'll fix that next.

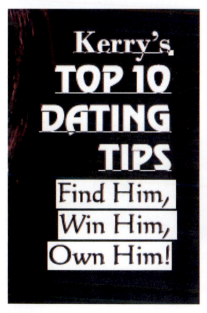

Figure 14-13: Yet another font family

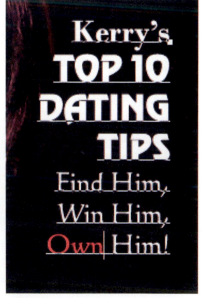

Figure 14-14: You can even change the color.

Line Them Up

Rather than try to line up all those blocks of text by eye, let's employ Elements' grid. From the menu, choose Edit | Preferences | Grid (on a Macintosh, Photoshop Elements | Preferences | Grid). In the Grid dialog, set the color to Green, the Style to Lines, and specify a gridline every 10 percent, as shown in Figure 14-16. Set the Subdivisions to 2 and click OK.

Figure 14-15: Text sloppily in place

Figure 14-16: Change your grid preferences.

Make the Grid visible by choosing View | Grid from the menu. Make sure that Snap to Grid (View | Snap to Grid) is enabled.

Select the Move tool from the Toolbox and turn on Auto Select Layer in the Options bar. One by one, select the different type layers in the Layers palette, and then use the arrow keys on your keyboard to nudge the text into position. Using the gridlines as a reference, I placed all my text 5% of the way in from the edge, as shown in Figure 14-17.

When you're happy, turn off the grid (View | Grid) and flatten your image (Layer | Flatten Image). Save your work.

Figure 14-17: The text is nicely aligned.

Figure 14-18: Copy the barcode.

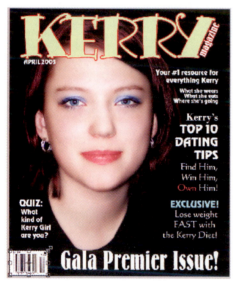

Figure 14-19: Position the barcode in a corner.

Add a UPC

Open a digital photograph or scan of a magazine cover that includes a UPC barcode. Use the Rectangular Marquee tool to select the UPC code, such as the one shown in Figure 14-18, and copy it to the clipboard (Edit | Copy). Return to the magazine.psd document and paste the bar code to a new layer (Edit | Paste).

Select the Move tool from the Toolbox and move the barcode into position in a corner of the image. SHIFT-click and drag on the corner handles to resize the barcode to fit your magazine, as shown in Figure 14-19. When you're satisfied with the results, press ENTER.

Flatten your image (Layer | Flatten Image) and save your work.

You can place any photo on the cover of a magazine but, as you can see in Figure 14-20, photos with busy backgrounds containing lots of contrast and color can make the text hard to read. Simple backgrounds work better.

Figure 14-20: Zoo Fun is hard to read.

Zoo Daze: Make a Poster by Tracing Bold Shapes

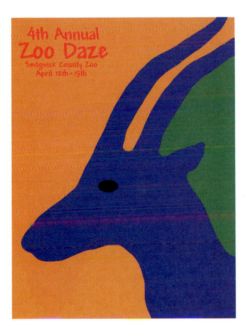

15

In This Project
You Will:

☐ Trace shapes on a new layer

☐ Use the Move tool to duplicate the contents of a selection

☐ Reposition layers within a document

☐ Use the Fill and Brush tools to add color

Let's create a simple poster using bold, colorful, hand-drawn graphics. Can't draw? No problem—we're going to trace. Don't worry about any shakiness of hand or perceived lack of artistic talent; it doesn't get any easier than this.

Start with a Gazelle's Head

Figure 15-1: A recumbent gazelle, photographed by Ned Benjamin

I've started with a lovely photo of a gazelle (Figure 15-1) by Ned Benjamin (admin@compdoctor.org). The poster will only use the gazelle's head, so I have cropped the photo to fit the composition of the poster I have in mind.

Open the photo gazelle-head.jpg and save it as gazelle-poster .psd. Select the Brush tool from the Toolbox. In the Options bar, select a hard, round, 13-pixel brush. Make sure that Opacity is set to 100%.

Set the Foreground Color to a dark blue (5,10,155).

Create a new blank layer (Layer | New | Layer) named Gazelle. With the Brush tool, begin to trace the outlines of the gazelle's head. Trace the near ear, the back of the neck, the front of the neck and the head, and, finally, the near horn, as shown in Figure 15-2. Only trace one ear and one horn. Make sure the outline doesn't have any gaps around the outside.

Figure 15-2: Trace around the gazelle's head with blue.

When the outline is complete, select the Paint Bucket tool from the Toolbox and click within the outline to fill it. You should have something like Figure 15-3. The silhouette should be completely filled in. If there are any gaps or lines remaining between the filled area and your original outline, as shown in Figure 15-4, paint over them with the Brush tool. Your final result should be a solid, filled silhouette like the one in Figure 15-5.

Figure 15-4: Gap around fill

Figure 15-3: Fill in the outline with the Paint Bucket tool.

One More Horn

I wanted the gazelle to sport two horns in the final poster but the two horns in the original photo are too close together to read in silhouette; they would look like a single, fat horn. So … let's cheat.

If you want, you can use the Brush tool to paint in a second horn. I chose to make a copy of the first horn instead.

Figure 15-5: Outline filled with blue

First, select the Polygonal Lasso tool from the Toolbox and use it to select the first horn as shown in Figure 15-6.

Now select the Move tool from the Toolbox. Hold down the ALT key (OPTION on a Macintosh), click within the selection, and drag to duplicate the contents of the selection. The ALT or OPTION key tells Elements to duplicate the contents of the selection, rather than just moving them. Position the horn as shown in Figure 15-7. Then turn off the selection (Select | Deselect). This places the horns one behind the other, as shown in Figure 15-8, which isn't really the way a gazelle wears them. But in a stylized graphic like this, it works.

Figure 15-6: Select the horn with a Polygonal Lasso.

Figure 15-7: Copy the selected horn.

Figure 15-8: A second horn

Fill in the Background

At this point, you're done with the background photo. Let's fill it with our new background color.

Set the Foreground Color to a dark orange (220,140,5). In the Layers palette, click on the background layer containing the photograph to select it. From the menu choose

Edit | Fill Layer. Set Contents to Use: Foreground Color and click OK. This covers the photo with your new background color, as shown in Figure 15-9.

Smooth It Out

Things may be looking rather rough at this point; they certainly are in my picture. Time to smooth things out a bit with the Brush and Eraser tools.

In the Layers palette, select the Gazelle layer. Select the Brush tool from the Toolbox. In the Options bar, select a hard, round, 13-pixel brush. Reset the Foreground Color to blue by holding down the ALT or OPTION key and clicking on the blue gazelle to sample its color. Paint with the brush to add to areas that need it. My gazelle was looking distinctly undershot, for example, so I used the Brush tool to extend the top and front of his snout, as shown in Figure 15-10.

Select the Eraser tool from the Toolbox. In the Options bar, select the same hard, round, 13-pixel brush as before. Erase areas that are rough, uneven, or stick out too far. I erased the front of the gazelle's neck, creating a smooth concave shape that follows the bottom of the jaw, as shown in Figure 15-11.

Figure 15-9: Our work so far

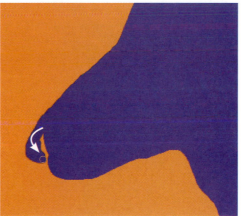

Figure 15-10: Paint a new nose.

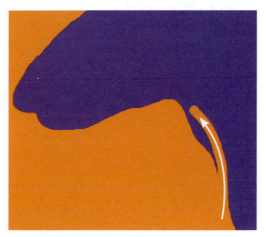

Figure 15-11: Erase the neck.

Figure 15-12: A cleaned up silhouette

Figure 15-13: Draw an arc.

Switch back and forth between the Eraser and Brush tools, adding and subtracting until you have a smooth, pleasing outline. Figure 15-12 shows what I wound up with.

This is a good time to save your work.

Background Color #2

In this step you'll create a second background color, to fill the orange area above and behind the gazelle's ear. You could just select the background layer and paint directly on that—and if you want to, I won't stop you—but there's a faster, easier way. Create a new layer (Layer | New | Layer) and name it Green.

Set the Foreground Color to a dark green (35,130,0). Select the Brush tool from the Toolbox and paint an outline that completely surrounds the area to be filled. Make sure your stroke stays within the blue silhouette of the gazelle as shown in Figure 15-13.

Now select the Paint Bucket tool from the Toolbox and click with the outlined area as shown in Figure 15-14.

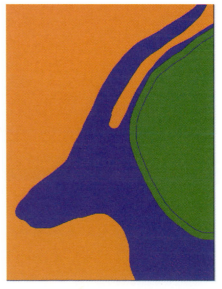

Figure 15-14: Fill the arc.

Finally, in the Layers palette, click the Green layer and drag it beneath the Gazelle layer, as shown in Figures 15-15 and 15-16. The results are shown in Figure 15-17.

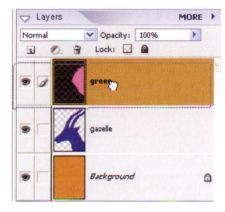

Figure 15-15: Grab the Green layer in the layers palette.

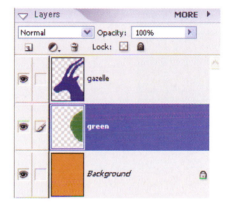

Figure 15-16: Drag the Green layer beneath the gazelle.

Making Eyes

Your gazelle needs an eye. Easy enough. In the Layers palette, click the Gazelle layer to select it. Now select the Ellipse tool from the Toolbox. Press D (for default) to restore the Foreground and Background Colors to black and white, and then click and drag to create an eye, as shown in Figure 15-18. If you need to reposition your eye, select the Move tool and then use the arrow keys to nudge the shape into place. When you're happy, flatten the image (Layer | Flatten Image). Save your work.

Figure 15-17: The green arc is in place beneath the silhouette.

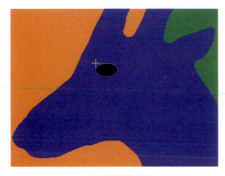

Figure 15-18: Draw an eye.

Add Some Text

The final step is to add some text (see the finished image at the beginning of this project). Set the Foreground Color to a bright red (240,8,0). Select the Type tool from the Toolbox, click on the image, and start typing. Use the Move tool to position the text in the empty top-left corner. I used the Andy font and a combination of 11, 34, and 23 point sizes to create my poster title with a variety of text sizes.

When your text is complete, flatten the image (Layer | Flatten Image), and save your work.

Nebulosity: Create a Starry Night Background

16

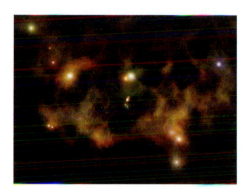

In Photoshop Elements, it's easy to quickly create a realistic picture of a deep space nebula suitable for all your deep space background needs. This project uses a blend of filters and brush strokes, guaranteeing that no two nebulae are the same.

In This Project You Will:

☐ Create a star field from scratch

☐ Create stars from lens flares

☐ Use the Smudge and Impressionist Brush tools to mix colors

☐ Use clouds to partially mask layers

☐ Use the Screen and Multiply blend modes to combine layers

Starry Sky

This first part is useful any time you need a starry sky for a project. Start by creating a new document. From the menu choose File | New | Blank File. Name the new file Nebula. Make it 1024 pixels wide by 768 pixels tall. Make sure the Color Mode is set to RGB color. Click OK.

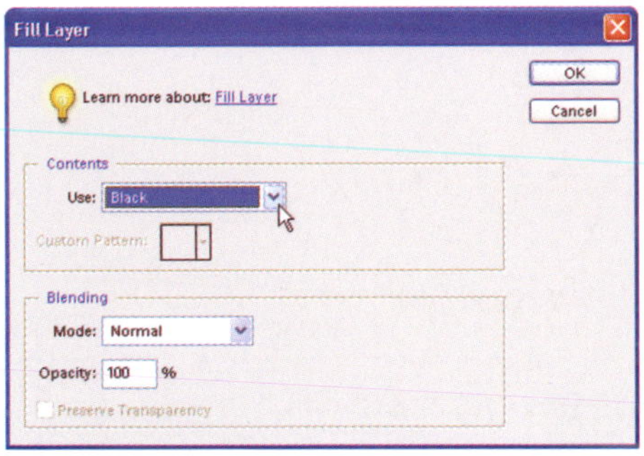

A night sky needs to be black, so let's fill the background with black. From the menu choose Edit | Fill Layer. When the Fill Layer dialog appears, set the Contents to use Black, as shown in Figure 16-1. Click OK.

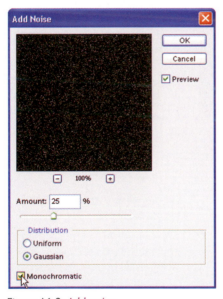

Figure 16-1: Fill the layer with black.

In the Toolbox, double-click on the Zoom tool to zoom in to 100%. Don't worry if you can't see the entire image; it's more important to be able to see your work up close.

Time to add some stars. From the menu choose Filter | Noise | Add Noise. Check both Gaussian and Monochromatic, and drag the slider to about 25%, as shown in Figure 16-2. Click OK. You should have something like Figure 16-3.

That, my friends, is too many stars. Let's tone it down a little. From the menu choose Enhance | Adjust Lighting | Levels. In the three Input Levels boxes near the top, type 50, 1.0, and 200. The first number is the black level. A value of 50 forces the dimmest one-fifth of the stars to black, making them disappear completely. The third value is the white level. A value of 200 forces the brightest one-fifth of the stars to pure white. The middle number is the gray value.

Figure 16-2: Add noise.

Figure 16-3: Too many stars

Fine-tune your star field by dragging the gray slider beneath the graph. Dragging it to the right darkens the overall image and reduces the number of stars; dragging to the left lightens the overall image, increasing the number of stars. I ended up with a middle number of about 0.35, as shown in Figure 16-4. Click OK to accept these changes.

Create another new layer (Layer | New | Layer). Name the new layer Stars, set its Mode to Screen (as shown in Figure 16-5) and click OK. Fill the layer with black (Edit | Fill Layer, Use: Black).

Add noise as before. From the menu choose Filter | Add Noise. Photoshop Elements remembers the last filter used and the settings chosen.

Adjust the levels (Enhance | Adjust Lighting | Levels), but this time, set the values in the Input Levels boxes at 175, 1.00, 207. Then click OK. This creates fewer, brighter stars.

You can repeat these steps as often as you want, using different Levels settings to create brighter or dimmer stars.

Make sure that all your star layers are in Screen mode. In Screen mode, the light parts of the current layer (the stars) shine through to the underlying image. Screen mode completely ignores the layer's black pixels.

When you're happy with the results, or at least tired of adding stars, choose Layer | Flatten Image to merge all the stars onto a single background layer.

Save your work.

Constellation

The results so far look pretty good, but they are too regular. Stars aren't spread that evenly across the heavens; there are bright clumps and dark patches.

From the menu choose Layer | New | Layer. Name the new layer Star Mask, and set it in Multiply mode, as shown in Figure 16-6. Click OK.

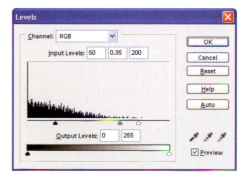

Figure 16-4: Adjust Levels to control the number and brightness of stars.

Figure 16-5: Create a new layer of stars.

Figure 16-6: Create a new layer to mask some stars.

Restore the default Foreground and Background Colors (black and white). From the menu choose Filter | Render | Clouds. This generates a random, cloudlike pattern of black and white, which darkens the stars unevenly, creating areas of light and dark, varying the density of the stars. Multiply mode is the opposite of Screen mode: the dark parts of the current layer darken the underlying image.

To make this pattern of light and dark stars more complex, use the Difference Clouds filter (Filter | Render | Difference Clouds). While the Clouds filter generates a new, random pattern every time it runs, Difference Clouds interacts with the existing image. Every time you run it, the pattern becomes more convoluted. Run the Difference Clouds filter again, just for good measure. In the Layers palette, reduce the Star Mask layer's opacity to about 40–50%, or wherever the effect looks best to you (see Figure 16-7).

When you're happy, choose Layer | Flatten Image, and save your work.

Figure 16-7: My work so far

Constellation 2

Select the Clone Stamp tool from the Toolbox. In the Options bar, set the tool's mode to Lighten and Opacity to 100%. Select a soft, round, 35-pixel brush.

ALT-click (on a Macintosh, use OPTION-click) on some stars in your image, to sample them, and then click and drag multiple times in relatively dense areas of stars. This clones the stars (but not the dark background), making the dense area even more dense. ALT-click or OPTION-click multiple times as you work, sampling from different areas, so that you don't wind up with recognizable duplicate patterns of stars.

Now reverse the process. In the Options bar, set the Clone Stamp's mode to Darken, and set the tool's Opacity down to about 30%. ALT-click or OPTION-click on part of the image with few or no stars, and then click and drag multiple times in areas with too many stars, to thin them out. Again, ALT-click or OPTION-click to reset the sample several times as you work, to keep from creating suspicious-looking patterns. My results are shown in Figure 16-8.

Figure 16-8: Stars after some judicious cloning

Nebula

All right, enough with the background. Time to create our nebula. From the menu choose Layer | New | Layer. Name the new layer Nebula and click OK.

Fill the new layer with black (Edit | Fill Layer, Use: Black).

Select the Brush tool from the Toolbox. In the Options bar, select a soft, round, 65-pixel brush with Opacity at 100%. Set the Foreground Color to bright orange (245,200,0). Use the Brush tool to paint a large squiggle. Here's mine in Figure 16-9, but yours needn't look anything like it. You can't do this part wrong.

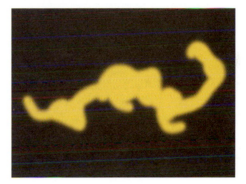

Figure 16-9: An ugly squiggle

From the Toolbox, select the Impressionist Brush tool. In the Options bar, choose a soft, round, 45-pixel brush. Under More Options, make sure Style is set to Tight Short, as shown in Figure 16-10.

Figure 16-10: More Impressionist Brush options

Drag the Impressionist Brush around the outside of your squiggle to distort and feather the edges, as shown in Figure 16-11.

Set the Foreground Color to pure yellow (255,255,0).

Select the Brush tool again. In the Options bar, choose a soft, round, 27-pixel brush. Paint the middle of your squiggle with the lighter color. It doesn't have to be very precise, but try to keep some of the darker original color around the edges, as shown in Figure 16-12.

Figure 16-11: A distorted squiggle

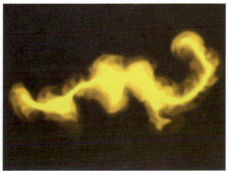

Figure 16-12: Add yellow to the inside.

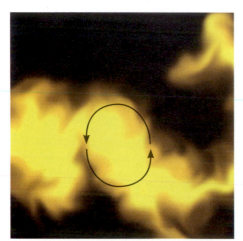

Figure 16-13: Use the Smudge tool to blend the two colors.

Figure 16-14: Paint the center white.

Figure 16-15: Add some final detail with the Smudge tool.

Now select the Smudge tool from the Toolbox. In the Options bar, choose a soft, round, 45-pixel brush. Set the Strength to 30%. Click and drag with the Smudge tool in large loops and figure eights, clockwise and counterclockwise, to smudge the two colors together and further distort the edges of the nebula, as shown in Figure 16-13. Again, have fun; you can't do this wrong.

Select the Brush tool again. In the Options bar, set the tool's opacity down to 50%. Set the Foreground Color to pure white (255,255,255). Use the Brush tool to paint white areas in the center of your nebula, as shown in Figure 16-14.

Return one last time to the Smudge tool. Make big circles and figure eights that run through the nebula to add more detail, as shown in Figure 16-15. Smudge in from the outside to pull dark swirls into the nebula. Smudge out from the inside to pull out little wisps.

Get the Dodge tool from the Toolbox. In the Options bar, select a soft, round, 35-pixel brush, set the Range to Highlights and the Exposure to 50%. Click and drag in short arcs around the edges of your nebula to create even more detail. Finally, set the Nebula layer to Screen mode to allow the stars to shine through.

Now would be a good time to save your work.

Nebula Clouds

It still looks a bit like a blob of paint thrown across the stars; to make it better fit in with the background, we'll use the same trick we used to add randomness to the stars: a cloud texture.

From the menu choose Layer | New | Layer. Name the layer Nebula Clouds. Set the Mode to Multiply and make sure that Group With Previous Layer is checked, as shown in Figure 16-16. Click OK.

Fill the new layer with black (Edit | Fill Layer, Use: Black). Press D (for default) to reset the Foreground and Background Colors to black and white, and then select the Difference Clouds filter (Filter | Render | Difference Clouds) three times. The darker parts of the Nebula Clouds layer now hide the corresponding parts of the nebula, making it wispier, as shown in Figure 16-17.

Wow! That looks pretty good. Hard to believe it started as an ugly orange squiggle. If the nebula still looks too bright for your tastes, reduce the Nebula layer's opacity somewhat in the Layers palette.

Save your work.

Large Stars

Let's add some large, prominent stars. In the Layers palette, select the Nebula Clouds layer. From the menu choose Layer | New | Layer to create a new layer above it. Name the new layer Large Star. Set it to Screen mode, and click OK.

Fill the layer with black (Edit | Fill Layer, Use: Black). Now choose Filter | Render | Lens Flare. Set the Brightness to 15%, and select 35mm Prime, as shown in Figure 16-18. Click OK. Use the Move tool to move your new star to a pleasing location.

Repeat these steps a few times, creating a new layer for each flare. Experiment with different lens flare types (such as 105mm Prime) and with changing the Brightness setting to make different size stars. Play with the layer opacity to make a star dimmer.

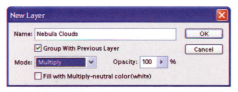

Figure 16-16: Create a cloud layer.

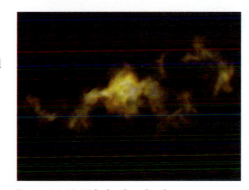

Figure 16-17: Nebula plus clouds

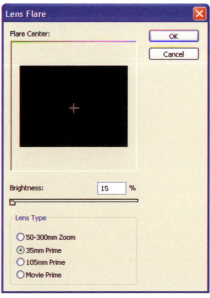

Figure 16-18: Create a lens flare.

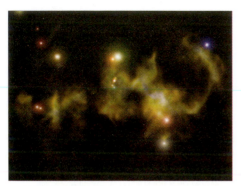

Remember that stars come in different colors. Change the colors of any of your stars by clicking on its thumbnail in the Layers palette, and then choosing Enhance | Adjust Color | Adjust Hue/Saturation. Drag the Hue slider to change the color of the star. Figure 16-19 shows my results so far.

You can call it done at this point or, if you're game, you can increase the density of detail of your nebula.

Either way, save your work.

Figure 16-19: Some big stars added to the mix

Extra Nebulae

Tip

To quickly create similar stars, copy existing stars with Layer | New | Layer via Copy, and then move the new stars into place.

In the Layers palette, click the Nebula Clouds layer to select it. From the menu choose Layer | Merge Down to combine the clouds and the nebula into a single layer. With the new combined Nebula layer selected, choose Layer | New | Layer via Copy. Repeat that step (Layer | New | Layer via Copy).

You now have three nebula layers. From the menu choose Filter | Distort | Polar Coordinates. Check Rectangular to Polar and click OK. This twists one nebula into a ring. Now, choose Enhance | Adjust Color | Adjust Hue/Saturation. In the Hue/Saturation dialog, drag the Hue slider left to about −20, making this nebula redder, and click OK.

In the Layers palette, select a different nebula layer. Choose Filter | Distort | Polar Coordinates again. This time, check Polar to Rectangular. Click OK. This rips your nebula apart and hangs it from the top of the canvas.

Again choose Enhance | Adjust Color | Adjust Hue/Saturation. This time drag the Hue slider right to about +20, making this nebula greener, and click OK.

Play with the opacity of the three nebula layers, making them as stark or as subtle as you want. I set my opacities to 80% (original), 70% (redder), and 25% (greener), respectively.

Save your work.

Color the Stars

Stars, as I've said before, come in all sorts of colors. But the background stars in this image are all white. It's easy and fun to add some color to them.

In the Layers palette, click the Background layer to select it. From the menu choose Layer | New | Layer. Name it Star Color and set its mode to Color. Click OK.

Grab the Brush tool from the Toolbox. In the Options bar, set the tool's Opacity to 100% and Choose a large, soft, round brush. Set the Foreground Color to blue (the exact color doesn't really matter) and paint in some broad swaths of color. Change the Foreground Color to add some areas of green and yellow and red as well. When you're done, reduce the Star Color layer's opacity to 20%. This adds subtle color to your starry background, as shown in Figure 16-20.

Save your work; you're done.

This project is based in part on a tutorial by Kier Darby at AP3D.com. Thanks for the inspiration, Kier!

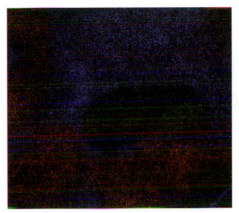

Figure 16-20: Multicolored stars on the background layer

Planet-Rise: Design a Space Scene from Scratch

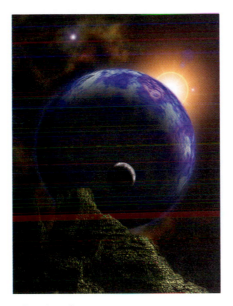

17

In This Project You Will:

- ☐ Create planets from scratch

- ☐ Apply texture with lighting effects

- ☐ Use Clouds and Difference Clouds filters

With Photoshop Elements, you can create realistic space scenes, featuring never-before-seen worlds. This project builds on Project 16, using that project as its background.

Create a Planet

To create the planet, we'll start in a new document. Choose File | New to create a new document. Name the document Planet. Set the Width and Height both to 600 pixels, make sure the Color Mode is set to RGB color, and click OK. Save the new document as planet.psd.

Set the Foreground Color to blue (100,0,255) and the Background Color to a light cyan (0,215,255). These colors will result in a vaguely Earth-like world. Feel free to choose other colors if you want something more alien. Choose black and white, or different shades of gray for a cold, dead moon.

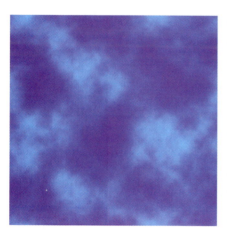

Figure 17-1: Some clouds

From the menu, choose Filter | Render | Clouds. This fills the canvas with a random, cloudlike mixture of your foreground and background colors, as shown in Figure 17-1. To add complexity, choose Filter | Render | Difference Clouds. This inverts the colors, but don't worry, they'll be back in a moment. Every time you run the filter, the image gets more complex and convoluted. Run Difference Clouds another nine times or so, to really mix things up again. Make sure you stop with the correct colors visible, as shown in Figure 17-2. (The Clouds filter produces random clouds, so your results won't look exactly like mine.)

From the Toolbox, select the Elliptical Marquee tool. Click near the top left of the image. Hold down the SHIFT key to constrain the selection to a circle, drag the cursor to near the bottom-right corner, and release. The selection should be pretty close to the center and be about as large as possible without going beyond the edge of the canvas, as shown in Figure 17-3.

From the menu, choose Layer | New | Layer via Copy, to copy the circle to a new layer. In the Layers palette, name the new layer Planet. Click the eye icon on the Background layer to hide it from view, as shown in Figure 17-4.

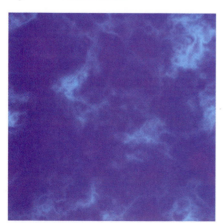

Figure 17-2: Difference Clouds

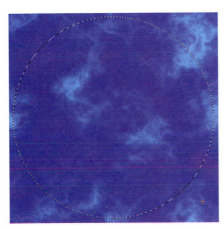

Figure 17-3: Select a circle.

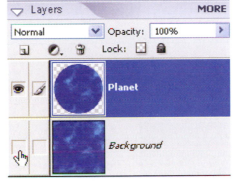

Figure 17-4: Hide the background.

Now to turn your planet into a ball. Make sure the Planet layer is selected in the Layers palette. From the menu, choose Filter | Distort | Spherize. In the Spherize dialog, set the Amount to 100% and click OK.

The planet needs a little 3-D texture to simulate mountains and whatnot. We'll add that with Elements' Lighting Effects. From the menu, choose Filter | Render | Lighting Effects. Choose Spotlight from the Light Type drop-down list. In the thumbnail at the left side of the dialog, click and drag on the light effects handles to pull the default oval shape into a circle the same size as your planet, as shown in Figure 17-5. Notice that the center handle is connected to one of the four outer handles by a line. Drag the outer handle until the line points "northeast," between 1 and 2 o'clock, as shown in Figure 17-5. This simulates light coming from the upper-right corner of the frame, where the rising sun will be.

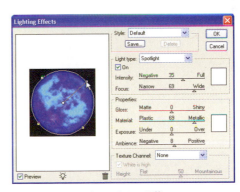

Figure 17-5: Apply Lighting Effects

Now, grab the center handle and move it up and to the right. Leave a small wedge of darkness at the bottom left of the planet, as shown in Figure 17-6.

Increase the Ambience to around 20%; this keeps that little wedge from being completely dark.

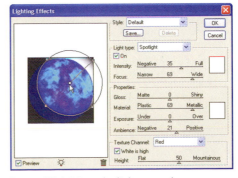

Figure 17-6: Move the light up and over.

Find the Texture Channel drop-down list at the bottom of the dialog. This is
where the real magic happens. Elements will simulate shadows and highlights in
your image based on the brightness of the image. The exact settings are, again,
largely a matter of personal taste, and of the way the light interacts with the clouds
in your image. Set the Texture Channel to Red, and drag the Height slider to 50.
Click OK to apply the Lighting Effects.

Figure 17-7: Paste the planet in place.

Open the Background

Open the final 1024×768 image from the previous project,
Nebulosity, or open the file nebula.jpg. Rotate the canvas 90° to
stand it on its end by choosing Image | Rotate | 90° Right (or
Left). Save the file under the new name planet-rise.psd.

Return to the Planet document. In the Layers palette, select the
Planet layer, and then CTRL-click (CMD-click on the Macintosh)
on that layer's thumbnail to select its contents. Choose Select |
Feather. Enter a value of 5 pixels and click OK. Feather softens
the transition between selected pixels and unselected pixels. This
will make the planet look less like it is just pasted in when we …
well … paste it in.

Copy the selection to the clipboard (Edit | Copy), and then
switch to the planet-rise.psd document and paste the planet to
the new layer (Edit | Paste), as shown in Figure 17-7.

Star Blocker

In the Layers palette, select the new Planet layer; then choose Layer |
New | Layer via Copy twice. This will give you a total of three planet
layers, as shown in Figure 17-8. Rename the three layers, from top to
bottom, to Planet, Atmosphere, and Star Blocker. The Planet layer will
continue to contain your planet. The Atmosphere layer will give the
glow of an atmosphere, and the Star Blocker layer will cause the stars
in the background to fade near the planet.

In the Layers palette, select the Star Blocker layer. CTRL-click or CMD-
click on the layer's thumbnail to select its contents, and then choose

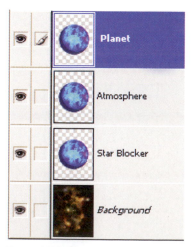

Figure 17-8: There are now three
planet layers.

Edit | Fill Selection from the menu. In the Fill Layer dialog, set the Contents to Black and click OK.

Set the Foreground Color to 85,110,170. This will be our atmosphere color.

With the selection still active, select the Atmosphere layer in the Layers palette. Again, choose Edit | Fill Selection. This time, set the Fill Layer's Contents to Foreground Color and click OK.

Remove the selection by choosing Select | Deselect.

So far, things still look about the same; the Atmosphere and Star Blocker layers are hidden behind the Planet layer, as shown in Figure 17-9. The next step will make them visible. In the Layers palette, select the black Star Blocker layer. From the menu, choose Filter | Blur | Gaussian Blur. Enter a Radius of 30 pixels and click OK. This smears the black out around the planet, making the background stars fade as they get near the planet, as shown in Figure 17-10.

In the Layers palette, select the Atmosphere layer and run the Gaussian Blur filter again (Filter | Blur | Gaussian Blur). This time, enter a Radius of 20 pixels and click OK. Set the Atmosphere layer in Screen mode to make it glow against the dark background, as shown in Figure 17-11, and reduce the layer's opacity to about 75%.

Figure 17-9: The atmosphere is invisible.

Figure 17-10: The nearest stars are dimmed.

Figure 17-11: A glowing atmosphere

In the Layers palette, select the Planet layer, and then choose Enhance | Adjust Color | Adjust Hue/Saturation. In the Hue/Saturation dialog, move the Hue slider around a bit, to see if any of the other color combinations appeal to you. Try reducing (or increasing) the saturation as well; I reduced the saturation of my planet by –50.

When you're happy, click OK. Now would be a good time to save your work.

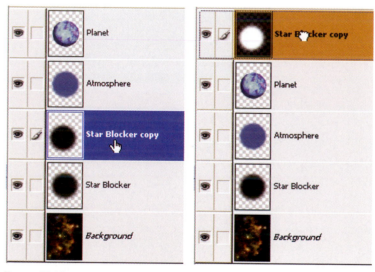

Figure 17-12: Reposition the layer to the top.

Shadow

We want to create a nice, crescent planet, mostly in shadow. We made a start on that with Lighting Effects. To complete the effect, select the Star Blocker layer in the Layers palette and choose Layer | New | Layer via Copy. In the Layers palette, drag the new, Star Blocker copy layer to a position above the Planet layer, as shown in Figure 17-12. Reduce the layer's opacity to 80%, and use the Move tool to slide the shadow down and to the left, as shown in Figure 17-13, to create a nice crescent planet. From the menu, choose Layer | Group with Previous. This keeps the shadow from falling across the stars in the background.

Figure 17-13: Move the shadow down and over.

Sunrise

The planet's in place; it's time for the sun. In the Layers palette, select the original Star Blocker layer, and then choose Layer | New | Layer. Name the new layer Sun and fill it with black (Edit | Fill Layer). From the menu, choose Filter | Render | Lens Flare. Select 35mm Prime and set the Brightness to 160%, as shown in Figure 17-14. Position the flare a little above and to the right of the center as shown, and click OK.

Set the Sun layer to Lighten mode and use the Move tool to slide the sun up and right until it just peaks over the edge of the planet, as shown in Figure 17-15. If Elements keeps selecting the wrong layer when you try to move the sun, turn off Auto Select Layer in the Move tool's Options bar.

Adjust the sun's color by choosing Enhance | Adjust Color | Adjust Hue/Saturation. Set the Hue to +55 and Saturation to +45 and click OK. Next, tweak its brightness by choosing Enhance | Adjust Lighting | Levels. Set the Input Levels to 0,0.40,250, as shown in Figure 17-16, and click OK.

Flatten the image (Layer | Flatten Image), and save your work.

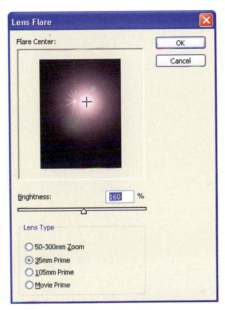

Figure 17-14: Create a lens flare.

Figure 17-15: Move the sun into position.

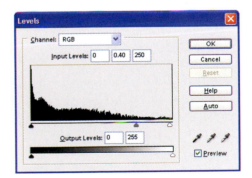

Figure 17-16: Tweak the sun's levels.

Mountains

Finally, let's add some alien landscape in the foreground for the planet to be rising above. Open the file mountains.jpg. (Thanks to Tom Szurkowski for this fine photo.) Copy the photo to a new layer in the document by choosing Layer | New | Layer via Copy from the menu. Hide the Background layer by clicking on its eye icon, and rename the new layer Mountain.

Select the Magic Eraser tool from the Toolbox. In the Options bar, set the tool's Tolerance to 32, and select Anti-aliased and Contiguous. Click on the sky and clouds above the mountains to erase them, as shown in Figure 17-17.

Figure 17-17: Erase the sky with the Magic Eraser.

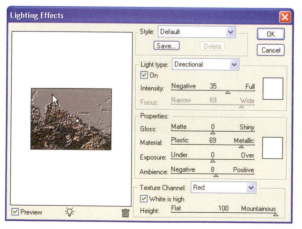

Figure 17-18: Lighting effects texture the mountains.

To obscure any telltale vegetation and add more texture, return to the Lighting Effects filter (Filter | Render | Lighting Effects). This time, set the Light type to Directional. Drag the light's white center handle to near the center, and drag its black square handle up toward 10 o'clock, as shown in Figure 17-18. The closer the handles are to each other, the brighter the lighting effect will be.

Set the Texture Channel to Red, and drag the Height slider all the way to 100. Click OK to apply the effect, shown in Figure 17-19.

To make the mountains even more alien, let's change their color. From the menu, choose Enhance | Adjust Color | Adjust Hue/Saturation. In the Hue/Saturation dialog, select Colorize, and then set the Hue to 70, the Saturation to 30, and the Lightness to −50, as shown in Figure 17-20. Click OK to tint the mountains a dark olive green.

Figure 17-19: The mountains with texture applied

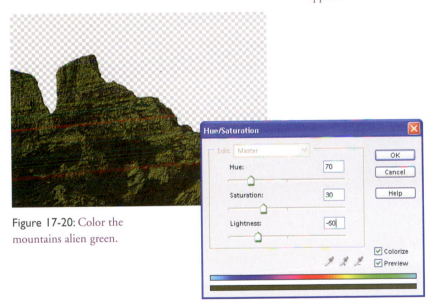

Figure 17-20: Color the mountains alien green.

In the Layers palette, CTRL-click or CMD-click on the Mountain layer's thumbnail to select that layer's contents. From the menu, choose Select | Feather. Enter a value of 5 pixels and click OK.

Copy the selection to the clipboard (Edit | Copy). Return to the planet-rise.psd document and paste the mountains (Edit | Paste) onto a new layer. In the Layers palette, rename the new layer Mountains. Select the Move tool and drag the Mountains layer to the bottom of the canvas, and then rotate, resize, and reposition it to suit your tastes, as shown in Figure 17-21.

Figure 17-21: Rotate and reposition the mountains.

Figure 17-22: Burn shadows into the landscape.

Select the Burn tool. In the Options bar, select a soft, round, 65-pixel brush. Set the tool's Range to Midtones, and its Exposure to 30%. Using multiple strokes, darken the mountains' shadows, especially those on the left side, away from the sunrise, as shown in Figure 17-22.

Change to the Dodge tool. Again, select a soft, round, 65-pixel brush. Set the tool's Range to Highlights, and its Exposure to 20%. Use multiple strokes to lighten the right edges of the mountains, where the distant sun would illuminate them.

Switch back and forth between the tools, lightening some areas and darkening others.

Flatten the image (Layer | Flatten Image), and save your work.

As a final touch, I added a small moon, made just like the planet but without an atmosphere or star blocker, to the final image.

Mock 3-D: Use Gradients to Create Simple 3-D Shapes

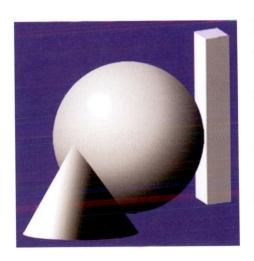

18

In This Project You Will:

☐ Create shapes with the Shape tool

☐ Create shapes by filling selections

☐ Use gradients to simulate 3-D shading

☐ Create custom gradients

Although Photoshop Elements is not a 3-D program, you can use it to produce shapes such as cones, balls, and boxes with a 3-D look. It's easier than you might think.

Custom Shape Picker

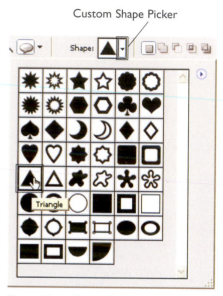

Figure 18-1: Choose the Triangle shape.

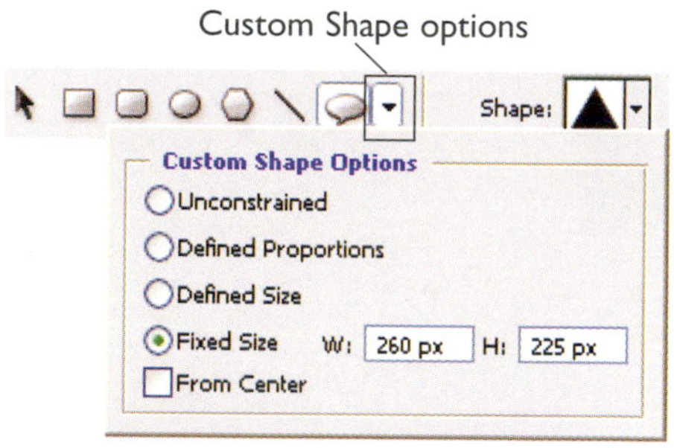

Custom Shape options

Figure 18-2: Define a fixed-size cone.

Figure 18-3: The start of a cone

Create a Background

Begin by setting the background color to 0,0,155 (a dark blue). We'll be working in black and white, and the blue background will make it easier to see what we're doing.

Create a new blank document (File | New | Blank File). Name the new document 3-D-shapes.psd, and make it 400 pixels wide by 400 pixels high. Make sure the Color Mode is set to RGB color, and the Background Contents are set to Background Color. Click OK to create the new document.

Make a Cone

Let's start with a cone. Select the Custom Shape tool from the Toolbox. In the Options bar, set the Color to white, and choose Triangle from the Shape drop-down, as shown in Figure 18-1. (If the triangle is not available, click the triangle at the top-right corner of the Shape palette and choose Shapes from the pop-up list.)

In the Options bar, open the Custom Shape options, as shown in Figure 18-2. Select Fixed Size and type in a width of 260 px and a height of 225 px (px stands for pixels). If you don't specify pixels, the measurement defaults to inches, and you don't want a triangle 260 inches wide, believe me.

Click on your canvas anywhere to create the triangle, as shown in Figure 18-3.

With the Custom Shape tool still selected, choose the
Oval shape from the Shape drop-down, as shown in
Figure 18-4.

In the Custom Shape options, leave Fixed Size selected,
but change the dimensions to 260 pixels wide by 50 pixels
high. Click on the canvas below the triangle to create
the oval.

The oval will form the bottom of the cone. By specify-
ing the width of both the oval and the triangle, you have
made sure that they will exactly match up at this point.
Select the Move tool from the Toolbox. Handles appear
around the oval shape. Use the arrow keys to nudge the
oval into position at the bottom of the triangle, as shown
in Figure 18-5.

In the Layers palette, link the two shape layers as shown
in Figure 18-6, and then merge the two shape layers
(Layer | Merge Linked). Rename the new merged
layer Cone.

Doesn't look very 3-D, does it? A little shading fixes
that. Restore the Foreground and Background Colors
to their default black and white. Select the Gradient
tool from the Toolbox. In the Options bar, select
Linear Gradient, and choose the Foreground to

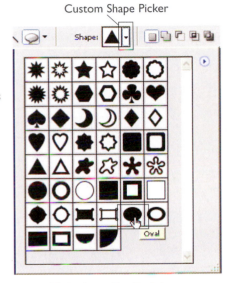

Figure 18-4: Choose the Oval shape.

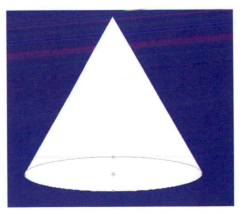

Figure 18-5: The oval forms the bottom of
the cone.

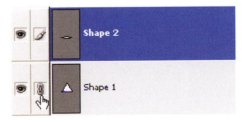

Figure 18-6: Link the layers together.

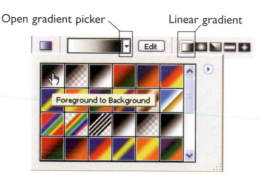

Open gradient picker   Linear gradient

Figure 18-7: Select the Foreground to Background gradient.

Background gradient from the Gradient drop-down, as shown in Figure 18-7.

In the Layers palette, CTRL-click (CMD-click on a Macintosh) on the Cone layer's thumbnail to select the filled pixels on that layer. This will keep the gradient within the cone shape in the next step. Now, click and drag from right to left within the selection, as shown in Figure 18-8, to fill it with the gradient. It should resemble Figure 18-9. If it comes out wrong, just click and drag again.

Remove the selection (Select | Deselect) and hide the Cone layer in the Layers palette by clicking on its eye icon.

Save your work.

Box Block

Next, let's make a box. Select the Rectangle tool from the Toolbox. In the Options bar, open the Custom Shape options and select Unconstrained. This will allow you to make your rectangle whatever size and shape you want.

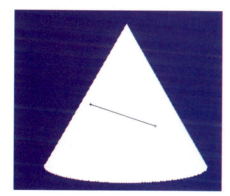

Figure 18-8: Click and drag within the selection.

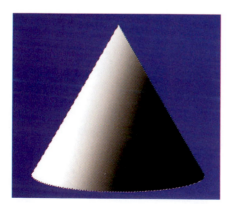

Figure 18-9: A faux 3-D cone

Set the shape color 40% gray from the color menu, as shown in Figure 18-10. Click and drag on the canvas to make a tall, thin box, as shown in Figure 18-11.

Figure 18-10: Choose 40% Gray as the shape color.

Select the Move tool from the Toolbox. Handles appear around the rectangle shape. Hold down SHIFT-CTRL (SHIFT-CMD on a Macintosh), and click and drag on the handle on the right side of the rectangle, as shown in Figure 18-12, dragging up slightly to skew the shape. Press ENTER (RETURN on a Macintosh) to save the change. This makes one side of your box.

From the menu, choose Layer | New | Layer via Copy. Select the Move tool from the Toolbox, and then use the arrow keys to move the new shape to the left until it emerges from beneath the first rectangle, as shown in Figure 18-13. From the menu, choose Image | Rotate | Flip Layer Horizontal. This creates the second side of your box.

To differentiate between the two sides, let's make this side lighter, and narrower. In the Layers palette, double-click on the thumbnail of the new shape layer to bring up the Color Picker dialog. In the Color Picker, set the color to white (255,255,255) and click OK. Use the Move tool to click and drag on the left handle to shrink the new shape's width by about half, and then use the arrow keys to nudge it into place against the first side, as shown in Figure 18-14.

In the Layers palette, link the two rectangle shape layers, and then choose Layer | Merge Linked from the menu to combine the two sides of the box. Rename the merged layer to Box.

Figure 18-11: Make a tall, thin box.　**Figure 18-12:** The first side of the box

Figure 18-13: The second side of the box　**Figure 18-14:** Slide the two sides together.

Figure 18-15: Our box top to be

One last step: the box top. It would be pretty tricky to create a skewed rectangle of just the right shape to fit on the top, so let's take an easier route. From the menu, choose Layer | New | Layer via Copy. In the Layers palette, CTRL-click or CMD-click on the thumbnail of the new layer to select all its filled pixels. Set the Foreground Color to light blue (200,200,255). From the menu, choose Edit | Fill Selection. In the Fill Layer dialog, choose Foreground Color for Contents and click OK to fill the shape with a pale blue as shown in Figure 18-15. Deselect the shape (Select | Deselect).

With the blue Box Copy layer selected in the Layers palette, choose Image | Rotate | Layer 180° from the menu. It doesn't look much like it now, but this is our box top.

In the Layers palette, click and drag on the top box shape, the one you've just filled with blue, and drag it beneath the original box shape layer, as shown in Figure 18-16.

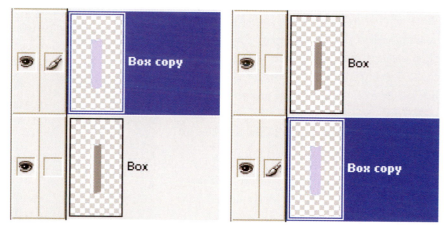

Figure 18-16: Drag the Box Copy layer beneath the Box layer.

Select the Move tool from the Toolbox, and then use the arrow keys to nudge the blue layer upwards until it forms the box top, as shown in Figure 18-17. In the Layers palette, select the Box layer, and then choose Layer | Merge Down from the menu to create a single Box Copy layer.

Making each side a different shade reinforces the idea that the object is solid, with highlights and shadows.

In the Layers palette, hide the Box Copy layer, and save your work.

Spheres

Finally, let's make a 3-D sphere. Create a new layer (Layer | New | Layer). Name it Sphere and click OK.

In the Toolbox, select the Elliptical Marquee tool. SHIFT-click and drag on the canvas to create a circular selection. Holding down the SHIFT key constrains the selection to a perfect circle. Select the default Foreground and Background Colors, and then press X to swap the Foreground and Background Colors (for a white foreground and black background).

Select the Gradient tool from the Toolbox. In the Options bar, select Radial gradient, as shown in Figure 18-18, and then choose the Foreground to Background gradient from the Gradient Picker. Click and drag within the circular selection from top left to bottom right, as shown in Figure 18-19.

That looks okay. But we can do better. The secret to creating a 3-D look is gradient shading. We can improve the look by tweaking the gradient.

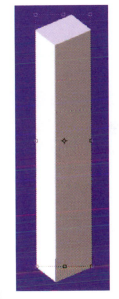

Figure 18-17: A faux 3-D box

Figure 18-18: Radial gradient

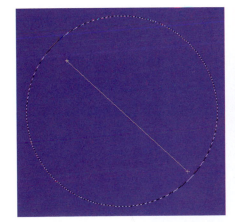

Figure 18-19: Click and drag within the selection to fill it with the gradient.

Gradient edit button

Figure 18-20: Edit the gradient.

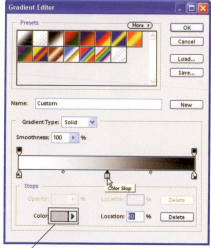

Color swatch

Figure 18-21: A new color stop

Figure 18-22: A second new color stop

In the Options bar, click the Edit button to open the Gradient Editor, as shown in Figure 18-20.

Click beneath the gradient bar to create a new color stop as shown in Figure 18-21. Drag the new color stop to the center, until Location reads 50%. Click the Color swatch to open the Color Picker. In the Color Picker, set the color to 190,190,190 (a light gray) and click OK. This will extend the lighter part of the gradient over more of the sphere.

Still in the Gradient Editor, click and drag the white color stop to the right, to 5%. This will give the sphere a wider, brighter highlight. Finally, find the small diamond color midpoint between the first and second color stops, and drag it left until its Location reads 15%, as shown in Figure 18-22. This stretches the gray middle color and makes the transition between it and the white highlight more abrupt. Click OK to close the Gradient Editor.

Click and drag again to fill the circle with the new, improved gradient. You'll wind up with something like Figure 18-23. Then remove the selection (Select | Deselect).

Leave the separate objects on their own layers, so that you can easily retrieve them for later projects.

Save your work.

Figure 18-23: The final, faux 3-D sphere

Marbles Poster: Make Faux 3-D Marbles

19

"Golf is just an expensive way of playing marbles."
G.K.Chesterton

In This Project You Will:

☐ Create a realistic 3-D ball

☐ Create clouds to add reflections

☐ Adjust hue and saturation to introduce variety among similar objects

The preceding project dealt with simple 3-D shapes. This project kicks it up a notch, creating 3-D marbles that look like the real thing.

A Basic Circle

Start by creating a new document. From the menu, choose File | New | Blank File. Set the Width and Height both to 400. Make sure that Color Mode is set to RGB color, and the Background Contents are set to White, and then click OK. Save the new document as marble.psd.

Create a new layer by choosing Layer | New | Layer from the menu. Name the new layer Circle and click OK.

Select the Elliptical Marquee tool from the Toolbox. In the Options bar, set the Mode to Fixed Size and enter both a Width and Height of 375 px, as shown in Figure 19-1. Click on the canvas to create a circular selection, as shown in Figure 19-2. Try to get the selection more or less centered.

Figure 19-1: Elliptical Marquee options

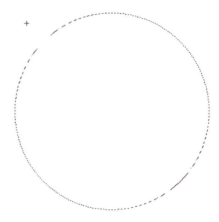

Figure 19-2: Select a circle.

Set the Foreground Color to 30,0,100 (a dark blue). From the menu, choose Edit | Fill Selection. In the Fill Layer dialog, choose Foreground Color for the Contents, and then click OK to fill the selection with blue as shown in Figure 19-3.

Figure 19-3: Fill the circle with blue.

Glow

Choose Layer | New | Layer via Copy to copy its contents to a new layer. In the Layers palette, rename the new layer Glow. Hide the Circle layer by clicking on its eye icon in the Layers palette, as shown in Figure 19-4.

Make sure the Glow layer is selected in the Layers palette, and then CTRL-click (CMD-click on a Macintosh) on its thumbnail to select its contents, as shown in Figure 19-5. From the menu, choose Select | Modify | Contract. In the Contract Selection dialog, enter a value of 32 and click OK. Now only the center of the circle is selected, as shown in Figure 19-6. Choose Select | Feather and enter a value of 25 pixels. Click OK, and then press DELETE to delete the contents of the selection, as shown in Figure 19-7. Feathering the selection gives you a nice, smooth transition between transparent and opaque.

Remove the selection (Select | Deselect).

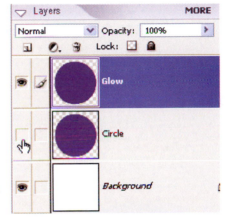

Figure 19-4: Hide the Circle layer.

Figure 19-5: CTRL-click or CMD-click to select the layer's contents.

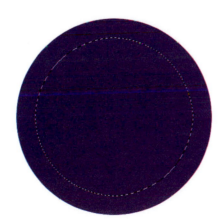

Figure 19-6: The selection is contracted.

Figure 19-7: A smooth transition between blue and transparent

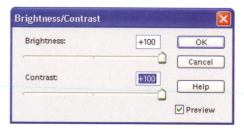

Figure 19-8: Turn up the brightness and contrast.

From the menu, choose Enhance | Adjust Lighting | Brightness/Contrast. Turn both Brightness and Contrast all the way up to 100, as shown in Figure 19-8, and click OK. This turns every pixel in the Glow layer pure white. In the Layers palette, set the Glow layer's blending mode to Screen and reduce the layer Opacity to 55%.

Since Screen mode lightens the underlying layers, the Glow layer is now invisible against the white Background. Unhide the Circle layer by turning on its eye icon in the Layers palette.

Shadow

Select the Glow layer in the Layers palette, and then create a new layer (Layer | New | Layer). Name the new layer Shadow. In the Layers palette, CTRL-click or CMD-click on the original Circle layer to select its contents. Make sure the Shadow layer is still selected, and then choose Edit | Fill Selection. In the Fill Layer dialog, set the Contents to use black and click OK.

Figure 19-9: A soft crescent shadow

Leave the selection active and select the Elliptical Marquee tool from the Toolbox. Hold down the SHIFT key and tap the left arrow key and the up arrow key six times each. With the SHIFT key down, each key press moves the marquee 10 pixels, rather than one, so this moves the selection 60 pixels each direction.

Feather the selection (Select | Feather) by 40 pixels. Press DELETE to delete the contents of the selection, leaving a nice, soft, crescent shadow as shown in Figure 19-9. Remove the selection (Select | Deselect), and then, in the Layers palette, set the Shadow layer's opacity to 40%.

Now is a good time to save your work.

Highlight

Create a new layer (Layer | New | Layer) called Highlight. Set the new layer's blending mode to Screen. CTRL-click or CMD-click on the Circle layer to select its contents. Make sure the Highlight layer is still selected in the Layers palette, and then fill the selection with black (Edit | Fill Selection). In Screen mode, the lighter areas of the layer lighten the underlying layers. Since the layer is currently all black, it has no effect at all.

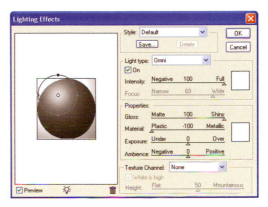

Figure 19-10: Lighting Effects

From the menu, choose Filter | Render | Lighting Effects. In the Lighting Effects dialog, set everything as shown in Figure 19-10. Set the Light Type to Omni and increase its intensity to 100. Set Gloss to 100 (Shiny), Material to –100 (Plastic), and Exposure and Ambience both to 0. Position the light in the upper-left corner of the image by dragging its center handle. Enlarge the light's radius by pulling on the outer handles. Click OK.

Remove the selection (Select | Deselect).

From the menu, choose Enhance | Auto Levels to increase the contrast of the resulting highlight. The results are shown in Figure 19-11.

Figure 19-11: Lighting Effects applied

Reflections

That's looking like a glass marble, all right. For a final touch, let's give it just a hint of a reflection. Set the Foreground to white (255,255,255) and the Background color to 100,175,230 (a sky blue).

In the Layers palette, select the Highlight layer. CTRL-click or CMD-click on its thumbnail to select the layer's contents. Now, create a new layer above it (Layer | New | Layer). Name the new layer Clouds.

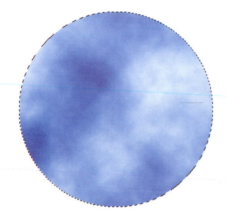

Figure 19-12: Handmade clouds

With the selection still active, choose Filter | Render | Clouds to fill the selection with blue and white clouds. From the menu, choose Enhance | Auto Contrast to bump up their contrast. Turn off the selection (Select | Deselect). Your results should resemble Figure 19-12.

Set the Clouds layer's blending mode to Linear Burn (which darkens the underlying layers) and reduce its opacity to 20%.

That's our marble. Save your work.

Into the Street

Open your favorite photograph of a street, driveway, or parking lot—or, if you don't have one handy, open the file street.jpg (Figure 19-13). Save the document as marbles-poster.psd.

Return to your original marble.psd document. Hide the Background layer by clicking its eye icon in the Layers palette. With only the marble showing, choose Select | All, and then Edit | Copy Merged to copy all the marble layers to the clipboard.

Figure 19-13: The street

Return to the new marbles-poster.psd document and paste the marble to a new layer (Edit | Paste), as shown in Figure 19-14.

Smooth It Out

The edge of the marble might look a little jagged, so let's smooth it out. In the Layers palette, CTRL-click or CMD-click on the new layer to select its contents. From the menu, choose Select | Modify | Contract. Enter a value of 2 pixels and click OK. This excludes the outermost pixels from the selection. Now choose Select | Feather. Enter a Feather Radius of 1 pixel, and click OK.

Figure 19-14: Paste a marble in the street.

Copy the selection to a new layer (Layer | New | Layer via Copy). Even though you can't see it just yet, the new layer has a much smoother edge than before, as shown in Figure 19-15. In the Layers palette, name the top layer Marble, and name the lower marble layer Shadow, as shown in Figure 19-16.

Figure 19-15: Feathering smoothes the edge.

Shadow

Shadows tie an object to its environment. Elements' drop shadows aren't the kind of shadows we can use here. Instead, we'll make some by hand.

In the Layers palette, select the Shadow layer. CTRL-click or CMD-click on its thumbnail and fill the selection with black (Edit | Fill Selection). You can't see the Shadow layer, but it should be solid black now. Remove the selection (Select | Deselect).

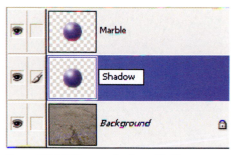

Figure 19-16: Rename the layer Shadow.

Select the Move tool from the Toolbox, and then click and drag on the top handle to squash the black shadow down to about one-third of its original height. Hold down the CTRL or CMD key and click and drag up on the right side handle, as shown in Figure 19-17, to skew the shadow. Drag the shadow into a believable position beneath the marble. Press ENTER (RETURN on a Macintosh) to accept the changes.

Figure 19-17: Skew the shadow.

Figure 19-18: Blur the shadow into the scene.

This shadow is far too sharp and black. To fix that, choose Filter | Blur | Gaussian Blur. Enter a Radius of 10 pixels and click OK to blur the shadow as shown in Figure 19-18. In the Layers palette, reduce the Shadow layer's opacity to 60%.

Making Marbles

In the Layers palette, select the Marble layer, and then duplicate it half a dozen times (Layer | New | Layer via Copy). You can use a shortcut, CTRL-J or CMD-J, to speed things along. Hide the original Marble layer.

Repeat the process with the Shadow layer, creating a matching half dozen copies of it, and hiding the original shadow layer.

In the Layers palette, link each Marble layer to its Shadow layer by first selecting the Marble layer, and then turning on the link icon in the corresponding Shadow layer: Marble copy 6 to Shadow copy 6, and so forth, as shown in Figure 19-19.

In the Layers palette, select any Marble layer. Select the Move tool, and then hold down the SHIFT key and click and drag on one of the top corner handles to resize the sphere and its shadow. (That's why we link them.) Click and drag within the handles to reposition the sphere and shadow in the image. Press ENTER to accept the changes.

Repeat the process to resize and reposition all of your marbles. Figure 19-20 shows my arrangement.

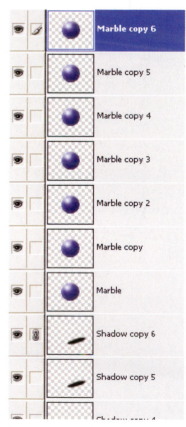

Figure 19-19: Link layers

Figure 19-20: An assortment of marbles

Colorizing

You've undoubtedly noticed that the marbles are all the same color. To change that, select any Marble layer in the Layers palette, and then choose Enhance | Adjust Color | Adjust Hue/Saturation. Drag the Hue slider around to change the color of the marble. Play around with the Saturation and Lightness values as well. Also try reducing a Marble layer's opacity a bit, to make it translucent. Figure 19-21 shows one possible result.

Figure 19-21: Marbles of different colors

Chalk Circle

Let's draw a chalk boundary for our sidewalk marble game. Set the Foreground Color to White. Select the Brush tool from the Toolbox. In the Options bar, choose the 17 pixel Chalk brush from the default brush presets, as shown in Figure 19-22. Click the More Options button at the far right of the Options bar. Set the Spacing to 50% and the Scatter to 4%, as shown in Figure 19-23. This will create a rougher, less consistent brush stroke.

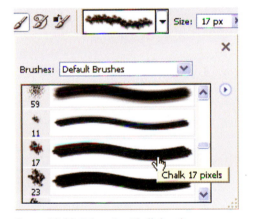

Figure 19-22: Select the Chalk brush.

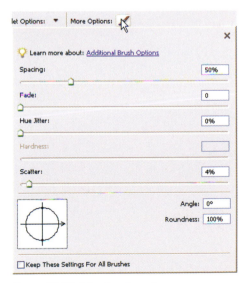

Figure 19-23: More brush options

Figure 19-24: A chalk circle

In the Layers palette, select the Background layer, and then create a new layer (Layer | New | Layer). Name the new layer Chalk. Use the Brush tool to sketch a crude chalk circle on the ground, as shown in Figure 19-24. Reduce the Chalk layer's opacity to about 70%.

Save your work, and then flatten the image (Layer | Flatten Image).

Frame It

To create a frame around your poster, select the Rectangular Marquee tool from the Toolbox. In the Options bar, set the Mode to Fixed Size and enter a Width of 796 px and a Height of 596 px. Click and drag to select your favorite portion of the image, and then copy it to the clipboard (Edit | Copy). Remove the selection (Select | Deselect), and then fill the layer with black (Edit | Fill Layer).

Paste from the clipboard onto a new layer (Edit | Paste). With no selection active, Elements automatically centers the contents within the new layer.

Choose the Move tool, and then hold down SHIFT and press the up arrow three times to make room for a motivational saying below the image. Set the Foreground Color to White, and then select the Type tool, click on the image, and type in your motivational saying. Mine's from G. K. Chesterton, in the KidTYPEPaint font.

When you're happy, flatten the image (Layer | Flatten Image) and save your work.

This project is based in part on a tutorial by Anson Vogt of phong.com. Thanks, Anson!

Circuit (Board) City: From Circuit Board to Futuristic City

20

In This Project You Will:

- ☐ Create random patterns with the Clouds filter

- ☐ Use the Extrude and Emboss filters to create faux 3-D effects

- ☐ Colorize a grayscale image

- ☐ Create lens flares

This project creates a circuit board, or a future city, or a cool abstract design, depending on how you look at it. It is one of the few projects in the book accomplished entirely with filters and adjustments … well, almost entirely.

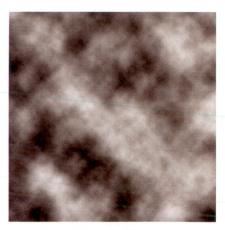

Figure 20-1: Effect of Difference Clouds

Figure 20-2: A mosaic grid

Getting Started

Start by creating a new document (File | New | Blank File). Set Width and Height both to 800 and make sure that the Color Mode is set to RGB color. Click OK to create the document. Save the document as circuit.psd.

Set Elements' Foreground and Background Colors to their default black and white. From the menu, choose Edit | Fill Layer. In the Fill Layer dialog, choose Black from the Contents, and click OK to fill the Background layer with black.

Now choose Filter | Render | Difference Clouds. You should have something like Figure 20-1. Yours won't be exactly the same because Difference Clouds' results are random.

From the menu, choose Filter | Pixelate | Mosaic. Set the Cell Size to 24 and click OK. This creates the basic grid that will form the basis of the circuit board, as shown in Figure 20-2.

Next, choose Filter | Blur | Radial Blur. In the Radial Blur dialog, set the Amount to 40, the Blur Method to Zoom, and the Quality to Best, as shown in Figure 20-3. Click OK to blur the grid outward from the center.

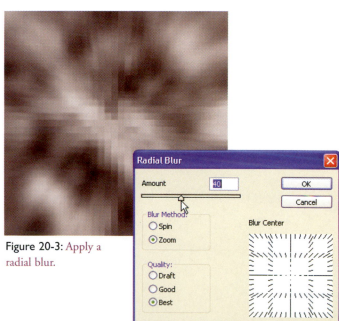

Figure 20-3: Apply a radial blur.

Filter | Stylize | Emboss. Set the Angle to 135°, the Height to 4 pixels, and the Amount to 200%, as shown in Figure 20-4, and then click OK. This adds a little faux 3-D to the grid, as shown in Figure 20-5.

To further accent the edges of the grid, use the Accented Edges filter (Filter | Brush Strokes | Accented Edges). Set the Edge Width to 4, the Edge Brightness to 50, and the Smoothness to 10, and then click OK to apply the filter. The results are shown in Figure 20-6.

The white lines are the only things we're going to use. To make them easier to find, choose Enhance | Auto Levels to increase the contrast between the edges and the background, as shown in Figure 20-7.

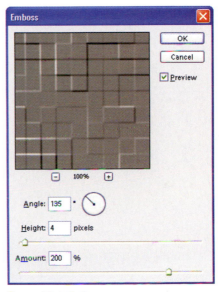

Figure 20-4: Emboss

Figure 20-5: Emboss adds 3-D.

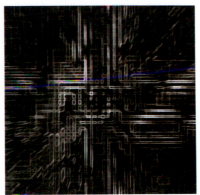

Figure 20-7: Auto Levels increases the contrast.

Figure 20-6: With accented edges

Figure 20-8: Find the edges.

Now, choose Filter | Stylize | Find Edges. This sharply picks out all the edges, as shown in Figure 20-8. It also inverts the colors in the image, but those are easily restored by choosing Filter | Adjustments | Invert, as shown in Figure 20-9.

There's our circuit board, boys and girls, although it's currently in black and white. To add some color, choose Enhance | Adjust Color | Adjust Hue/Saturation. In the Hue/Saturation dialog, check the Colorize box at lower right, and then set Hue to 80, Saturation to 40, and Lightness to –10, as shown in Figure 20-10. Click OK to apply the color.

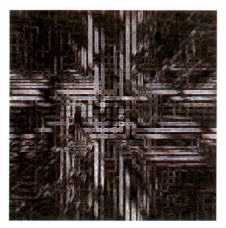

Figure 20-9: Invert the colors back to white on black.

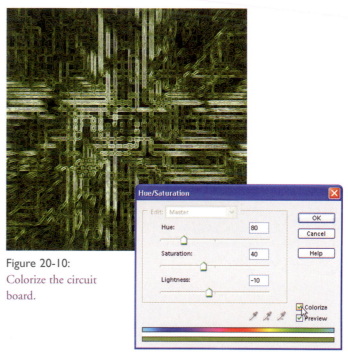

Figure 20-10: Colorize the circuit board.

Save your work. If you're just after a circuit board pattern, you can call it done now. The central part of the pattern looks more circuit-boardish than does the outside. You can often make the image look more like a real circuit board by cropping it down a bit, as shown in Figure 20-11.

Future City

You can turn this basic circuit board into a nighttime aerial view of a futuristic city. Start by copying the Background layer to a new layer: from the menu, choose Layer | New | Layer via Copy. In the Layers palette, rename the new layer Buildings. From the menu, choose Filter | Stylize | Extrude. In the Extrude dialog, set Type to Blocks, Size to 10 pixels, and Depth to 30. Select Level-Based, Solid Front Faces, and Mask Incomplete Blocks, as shown in Figure 20-12, and then click OK. This filter extrudes the image into blocks, 10 pixels wide, whose height is based on the brightness of the base image, as shown in Figure 20-13.

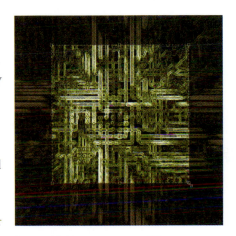

Figure 20-11: A crop can yield a more circuit board–like result.

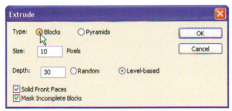

Figure 20-12: Extrude

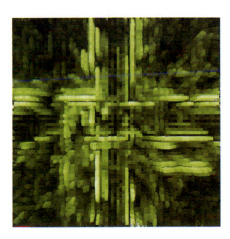

Figure 20-13: Extruded buildings

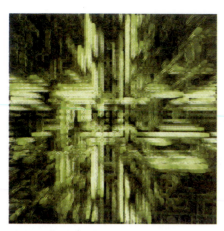

Figure 20-14: Lighten mode lets the streets show through.

Figure 20-15: From green to blue

Now, in the Layers palette, set the Buildings layer's blending mode to Lighten. This allows the underlying circuit board to show through, like lighted streets beneath the new layer of buildings, as shown in Figure 20-14. Flatten the image by choosing Layer | Flatten Image.

For a cityscape, I don't think that circuit board green works very well. To change it, call up the Hue/Saturation adjustment dialog again (Enhance | Adjust Color | Adjust Hue/Saturation). Select Colorize, and then slide the Hue to 210 and the Saturation to 60, and then click OK (Figure 20-15).

To add some more color, create a new layer above the background (Layer | New | Layer). Name the new layer Hue and set its Mode to Hue. Click OK.

Select the Brush tool from the Toolbox. In the Options bar, choose a soft, round, 300-pixel brush. Set the Foreground Color to red (255,0,0) and paint in the corners to tint the underlying city. Switch the Foreground Color to yellow (255,255,0) and add some additional touches of color, as shown in Figure 20-16. If the effect is too strong for your tastes, lower the Hue layer's opacity.

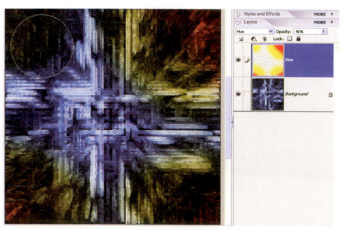

Figure 20-16: Paint in additional colors.

You can add more colors, or strategically erase parts of the Hue layer to suit your personal tastes. When you're happy, flatten your image (Layer | Flatten Image).

Save your work.

Street Lights and Flying Cars

For a final touch, you add a cool few lights floating here and there. Start by creating a new layer (Layer | New | Layer). Name the layer Flare and set its Mode to Screen. Click OK. Fill the new Flare layer with black (Edit | Fill Layer). Black has no effect in Screen mode, so you won't see anything just yet.

Figure 20-17: The Lens Flare dialog

Choose Filter | Render | Lens Flare. In the Lens Flare dialog, set the Brightness to 100% and select 50–300mm Zoom from the Lens Type. In the dialog's preview window, click as near the center as possible to minimize the lens flare artifacts, as shown in Figure 20-17. Click OK to apply the lens flare. The flare will now be visible above the cityscape, while the black background will remain invisible. To make the flare stand out more brightly, choose Enhance | Adjust Lighting | Levels. Set the Input Levels to 0, 0.60, 225, as shown in Figure 20-18 and click OK. This sharply increases the flare's contrast, as shown in Figure 20-19.

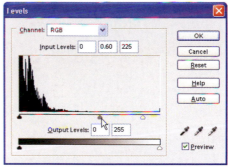

Figure 20-18: Change the Lens Flare levels.

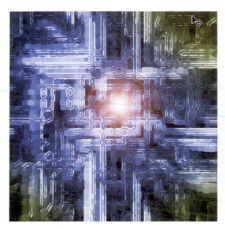 

Figure 20-19: The lens flare has gained contrast.

You can change the color of the lens flare with the Hue/Saturation adjustment (Enhance | Adjust Color | Adjust Hue/Saturation). Drag the Hue slider around to try out different colors.

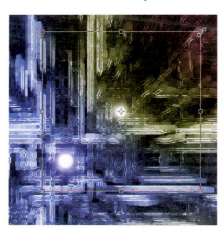

Duplicate the Flare layer (Layer | New | Layer via Copy) and use the Move tool to reposition the new flare. SHIFT-click and drag on one of the corner handles to resize the flare, as shown in Figure 20-20. If you can't see the handles, choose View | Zoom out until you can. Press ENTER (RETURN on a Macintosh) when you're satisfied with the results.

Repeat this process as many (or few) times as you please, to create strings of lights. When you're happy, flatten your image (Layer | Flatten Image), and save your work.

This project is based in part on a tutorial by Man1c M0g at www .biorust.com. Thanks, Man1c!

Figure 20-20: Move and resize additional flares.

Vector Greeting Card: Assemble Santa from Simple Vector Shapes

21

In This Project You Will:

☐ Select and create shapes from Elements' shape libraries

☐ Use grouped layers to control visibility

☐ Create a complete illustration from simple shapes.

You can build delightful and surprisingly complex images in Photoshop Elements by simply combining shapes from Elements' built-in collection of shapes. This project creates a greeting card, featuring Santa, from simple shapes. It's reminiscent of many a grade school composition made with construction paper and scissors.

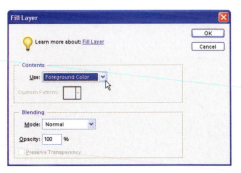

Figure 21-1: Fill the canvas with the foreground color.

Figure 21-2: Change the grid preferences.

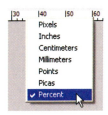

Figure 21-3: Set the rulers to Percent.

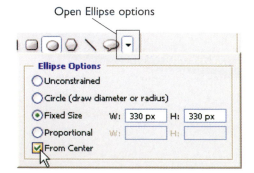

Figure 21-4: Set new Ellipse options.

Getting Started

Start by creating a new document (File | New | Blank File). Make it 700 pixels wide by 750 pixels tall. Make sure Color Mode is RGB Color, and click OK to create it. Save the new document as santa-card.psd.

In the Toolbox, set the Foreground Color to 35,90,145 (a dark blue). From the menu choose Edit | Fill Layer. In the Fill Layer dialog, set the Contents to Foreground Color, as shown in Figure 21-1. Click OK.

Let's turn on the grid, so you can follow along more easily. If you are using Windows, choose Edit | Preferences | Grid from the menu. On a Macintosh, choose Photoshop Elements | Preferences | Grid. Set the grid Color to Cyan, and the Style to Lines. Set a gridline every 10 percent, with 1 subdivision, as shown in Figure 21-2. This will show a gridline at 10%, 20%, 30%, and so forth. Click OK. Turn the grid on by choosing View | Grid from the menu. Also make sure Snap to Grid is enabled (View | Snap to Grid).

Turn on the rulers, as well (View | Rulers). Set the rulers to percent by right-clicking (CONTROL-click for Macintosh users) on a ruler and choosing Percent from the pop-up list, as shown in Figure 21-3.

Choose View | Fit on Screen so you can see your entire document.

Big Belly

Time for Santa. Let's start with his big fat belly. In the Toolbox, set the Foreground Color to pure red (255,0,0).

In the Toolbox, select the Ellipse tool. In the Options bar, click the triangle to open the Ellipse Options pop-up, as shown in Figure 21-4.

In the Ellipse options, select Fixed Size, and enter a width and height of 330 pixels. Select From Center. This will create a circle, 330 pixels across, centered wherever you click in the document. Move the cursor to a point about 70% of the way to the right, and 60% of the way down, as shown in Figure 21-5. Click to create your circle.

In the Layers palette, name the new layer Belly. It's a really good idea to rename each layer as you create it—Left Shoe, Hat, Right Eye, and so forth. It'll make it much, much easier to find individual elements later on, believe me.

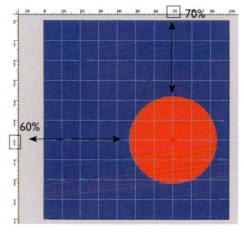

Figure 21-5: Creating Santa's belly

Legs and Arms

Santa's legs and arms are created with the Rectangle tool, as shown in Figure 21-6. (Actually, our Santa only has one arm ... don't tell him.) I've added the white outlines around the rectangles to make the figure clearer; you won't see these outlines in your document.

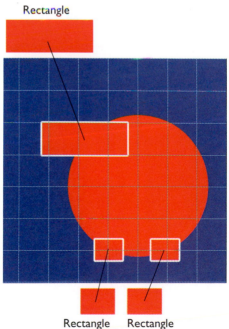

Figure 21-6: Creating Santa's arms and legs

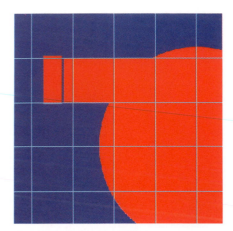

Figure 21-7: Create a cuff.

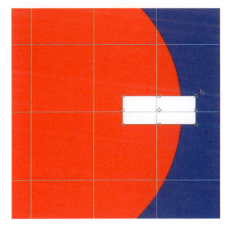

Figure 21-8: A second cuff

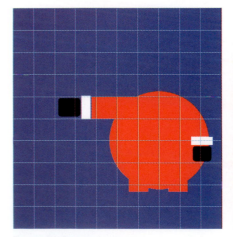

Figure 21-9: Santa's mittens

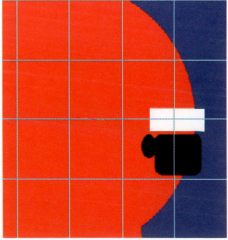

Figure 21-10: Adding a thumb

With the Rectangle tool, click and drag to create the left cuff at the end of the arm. Make it a bit taller than the sleeve, as shown in Figure 21-7. Change the shape's color to white in the Options bar. To create the right cuff, copy the first Cuff layer (Layer | New | Layer via Copy), and then select the Move tool. Drag the cuff over to the right side, and then click and drag outside of a corner handle to rotate the cuff 90 degrees, as shown in Figure 21-8. Hold down the SHIFT key while dragging to constrain the rotation to 15 degree intervals.

Santa's mittens are made with the Rounded Rectangle tool. Select it and then, in the Options bar, set the Radius to 10 pixels, and change the color to black. Click and drag to create the mittens, as shown in Figure 21-9.

Choose the Ellipse tool from the Toolbox. In the Options bar, change the tool's color to black. Open the Ellipse options and deselect Circle. Click and drag near Santa's left mitten to create a thumb, as shown in Figure 21-10.

Face, Beard, and Shoes

Santa's face, beard, and shoes are all made of simple circles, as shown in Figure 21-11. Select the Ellipse tool from the Toolbox.

In the Options bar, open the Ellipse Options drop-down, as shown in Figure 21-12, and select Circle and From Center. This will allow you to draw perfect circles centered on your initial click without holding down lots of extra keyboard keys.

Start with the face. Click at the top center of Santa's belly and drag outward to create the face. In the Options bar, set the color to Santa's skin tone. I chose 255,180,130.

Click beneath Santa's chin and drag outward until the beard almost reaches his eyes. In the Options bar, change the tool's color to white.

Finally, let's create Santa's shoes. Click at the intersection of the two gridlines beneath Santa's left leg, and drag outward until the circle almost meets the bottom of his leg. In the Options bar, change the color to Black. Copy this Shoe layer (Layer | New | Layer via Copy). Now, select the Move tool from the Toolbox and move the duplicate shoe into place beneath the other leg. In the Layers palette, select one of the Shoe layers and choose Layer | Simplify Layer from the menu. Repeat this step with the other shoe. In the Layers palette, select the topmost of the two Shoe layers. From the menu, choose Layer | Merge Down to combine the two shoes into a single layer.

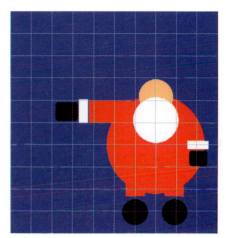

Figure 21-11: Face, beard, shoes … just circles

Open Ellipse options

Figure 21-12: Changing Ellipse options.

Choose the Rectangular Marquee tool from the Toolbox and select the bottom half of the shoes as shown in Figure 21-13. Press DELETE to delete the selected area. Then turn off the selection (Select | Deselect).

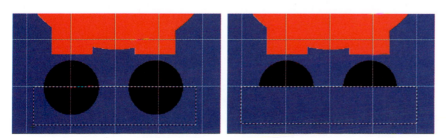

Figure 21-13: Cut the shoes down.

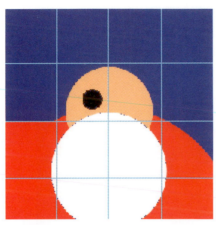

Figure 21-14: Start an eye.

Figure 21-15: Add a pupil.

Figure 21-16: Santa's mouth

Eyes

To give Santa his eyes, return to the Ellipse tool. Click and drag to create Santa's eye, as shown in Figure 21-14. In the Options bar, set the color to white. In the Layers palette, select the Eye layer and duplicate it (Layer | New | Layer via Copy). Use the Move tool to move it into position on the other side of Santa's face. Click on the Ellipse tool again. Click and drag to create a smaller circle for Santa's pupil, as shown in Figure 21-15. Then change the color in the Options bar to black. In the Layers palette, select the black Pupil layer and duplicate it (Layer | New | Layer via Copy). Use the Move tool to move it into position on the other side of Santa's face to give him two eyes.

Click on the Ellipse tool again. In the Options bar, change the tool's color to red. Give Santa a round mouth, about the size of one of his eyes, and then in the Options bar change the shape's color to red, as shown in Figure 21-16.

Moustache

Next, Santa needs a moustache. In the Ellipse options dropdown, choose Unconstrained. Click near the center of Santa's mouth and pull outward to create an oval, taller than it is wide, as shown in Figure 21-17. In the Options bar, change the color

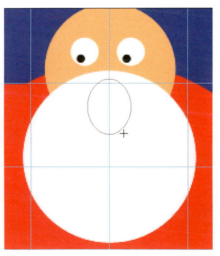

Figure 21-17: Draw a moustache.

to white. In the Layers palette, choose Layer | Simplify Layer from the menu. In the Layers palette, reduce the new layer's opacity to about 50%, allowing you to see the mouth underneath.

Select the Rectangular Marquee tool from the Toolbox and select the bottom half of the moustache, as shown in Figure 21-18, and then press DELETE to delete it. Turn off the selection (Select | Deselect). In the Layers palette, restore the Moustache layer's opacity to 100%. CTRL-click (CMD-click on a Macintosh) on the Moustache layer thumbnail to select the moustache pixels. From the menu, choose Edit | Stroke (Outline) Selection. In the Stroke dialog, set the Width to 2 px, Color to black, and Location to Outside, as shown in Figure 21-19. Click OK, and then turn off the selection (Select | Deselect).

This would be a good time to save your work.

Hat and Belt

Santa's hat is made from a white rectangle, a red triangle, and a white circle, as shown in Figure 21-20. Use the Rectangle tool to create the white trim.

Figure 21-18: Trimming the moustache

Figure 21-19: Stroke the moustache.

Figure 21-20: Santa's hat

Open Shape palette

Triangle

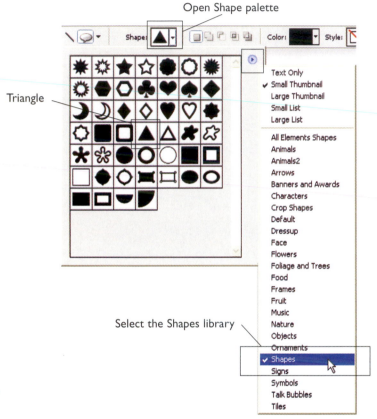

Select the Shapes library

Figure 21-21: Select the Shapes library.

Use the Custom Shape tool to create the red triangle part of the hat. With the Custom Shape tool selected, open the Shape Picker in the options bar, and then click the small triangle at the upper right of the palette, and select Shapes from the pop-up list, as shown in Figure 21-21. Select the Triangle shape from the Shape Picker. Click and drag to create the hat, and then use the Move tool to position it.

Use the Ellipse tool to create the pom-pom: hold down the SHIFT key to constrain the pom-pom to a perfect circle, and then change its color to white.

To make Santa's belt, first select his Belly layer in the Layers palette. Use the Rectangle tool to create a thin black rectangle, as shown in Figure 21-22. Select the new Belt layer in the Layers palette, and then choose Layer | Group with Previous from the menu. The Belt layer is now "clipped" by the Belly layer; it is only visible where it overlaps Santa's belly, as shown in Figure 21-23.

Save your work.

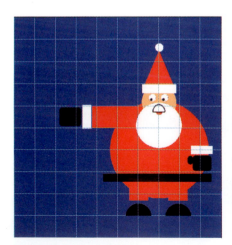

Figure 21-22: Start the belt.

Figure 21-23: Clip the belt to Santa's belly.

Snow and Tree

To create snow on the ground, first turn off Snap to Grid (View | Snap to Grid). Select the Brush tool and in the Options bar, select a hard, round, 50-pixel brush. Set the Foreground Color to 200,190,240 (a light lilac).

In the Layers palette, select the Background layer and use the Brush to paint in a snowy hill, as shown in Figure 21-24.

To create the Christmas tree, select the Custom Shape tool. In the Options bar, set the tool color to 25,75,25 (a dark green). Open the Custom Shape Picker and choose the Foliage and Trees library. Select Tree 1, as shown in Figure 21-25. Select the topmost layer in the Layers palette—the layer farthest above the Background layer.

Figure 21-24: Paint in some snow.

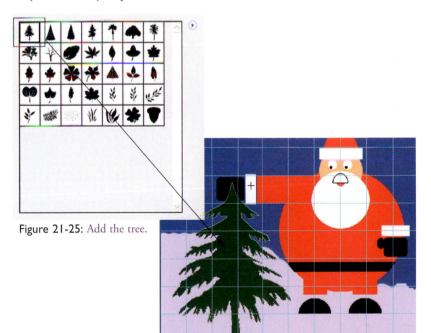

Figure 21-25: Add the tree.

Then click and drag to create the Christmas tree. Use the Move tool to resize and reposition the tree, if you need to.

From the menu, choose Layer | New | Layer via Copy, to copy the tree. In the Layers palette, double-click the thumbnail of the lower of the two Tree layers. When the Color Picker appears, select white (255,255,255) and click OK. Choose the Move tool and press the up arrow four times to raise the white layer and create the effect of snow lying on the boughs.

Figure 21-26: Paint some foreground snow.

To create some snow in the foreground for Santa to stand on, select the topmost layer in the Layers palette—the layer farthest above the Background layer. Create a new layer (Layer | New | Layer). Set the foreground color to 220,255,255 and use the Brush tool to paint in a little foreground snow, as shown in Figure 21-26.

I placed a yellow star atop the tree with the Custom Shape tool, using the 5 Point Star from the Shapes library.

There's a nice space at the top for you to add your holiday greeting with the Type tool. Mine is in 96 point Script MT Bold. I used the same color (220,255,255) as I did for the foreground snow. When the text's in place, flatten your image (Layer | Flatten Layers).

Finally, create a flurry of snowflakes using the Custom Shape tool; Elements includes four different snowflake shapes in the Nature library.

When you're feeling sufficiently festive, flatten the image (Layer | Flatten Image) and save your work.

Wine Bottle: Create Photoreal Composite Vector Shapes

In This Project
You Will:

- ☐ Create a composite shape from simple Photoshop Elements shapes

- ☐ Use shading to create photo-real glass

- ☐ Use filters to bend a label around a bottle

As the last project shows, you can create complex pictures from simple shapes. But while the last project was reminiscent of construction paper art, this project will show you how to create a surprisingly realistic glass from the same basic shapes.

Getting Started

Begin by creating a new file: choose File | New | Blank
File. Name the document bottle.psd, set the Width to
1024 pixels, the Height to 768 pixels, the Color mode to
RGB color, and the Background Contents to White.

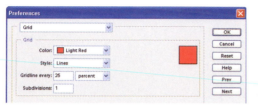

Figure 22-1: Grid preferences

This project requires a lot of shapes to line up with each
other. To make that easier to accomplish, let's start by
setting up Elements' grid. From the menu, choose Edit
| Preferences | Grid (on a Macintosh,
choose Photoshop Elements | Preferences
| Grid). In the Grid dialog, set the Color
to Light Red, and the Style to Lines.
Specify a gridline every 25 percent, and
enter 1 for the number of subdivisions, as
shown in Figure 22-1. Click OK.

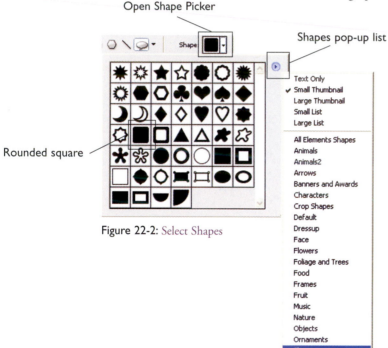

Figure 22-2: Select Shapes

Turn on the grid (View | Grid) and
enable snapping to the grid (View | Snap
to Grid). Now we're ready to create our
bottle.

Custom Shapes

Select the Custom Shape tool. In the
Options bar, open the Custom Shape
Picker, as shown in Figure 22-2, and then
click the arrow at the top right of the
palette and choose Shapes from the pop-
up list. Select the Rounded Square shape
from the Custom Shape Picker.

In the Custom Shape Options drop-down, select From Center and Fixed Size,
and then set Width to 157 px and the Height to 310 px, as shown in Figure 22-3.
Finally, set the tool to a nice, bright blue as shown in Figure 22-4.

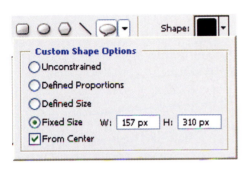

Figure 22-3: Custom Shape options

Figure 22-4: Set the shape's color to blue.

Click near the center of the canvas to create the shape. In the Layers palette, name the new layer Body Upper. If necessary, use the Move tool to slide the shape a bit to the left or right until it snaps into place in the very center of the canvas, as shown in Figure 22-5.

Duplicate this layer by choosing Layer | New | Layer via Copy from the menu. In the Layers palette, name the new layer Body Lower.

Select the Move tool. Hold down the SHIFT key and tap the down arrow nine times. When you hold the SHIFT key, each press of an arrow key moves the selected object 10 pixels, rather than just one. So this last step moved the shape down by 90 pixels, as shown in Figure 22-6.

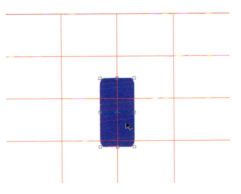

Figure 22-5: Place the first shape.

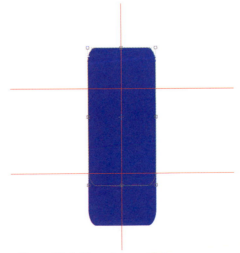

Figure 22-6: Place the second shape.

Necking

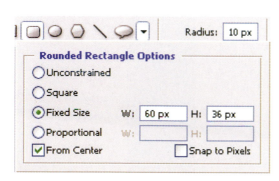

That's the bottle's body; for the neck, we'll again use the Custom Shape tool. With the Rounded Square shape still selected, open the Custom Shape Options drop-down and change the Width to 55 px, and the Height to 222 px.

Click on the canvas to create the shape, and then use the Move tool to snap the shape to the center line and move it down until its bottom curve is just hidden in the top of the bottle, as shown in Figure 22-7. Name the shape layer Neck.

Return to the Custom Shape tool. In the Options bar, switch to the Rounded Rectangle tool, as shown in Figure 22-8. Set the tool's Radius to 10 px. In the Rounded Rectangle options, choose From Center and Fixed Size. Change the Width to 60 px and the Height to 36 px, as shown in Figure 22-9.

Click to create the shape and position it slightly below the top of the neck, as shown in Figure 22-10. Name the layer Bottle Mouth.

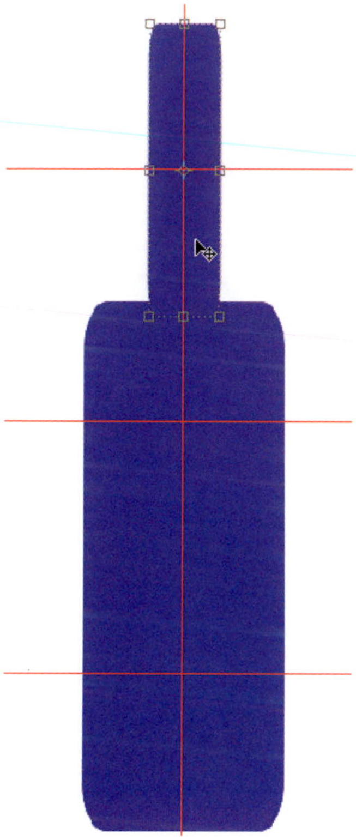

Figure 22-8: The Rounded Rectangle tool

Figure 22-7: Place the neck.

Figure 22-9: Rounded Rectangle options

Figure 22-10: Position the bottle mouth.

Rounding It Off

It's starting to look like a bottle, but there are some unnaturally square corners on it. Let's round them off now.

Choose the Ellipse tool from the Toolbox. In the Ellipse options, select Fixed Size, set the Width to 126 px, and the Height to 12 px, leaving From Center checked. Click near the bottom of the bottle to create a new shape. Name this shape Bottom Rim.

Zoom way in on the bottom of the bottle, and then select the Move tool and use the arrow keys to nudge the ellipse up (or down) until it meets with the curve of the bottle, as shown in Figure 22-11. Figure 22-12 shows the bottle so far.

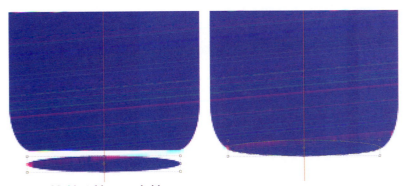

Figure 22-11: Add a rounded bottom.

The biggest problem is the area where the neck joins the body; it's much too square. Zoom out so you can see the entire bottle. Then grab the Custom Shape tool again. In the Custom Shape Picker, click the arrow at the top right of the palette and choose Signs from the pop-up list. Select the Sign 10 shape from the Custom Shape Picker, as shown in Figure 22-13. In the Custom Shape options,

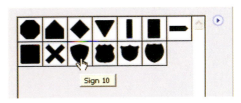

Figure 22-13: Choose Sign 10.

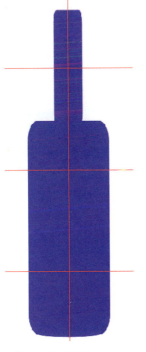

Figure 22-12: Your work so far

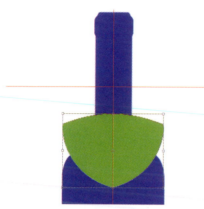

Figure 22-14: Add the sign shape.

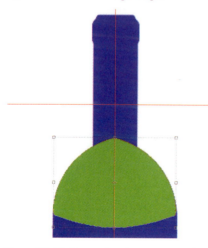

Figure 22-15: Rotate the sign to merge the neck and body.

change the Width to 153 px and the Height to 110 px, leaving From Center checked. Click on the canvas to create the new shape, as shown in Figure 22-14. I've made mine bright green, so you can more easily see what I'm doing, but you can leave yours blue. Name this shape Bottle Top.

Select the Move tool. Make sure that the new shape is snapped to the center line. From the menu, choose Image | Rotate | Layer 180°. With the Move tool still selected, use the arrow keys to nudge the shape up (or down) until it just blends into the curve at the top of the bottle, as shown in Figure 22-15.

A Pair of Pears

The area where the rounded top of the body meets the neck still needs a little work. What's really called for is a nice concave curve. None of the standard shapes gives us that, so we'll use … a pear! Select the Custom Shape tool again. In the Custom Shape picker, click the arrow at the top right of the palette and choose Fruit from the pop-up list. Select the Pear shape from the Custom Shape Picker. In the Custom Shape options, enter a Fixed Size of 76 px wide by 118 px high; leave From Center checked. Click on the canvas to create a new shape layer. Name it Pear. Use the Move tool to drag the pear over to where the neck joins the body, so that it smoothes out the transition, as shown in Figure 22-16. Again, I've made mine green for better visibility, but you can leave yours blue.

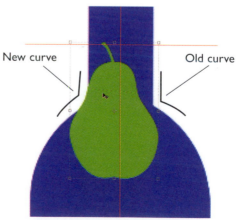

New curve   Old curve

Figure 22-16: Place the pear to smooth the curve.

Copy the Pear layer (Layer | New | Layer via Copy).

Flip the new pear sideways to smooth the curve on the other side of the bottle. First, simplify the Pear layer (Layer | Simplify). Select the entire canvas (Select | All), and then flip it (Image | Rotate | Flip Selection Horizontal). Turn off the selection (Select | Deselect).

By first simplifying the layer, and then selecting the entire canvas, you compel Elements to flip the pear around the center of the canvas, rather than around its own center. This should put the new pear in the proper position on the right side of the bottle. If it needs adjustment, select the Move tool, and then use the arrow keys to nudge it into position.

There's your bottle (Figure 22-17)! Let's merge it into a single shape. In the Layers palette, hide the white Background layer by clicking on its eye icon, as shown in Figure 22-18. Leave all the other layers visible and choose Layer | Merge Visible from the menu to combine them into a single layer. Name the new layer Bottle and unhide the Background layer again. Save your work.

Glass

The shading leaves something to be desired, I'll admit. We'll fix that next, starting with a custom gradient. Select the Gradient tool from the Toolbox. In the Options bar, choose the Linear gradient style, and then click the Edit button to open the Gradient Editor. Choose the Black, White gradient in the top row of the Presets.

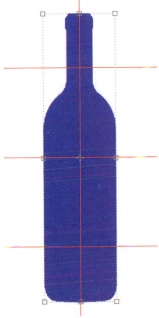

Figure 22-17: It looks like a bottle!

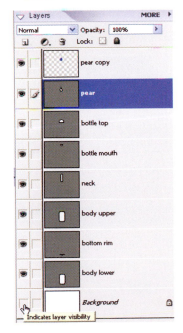

Figure 22-18: Hide the Background.

Double-click on the left Color Stop beneath the gradient bar as shown in Figure 22-19. Set the stop's color to 150,135,145. Next, double-click the right Color Stop and set its color to 45,40,40. Click between the two existing stops to create a new stop. Set its location to 50%, and its color to 55,45,45, as shown in Figure 22-20. Add a fourth stop at 25% and set its color to 50,45,45. Finally add a stop at 75%, with a color of 165,155,160. You should have the gradient in Figure 22-21. Click OK.

Turn off the grid (View | Grid) for a better view.

CTRL-click (CMD-click on a Macintosh) on the Bottle layer's thumbnail in the Layers palette to select that layer's contents; this will keep the gradient inside of

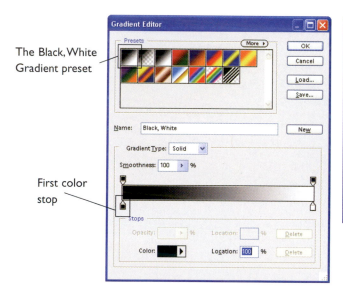

The Black, White Gradient preset

First color stop

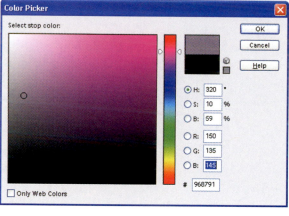

Figure 22-19: Edit the first color stop.

Figure 22-20: Add a third color stop.

Figure 22-21: The final gradient

the bottle's shape in the next step. Hold down the SHIFT key and click and drag from the far left edge of the bottle to the far right, to fill it with the gradient, as shown in Figure 22-22.

With the bottle still selected, grab the Brush tool from the Toolbox. Hold down the ALT key (OPTION on a Macintosh) to temporarily switch to the Eyedropper tool and click in the center of the bottle to sample the color. In the Options bar, choose a soft, round, 21-pixel brush in Normal mode and at 100% opacity. Use the Brush to paint out the lighter parts of the reflections at the top of the bottle, the bottom, and along the neck, as shown in Figure 22-23. Turn off the selection (Select | Deselect). Then save your work.

Label It

Open the file label.jpg (Figure 22-24). Copy the label to a new layer (Layer | New | Layer via Copy) and hide the Background layer by clicking on its eye icon in the Layers palette. To get a little room to work, increase the canvas size by choosing Image | Resize | Canvas Size. Turn off the Relative checkbox. Enter a new value of 500 pixels for both Width and Height and click OK.

Figure 22-22: Pour the gradient in the bottle.

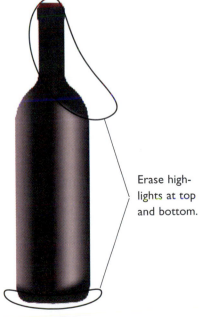

Erase highlights at top and bottom.

Figure 22-23: Paint out some highlights.

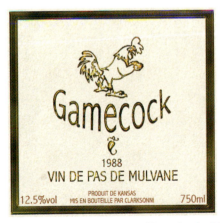

Figure 22-24: The image you'll use for the label

Rotate the label by choosing Image | Rotate | Layer 90° Right, as shown in Figure 22-25. The reason will be apparent in a minute.

From the menu, choose Filter | Distort | Spherize. In the Spherize dialog, set the Mode to Vertical Only and the Amount to 100%, as shown in Figure 22-26, and click OK. This simulates the distortion you'd see if the label was wrapped around a bottle.

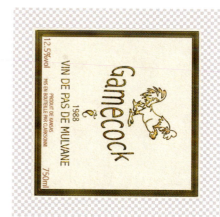

Figure 22-25: Turned on its side

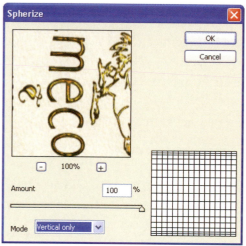

Figure 22-26: Distort the label.

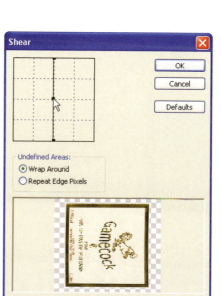

Figure 22-27: Apply a slight shear.

To give the label a little downward bend, we're going to use Elements' Shear filter. The problem is that Shear only bends things sideways. That's why we flipped the label on its side in the first place. From the menu, choose Filter | Distort | Shear. In the Shear dialog, click in the center of the control line to create a new handle. Now, pull a tiny, *tiny* little bit to the left, as shown in Figure 22-27. The results are shown in Figure 22-28.

Rotate the label back to vertical (Image | Rotate | Layer 90° Left), and then select the whole thing (Select | All) and copy it to the clipboard (Edit | Copy). Return to the bottle.psd document (Window | bottle.psd) and paste the label to a new layer. Select the Move tool and use it to resize and reposition the label, as shown in Figure 22-29. Zoom way in to check your work. When you're happy, press ENTER (RETURN on a Macintosh) to accept the changes. Merge the label with the Bottle layer (Layer | Merge Down). Then save your work.

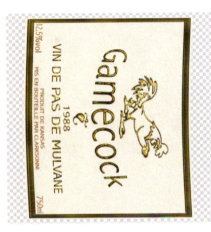

Figure 22-28: The nearly finished label

Final Touches

A few reflections will help to tie everything together. Create a new layer (Layer | New | Layer) and name it Reflections. Set the Foreground color to white (255,255,255).

CTRL-click or CMD-click on the Bottle layer's thumbnail to select its contents but leave the Reflection layer selected. Use the Brush tool with a soft, round, 17-pixel brush to paint along the left side of the bottle, as shown in Figure 22-30. Choose Filter | Blur | Motion Blur, enter a Distance of 30 pixels, be sure the Angle is set to 0°, and click OK.

Figure 22-29: Resize the label to fit.

Figure 22-30: Paint a reflection down the left.

Increase the size of the brush to 27 pixels and paint down the right side of the neck, as shown in Figure 22-31.

Increase the brush size to 45 pixels and paint a white stripe down the right side of the bottle, following the broad reflection there, as shown in Figure 22-32. Reduce the Reflection layer's opacity to 40%.

Zoom in on the mouth of the bottle. Select the Eraser tool and choose a hard, round, 3-pixel brush. Click to the right of the mouth of the bottle, hold down the SHIFT key, and then drag left to erase a straight line through the reflection, as shown in Figure 22-33. Repeat the process to erase a second line just below the mouth of the bottle, as shown. If you SHIFT before you click, you'll get a diagonal line connecting the two horizontal ones. Just Edit | Undo and click *first*.

Select the Rectangular Marquee tool. In the Options bar, change the Mode to Normal. Select the reflections remaining on the bottle's mouth, as shown in Figure 22-34. Hold down the CTRL or CMD key and press the right arrow key three times to nudge the reflections to the right. Remove the selection (Select | Deselect). Use the Smudge tool with a 9-pixel soft brush in Normal mode with a Strength of 30% to distort the reflection a bit, if you want.

Save your work.

Figure 22-31: Add some glare to the neck.

Figure 22-32: Yet more reflected glare

Figure 22-33: Erase two lines across the mouth.

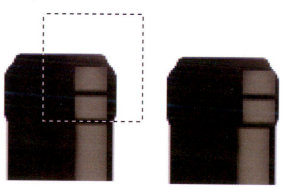

Figure 22-34: Select the top reflections and nudge them to the right.

Making the Band

In the Layers palette, select the Bottle layer, and then create a new blank layer (Layer | New | Layer). Name the layer Band.

Select the Rectangular Marquee tool. Click and drag to select a short area at the bottom of the neck, as shown in Figure 22-35.

Select the Gradient tool. Choose a Linear gradient. In the Gradient Picker, select the Copper gradient and click OK. Hold down the SHIFT key and drag from *right to left* across the neck to fill the selection with the gradient, as shown in Figure 22-36. Now, choose Layer | Group with Previous from the menu. This "clips" the band, so that it's only visible where it overlaps the bottle, as shown in Figure 22-37.

Remove the selection (Select | Deselect), and then copy the Band layer (Layer | New | Layer via Copy). Again, choose Layer | Group with Previous. Select the Move tool. Hold down the SHIFT key and drag the new layer up above the first, as shown in Figure 22-38. Click and drag on the top-center handle to

Figure 22-35: Select an area.

Figure 22-36: Fill the selection with a gradient.

Figure 22-37: Clip the band to the bottle.

Figure 22-38: Duplicate the existing band.

Figure 22-39: Resize
the new band.

Figure 22-40: Recolor
the new band.

Figure 22-41: The beginnings of a
background

squash the new band down, as shown in Figure 22-39, and press ENTER. Finally, choose Enhance | Adjust Color | Adjust Hue/Saturation. In the Hue/Saturation dialog, move the Hue slider to 55 and click OK. This colors the thin band a yellow-green, as shown in Figure 22-40.

In the Layers palette, hide the Background layer by clicking its eye icon and choose Layer | Merge Visible to merge all the bottle layers into one. Rename the layer Bottle and save your work.

A New Background

Finally, let's create a new background. Adjust your view so you can see the entire bottle (View | Fit on Screen). Unhide the Background layer and make sure it is the selected layer. Select the Gradient tool and, in the Gradient Picker, select the Black to White gradient. Select Radial Gradient in the Options bar, and then click and drag from the center of the canvas to one side to fill the Background with the gradient, as shown in Figure 22-41. Invert the colors by choosing Filter | Adjustments | Invert. Now choose Enhance | Adjust Lighting | Levels, set the Input Levels to 0, 1.70, 255, and click OK. This lightens up the background a bit.

Now to create a table for the bottle to set on. Set the Foreground Color to white (255,255,255) and the Background Color to 200,200,200. Use the Rectangular Marquee tool to select the bottom sixth or so of the canvas. Select the Gradient tool. In the Options bar, click the

Linear Gradient and choose the Foreground to Background gradient from the Gradient Picker. SHIFT-click and drag from the top of the selection to the bottom to create the tabletop, as shown in Figure 22-42. Deselect the tabletop (Select | Deselect), and then blur the background by choosing Filter | Blur | Gaussian Blur and entering a value of 3 pixels.

Create a new layer (Layer | New | Layer) and name it Shadow. Select the Brush tool and choose a soft, round, 45-pixel brush. Set the Foreground Color to black, and paint in a rough shadow, as shown in Figure 22-43. Make the shadow bend where the table meets the wall.

Use the Gaussian Blur filter (Filter | Blur | Gaussian Blur) to apply a blur of 8 pixels, and then reduce the Shadow layer's opacity to 15–20%.

Flatten your image (Layer | Flatten Image), and save your work.

Figure 22-42: Create a tabletop.

Figure 22-43: Paint a rough shadow.

Picture Puzzle: Turn Your Favorite Photo into a Jigsaw Puzzle

23

You can add a little interest to any photograph by cutting it up and putting it back together again … digitally, anyway. Let's look at how to turn your favorite photo into a virtual picture puzzle.

In This Project You Will:

- ☐ Use the Texturizer to apply a jigsaw texture

- ☐ Combine multiple layers into a single image

- ☐ Apply layer effects to create shadows

- ☐ Use Perspective and Free Transform to place the puzzle into a real-world scene

Digital Jigsaw

Start by opening the file beach-scene.jpg (Figure 23-1)—or your own photo—and save it as puzzle.psd in Elements. Copy the photo to a new layer: select Layer | New | Layer via Copy. This preserves the original photo in the Background layer, always a good idea in case something goes wrong later. In the Layers palette, rename the new layer Jigsaw.

Figure 23-1: The original beach photo

Making a photo look like a jigsaw puzzle is super-easy in Elements. From the menu choose Filter | Texture | Texturizer. This brings up the Texturizer dialog as shown in Figure 23-2. Set Scaling to 100% and Relief to 8. Choose Top Left from the Light drop-down list. Select Puzzle from the Texture drop-down list.

Figure 23-2: Apply the Puzzle texture.

If Puzzle doesn't appear in the Texture drop-down list, you'll need to load that texture into Elements. To do that, click on the triangle to the right of the Texture drop-down, and click Load Texture as shown in Figure 23-3. Browse to the Elements install folder (e.g., C:\Program Files\Adobe \Photoshop Elements 3.0 in Windows; Applications | Adobe Photoshop Elements 3.0 on a Macintosh). Within the Elements install folder, open the Presets folder, then the Textures folder. Select the file puzzle.psd from the Textures folder and click Open or Load.

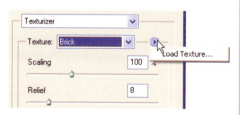

Figure 23-3: Load texture.

Figure 23-4: A puzzled picture

Click OK to apply the puzzle texture to the photo. The results should look something like Figure 23-4.

Cut Out a Piece

To reinforce the idea that this is a puzzle, let's take a piece out of it. From the menu choose Layer | New | Layer via Copy. This creates a new layer called Jigsaw Copy. In the Layers palette, click the eye icons to hide the Background layer and the original Jigsaw layer so that only the new Jigsaw Copy layer is visible, as shown in Figure 23-5. Grab the Eraser tool from the Toolbox and, in the Options bar, set it to a soft, round, 9-pixel brush. Pick a puzzle piece, any puzzle piece, and zoom way in on it. Using the Eraser tool, carefully erase your chosen piece from the photo. I've chosen a piece of blue sky, as shown in Figure 23-6, but suit yourself.

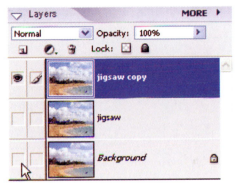

Figure 23-5: Hide the bottom layers.

Figure 23-6: Carefully erase your chosen piece.

When the piece is erased, open the Styles and Effects palette (Window | Styles and Effects). Choose Layer Styles and Drop Shadows from the two drop-down lists at the top of the palette. Click on the Hard Edge thumbnail to apply a hard-edged drop shadow to the Jigsaw Copy layer, as shown in Figure 23-7. This shadow is *only* visible under the missing piece, as shown in Figure 23-8; everywhere else, its effect is outside of the canvas and can't be seen.

Figure 23-7: Add a drop shadow.

Figure 23-8: The drop shadow in place

Figure 23-9: Select layer effects.

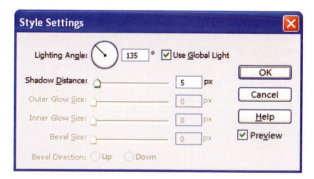

Figure 23-10: Set global shadows.

In the Layers palette, double-click on the (f) symbol in the Jigsaw Copy layer, as shown in Figure 23-9. When the Style Settings dialog appears, make sure that the Use Global Light is checked and that the Lighting Angle is set to 135 degrees, as shown in Figure 23-10. Leave the Shadow Distance set to 5 and click OK.

Add a Table

With that piece missing, we can see through the puzzle and see that there's nothing underneath it. Time to fix that. Let's create a simple texture to represent the table underneath the puzzle.

Double-click the Hand tool to see the entire puzzle. In the Layers palette, click on the Background layer to select it. From the menu choose Layer | New Fill Layer | Pattern. Name the new layer Table and click OK. When the Pattern Fill dialog appears, select the Wood pattern, as shown in Figure 23-11. (If the wood pattern isn't there, click the little arrow to the right of the pattern thumbnails and choose Reset Patterns from the pop-up list.) Click OK to fill the new layer with the wood pattern. Now the hole in the puzzle reveals the wood surface of the table beneath.

This is a good place to save your work.

Looking for My Missing Piece

Now let's add in that missing piece back, laying it on top of the puzzle. Just for yuks, I decided to make the last piece the *wrong* piece. It doesn't fit, the puzzle can't be finished, the pointlessness of our existence goes on, unabated. (If you're of a kinder, more optimistic bent, you can give the viewer the right piece. Up to you.)

In the Layers palette, select the Jigsaw Copy layer. Choose the Rectangular Marquee tool from the Toolbox. Find a piece of the puzzle that definitely doesn't match the hole: wrong shape, wrong color. Since I left out a piece of blue sky, I chose a piece of brown beach for contrast. Click and drag with the Rectangular Marquee tool to create a selection border around your chosen piece. Make sure you get all of it in there; don't worry about some extra bits around the edges, as shown in Figure 23-12.

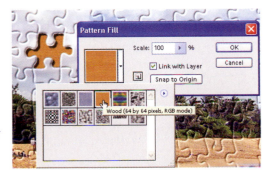

Figure 23-11: Set pattern fill with the Wood pattern.

Figure 23-12: Select your missing piece.

> **Note**
>
> If you want to portray the right piece, rather than the wrong piece, you'll need to copy it from the original Jigsaw layer.

From the menu choose Layer | New | Layer via Copy. This copies the selected piece to a new layer. In the Layers palette, rename the new Layer 1 to Missing Piece.

Notice that the drop shadow style is copied along with the piece. The shadow can make it a little hard to see what you're doing in this next step, so let's get rid of it temporarily. In the Layers palette, right-click (CONTROL-click on a Macintosh) on the name of the Missing Piece layer and choose Clear Layer Style from the pop-up menu, as shown in Figure 23-13.

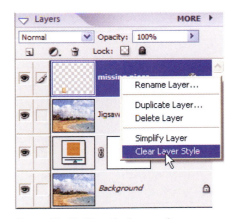

Figure 23-13: Clear the layer style.

In the Layers palette, ALT-click (OPTION-click on a Macintosh) on the eye icon in the Missing Piece layer. This hides every layer *except* that one.

Zoom in on the piece. Select the Eraser Tool with a soft, round, 9-pixel brush and carefully erase all around the edges of the piece, removing every pixel that's not part of your chosen piece, as shown in Figure 23-14. When you're done, put the drop shadow back by reselecting the Hard Edge shadow from the Styles and Effects palette.

Click on the eyes for the Jigsaw Copy and Table layers to make the rest of the puzzle visible. Double-click the Hand tool to see the whole puzzle. Use the Move tool to shift the last piece into a pleasing position, somewhere it'll be noticed. You can rotate it a bit, too, if you like. You should have something like Figure 23-15. Congratulations!

Figure 23-14: Erase all around the edges of your chosen puzzle piece.

If there are any stray pixels where they shouldn't be, use the Eraser tool to clean them up. Save your work.

Figure 23-15: The finished puzzle

Lay It on the Table

That looks pretty cool and you can stop right here. Or you could place your newly created puzzle into a larger, real-world scene, making it seem even more real.

Open a photo of a table or floor, such as table-top.jpg, shown in Figure 23-16. Save the photo with a new name, such as puzzle-table.psd. Return to your puzzle document. In the Layers palette, click the eye icon in the Table layer, hiding it. Also in the Layers palette, click the Jigsaw Copy layer to select it. Right-click or CONTROL-click on the layer's name and choose Clear Layer Style from the pop-up list. From the menu choose Select | All and then Edit | Copy Merged to copy the puzzle and extra piece, but not the background table pattern.

Switch back to the puzzle-table document and select Edit | Paste (or CTRL-V, or CMD-V on a Macintosh) to paste the merged puzzle layers on a new layer above the table. If the rulers are not visible, turn them on now (View | Rulers). Right-click or CONTROL-click on one of the rulers and select Percent from the pop-up list, as shown in Figure 23-17.

Figure 23-16: A table top

Time to introduce some real-world perspective. From the menu choose Image | Transform | Perspective. Click and drag on the upper-left corner handle until the corner is about 12% of the way in from the left edge, as indicated by the top ruler bar, and then double-click on the puzzle to accept the change. The results should look like Figure 23-18.

If you are using your own background image in place of table-top .jpg, you may need to add more or less effect to match any obvious lines of perspective in the background.

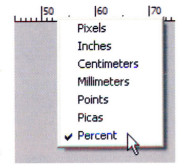

Figure 23-17: Set rulers to percent.

This operation makes the puzzle look far too tall. Time to shorten it. From the menu choose Edit | Transform | Free Transform. ALT-click or OPTION-click and drag on the top center handle to shrink the puzzle, top to bottom. Holding down the ALT or OPTION key shrinks the photo from the center, rather than from the edge, keeping the puzzle more or less centered in the canvas. Watch the Options bar and drag until the Height field (labeled H) reads about 50%, as shown in Figure 23-19. It should resemble Figure 23-20.

Figure 23-18: Use perspective distort.

Figure 23-19: The Free Transform option bar

Figure 23-20: Resize from center.

Figure 23-21: A final crop

Double-click on the puzzle to accept the transformation.

Reapply the drop shadow by choosing the Soft Edge shadow from the Styles and Effects palette. I chose the Soft Edge shadow because it better blended with the new background. In the Layers palette, double-click on the (f) symbol in the Puzzle layer. When the Style Settings dialog appears, make sure that the Lighting Angle is set to 135 degrees to match the shadow for the missing puzzle piece. Click OK.

Select the Crop tool from the Toolbox and use it to remove any extraneous table top, placing the emphasis on the puzzle, where it belongs, as shown in Figure 23-21. Save your work; you're done.

You can use any image as the basis for this fun and easy project, from family portraits to vacation snapshots to original creations (see Figure 23-22).

Figure 23-22: An alternate puzzle

Pixel Tagging: Create Digital Graffiti

24

Y ou can use Photoshop Elements to create a spray-painted graffiti effect for web page banners, document covers, or wherever you fancy a little faux vandalism.

In This Project You Will:

☐ Use Free Transform to scale, skew, and rotate letters and shapes

☐ Paint within a selection

☐ Use the gradient tool to fill a selection

☐ Create glows and special effects with layer styles

Create Some Text

Start by creating a blank file. From the menu, choose File | New | Blank File, and choose 640×480 from the presets.

Next, select the Type tool from the Toolbox. In the Options bar, choose black as your text color. Don't worry about alignment, size, and font just now; just type in your text. Press CTRL-ENTER (CMD-RETURN on a Macintosh) to finish typing.

With the Text tool still active, click within the Font Family box in the Options bar, as shown in Figure 24-1. Use your arrows keys or your mouse wheel to browse through your installed fonts to find the one that looks the most graffiti-like. As you scroll through the fonts, the text you entered in the last step will change. I used the Franciscan font, which has simple lines and looks handwritten. In the Options bar, change the font size until the letters more or less fill the space. You'll probably have to set the size up to 200 points or so. If necessary, click on your text with the Type tool and insert line breaks between words by pressing the ENTER key (RETURN on a Macintosh).

Font family   Font size

Figure 24-1: Click in the Font Family box.

It is important that each letter is clearly separated from all the others. If two letters overlap, edit the text to add spaces between the letters, as shown in Figure 24-2. The extra spaces won't matter; you'll be moving all the characters later.

Commit any changes to your text by pressing CTRL-ENTER or CMD-RETURN. From the menu choose Layer | Simplify Layer. You can no longer edit the text with the Type tool, but you can paint on it, erase it, and so forth. This will allow you to cut up individual letters and move them around the screen later on.

**Frodo
Lives!**

Figure 24-2: Your text message

Move the Letters

Select the Magic Wand tool from the Toolbox. In the Options bar, set the Tolerance to 8 and make sure that both Anti-aliased and Contiguous are checked. Make sure that Use All Layers is not checked. Click on a letter to select it, as shown in Figure 24-3. Now the fun begins.

Select the Move tool from the Toolbox. As shown in Figure 24-4, you can use any combination of the following techniques to distort the selected letter:

- Click and drag on the handles to resize the letter.
- Click and drag outside of the handles to rotate the letter.
- Click and drag on the letter to move it to a new position on the screen.
- CTRL-click (CMD-click on a Macintosh) and drag on the top, bottom, or side handles to skew the letter.
- CTRL-click or CMD-click and drag on any of the corner handles to drag that corner to a new position while leaving the other three corners anchored in place.

If at any time you don't like where you've gotten to, press ESC to cancel the transformation, and start again. When you're happy with a transformation, press ENTER to accept it.

Figure 24-3: Select a letter with the Magic Wand.

Note

If you don't see handles around your letter, select Show Bounding Box in the Options bar.

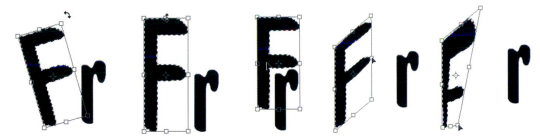

Figure 24-4: Rotate, resize, move, skew, distort

Repeat the process for every letter. At this point, you can overlap letters if you want to, but remember that once two letters overlap, they'll become stuck together; you won't be able to move or transform them separately again.

Figure 24-5: My transformed graffiti text

Figure 24-6: Quotes made from an exclamation mark!

Figure 24-7: Select part of a letter.

Figure 24-8: Duplicate the selection.

You should wind up with something vaguely like Figure 24-5.

Add Some Doodads

Time to add some extra bits here and there, to break up the letters and complicate the look a bit. There are several sources for the shapes. The first is the letters themselves. The top stroke of the exclamation mark, for example, can be squashed, tweaked and duplicated to form quotes, as shown in Figure 24-6.

I used the Magic Wand tool to select the top stroke of the exclamation point, and then used CTRL-ALT and drag (CMD-OPTION and drag on a Macintosh) to duplicate the selected pixels. Finally, I used the Move tool as described earlier, to resize and reshape it.

You can also use chunks cut off the letters. In Figure 24-7 I've used the Polygon Lasso tool to select the bottom portion of the L. Then I used CTRL-ALT and drag (CMD-OPTION and drag) on the contents of the selection to duplicate them elsewhere, as shown in Figure 24-8.

You can also make use of Element's stock of custom shapes, such as arrows and hearts. To create a custom shape, choose the Custom Shape tool from the Toolbox. In the Options bar, choose a shape from the Shape drop-down menu, as shown in Figure 24-9. Set the Color to black in the Shape tool's option bar. Click and drag on your image to create the shape at whatever size and proportion appeals to you. Use the Move tool to move your new shape into place, as shown in Figure 24-10. To fine-tune your shape, select the Move tool from the Toolbox, and use the handles to tweak the shape as you did the letters in the previous step.

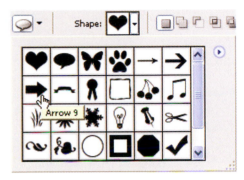

Figure 24-9: Custom shapes

Figure 24-10: Placing a custom shape

You might notice that the Custom Shape tool does not draw this shape on the same layer as your letters; rather, it creates a new Shape layer above the current layer as shown in Figure 24-11. When you're happy with your shape, choose Layer | Merge Down from the menu (or press CTRL-E or CMD-E). This merges your shape into your letters and eliminates the separate Shape layer.

Repeat these steps to create as many little doodads as you want. It doesn't have to be perfectly legible; remember, it's graffiti! You'll end up with something more or less like Figure 24-12.

Make sure that all of your extra layers have been merged. In the Layers palette, make sure you have only two layers: one black Graffiti layer and the original white Background. If you have more than that, no worries; we'll get rid of them now. In the Layers palette, click the eye icon on the Background layer to hide that layer. Click on any of the graffiti layers to select it. From the menu, choose Layer | Merge Visible to merge all your graffiti layers into one. In the Layers palette, rename the layer containing your graffiti to Graffiti.

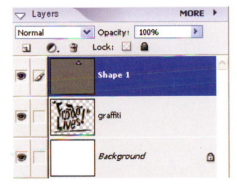

Figure 24-11: Shapes are created on separate layers.

Figure 24-12: Initial graffiti

Figure 24-13: Foreground
and background set to two
shades of blue

Figure 24-14: Choose the Foreground to
Background gradient.

Add the Paint

Now you'll add the final effects to make it look like spray paint rather than a
jumbled bunch of pure black lettering.

Choose new foreground and background colors. Make them similar; for example, I chose two shades of blue: 0,225,255 and 65,145,255, as shown in Figure
24-13.

Select the Gradient tool from the Toolbox. In the Options bar, click the
Gradient Picker, and select the Foreground to Background gradient from the
presets, as shown in Figure 24-14.

In the Layers palette, CTRL-click or CMD-click on the Graffiti
layer thumbnail. This selects only the filled pixels in the layer,
as shown in Figure 24-15. Anything you do with this selection active will only affect the black graffiti.

Click and drag on your image with the Gradient tool, starting at the top-left corner and dragging to the bottom right
before releasing the mouse button. This paints over the black
text with your new gradient, as shown in Figure 24-16. Click
and drag from different locations, and in different directions,
to experiment with different gradients. When you're happy,
remove the selection
by choosing Select |
Deselect (or pressing
CTRL-D or CMD-D)
from the menu.

Figure 24-15: Graffiti text selected

Figure 24-16: Gradient-filled graffiti

Add an Inner Outline

In the Layer Styles palette, choose Layer Styles from the first drop-down list, and Inner Glows from the second drop-down list. Click the Small Border thumbnail, as shown in Figure 24-17, to create a white border inside of your text. It will probably be too large (or too small) but we'll fix that next.

In the Layers palette, locate the Layer Styles button (it looks like a lowercase "f") in the Graffiti layer. Double-click on this button to open the Style Settings dialog. Drag the Inner Glow Size slider left or right (or type in a new value) to change the size of the glow until it better resembles a white outline within your letters. I went with a size setting of 5 pixels, as shown in Figure 24-18.

When you're happy, click OK. From the menu choose Layer | Simplify Layer. This merges the highlight with the underlying "paint." If you skip this step, the Inner Glow effect would also be applied to the additional elements you're about to add. And trust me, nobody wants that.

Figure 24-17: Choose Small Border from Layer Styles.

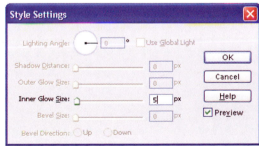

Figure 24-18: Adjust the Inner Glow size.

Lines and Stenciled Designs

Next, let's stencil in some small designs. Choose a new, contrasting foreground color. Since I have a blue background, I went with a bright reddish orange.

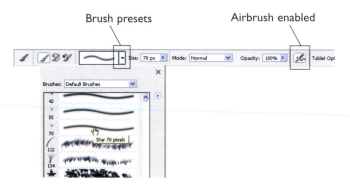

Brush presets

Airbrush enabled

Figure 24-19: The Star brush

Reselect the graffiti by using CTRL-click or CMD-click on the Graffiti layer thumbnail in the Layers palette. Select the Brush tool from the Toolbox. In the Options menu, select the 70-pixel star brush from the Brush presets drop-down, as shown in Figure 24-19. Make sure Airbrush is enabled in the Options bar.

Figure 24-20: Filling the text with stenciled shapes

Click on your graffiti with the Brush tool to paint your contrasting stars—or circles or whatever brush shape you've chosen, as shown in Figure 24-20. Do not drag; you're not painting lines, you're placing "stenciled" shapes. Adjust the size up or down as needed, depending on the size of shape you want to paint. Because you've enabled the Airbrush option, the star will become larger and denser the longer you hold down the mouse button.

Experiment with different brush shapes, if you want to.

Next, choose a soft, round, 17-pixel brush. Click once outside of your selection on the left. Nothing happens yet, but don't panic. Hold down the SHIFT key and click again, this time outside of your selection on the right side. Elements paints a perfectly straight line between the two points. If you don't like it, press CTRL-Z or CMD-Z to undo it, and repeat the process to draw a new line. Try it a few times to get the hang of it, and then lay down as many lines as you want.

The active selection prevents Elements from painting outside the lines, as it were. You should wind up with something like Figure 24-21.

Create a Black Outline

In the Layers palette, click on the Graffiti layer to make certain it is selected, and then choose Layer | New | Layer via Copy (or use CTRL-J or CMD-J) to create a duplicate Graffiti layer. If the graffiti is not still selected, select it now by using CTRL-click or CMD-click on the new layer's thumbnail in the Layers palette. From the menu, choose

Figure 24-21: Graffiti with lines

Edit | Stroke (Outline) Selection. In the Stroke dialog, set the Width to 6 pixels, set the Color to black, and select Outside to place the outline around the outside of each letter, as shown in Figure 24-22. Click OK. You should get something like Figure 24-23.

Add the Final Outer Glow

Almost there. One last step to go. If the graffiti is still selected, deselect it now by choosing Select | Deselect from the menu (or use CTRL-D or CMD-D).

In the Layers palette, hide the layer you've been working on—the Graffiti Copy layer—by clicking on its eye icon in the Layers palette. Hide the white background layer, as well, by clicking on its eye icon. This leaves you with one layer visible, the layer containing the graffiti *without* the dark outline. Click on that layer in the Layers palette to select it.

In the Styles and Effects palette, select Layer Styles from the first drop-down list and Outer Glows from the second drop-down list. Select Heavy from the presets. You'll see a faint yellow glow around your text now, as shown in Figure 24-24. Yellow doesn't look very good, but you'll fix that momentarily.

The glow will serve as a final, soft outline around the graffiti, but it's much too big. Let's resize it. In the Layers palette, double-click the Graffiti layer's Layer Styles button (f). Adjust the Outer Glow Size to better suit your tastes. I think a setting of around 10–20 works best. When you're happy, click OK.

The last step is to fix that sickly yellow outer glow. From the menu choose Layer | Simplify Layer. This merges the glow effect into the layer. Now you can modify it, as you'll see.

Figure 24-22: Stroke the selection.

Figure 24-23: Black outline in place

Figure 24-24: A nasty yellow glow

In the Layers palette, unhide all layers. Click the middle Graffiti layer to select it. From the menu choose Enhance | Adjust Color | Adjust Hue/Saturation. In the Hue/Saturation dialog, select Colorize, set Saturation to 100, and Lightness to −45 or so to get a nice, deep color. Now use the Hue slider to change the color itself. I used 360, which renders the outer glow as red. This actually turns the entire layer red, but since the outer glow is all that shows, we don't really care. When you're happy with the settings, press OK to accept them.

Click the topmost graffiti layer, Graffiti Copy, in the Layers palette. From the menu choose Layer | Flatten Image to merge the layers together.

That's it. You're done. Save your work.

This project is based in part on a tutorial by my friend Bas Hijmans (besideslife.com). Thanks, Bas!

Elements Noir: Combine Diverse Elements into a Nighttime Scene

Y ou can combine elements and effects from a variety of sources to create seamless composite scenes. The scene in this project is composed of four very different layers. Let's look at how to make one like it.

In This Project You Will:

☐ Use Levels to simulate darkness in a daytime scene

☐ Resize a photo by pasting it into a new document

☐ Use Free Transform to resize elements and alter their perspective

☐ Use layer blend modes to combine different elements

☐ Tint a picture with a Fill Layer

Figure 25-1: A generic warehouse

Select a Base Photograph

The first thing you'll need is a wall. It doesn't have to be a nighttime photo, but some moody shadows wouldn't hurt. I started with a photo of a warehouse (Figure 25-1).

It's actually a 3-D render, rather than a photograph, and way too bright, but it'll work just fine.

> **Note**
>
> When creating a composite scene, it's best to start with a photo or other image that's bigger than the final image will be. This gives you room to crop, trim, and resize to focus on the elements you want. The warehouse photo was originally larger; I cropped it down to the 640×480 size of the final image.

Open the photo warehouse.jpg, or your own photo, in Elements. Save the new document as noir.psd.

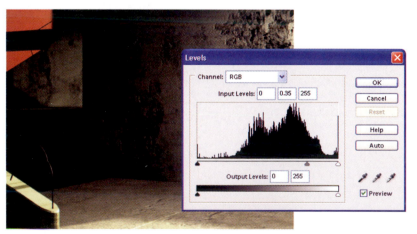

Figure 25-2: Stretching the shadows to simulate nighttime

Darken It Up

If your photo is already of a night scene, you can skip this next step. But if your photo, like mine, is too brightly lit, you'll have to tweak it a bit. From the menu choose Enhance | Adjust Lighting | Levels. In the Levels dialog, click on the middle slider beneath the histogram and drag it to the right, as shown in Figure 25-2. This stretches the dark values in the image, deepening the shadows and making things darker overall. Don't go too far, just enough to suggest nighttime rather than day. It's best to err on the side of brightness at this point; darkening costs you detail. You can always make it darker later on, if you feel it's warranted. I went with a value of 0.35.

Lay On the Graffiti

Create the graffiti to adorn the wall, as shown in Project 24. Make the graffiti big enough to fill the space you have in mind for it in this new scene. If in doubt, make it *too* big.

In the graffiti document, turn off the background color, leaving only the graffiti itself visible, as shown in Figure 25-3.

From the menu choose Select | All to select the entire canvas, and then choose Edit | Copy Merged. This copies all visible elements to the clipboard as a single layer.

Return to your nighttime composite document and paste the graffiti into the document on a new layer (Edit | Paste). It should look something like Figure 25-4.

Save your work.

In the Layers palette, name the new layer Graffiti.

Align the Graffiti

To resize the graffiti and align it with the wall, choose Image | Transform | Free Transform. Begin by dragging the graffiti into position and resizing it to fit. Click and drag on the graffiti to move it to a new position on the screen. Click and drag on the handles to resize the graffiti. SHIFT-click and drag on the handles to resize the graffiti while preserving its proportions.

Next, you'll want to tweak the graffiti's alignment to match the perspective of the wall, as shown in Figure 25-5. Click and drag outside of the handles to rotate the graffiti. CTRL-click (CMD-click on a Macintosh) and drag on the top, bottom, or side handles to skew the letter. CTRL-click or CMD-click and drag on any of the corner handles to drag that corner to a new position while leaving the other three corners anchored in place.

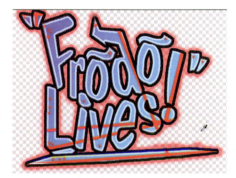

Figure 25-3: Graffiti with no background

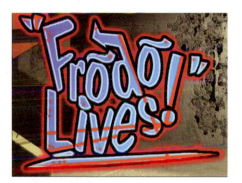

Figure 25-4: Graffiti on a new layer

Figure 25-5: Use Free Transform to position the graffiti in the scene.

The perspective of my image dictates that the graffiti should appear larger on the right than it does nearer the center. I stretched the top-right and bottom-right corner handles to accommodate this.

I dragged the bottom-right corner farther down than was strictly dictated by the perspective of the shot because I preferred the effect. Remember, it's graffiti; perfect alignment isn't necessary. When you're satisfied with how the graffiti looks, press ENTER (RETURN on a Macintosh) to finalize the transformation.

Changing the Mode

At this point the graffiti probably doesn't look like a part of the wall at all. That's because the layer is in the so-called Normal blend mode; it just sits there above the wall, not blending in at all. In the Layers palette, select the Graffiti layer and change its blend mode to Multiply.

No one blend mode will work best for all images. Black graffiti on a white wall is going to require a different blend mode than white graffiti on a black wall. Browse through all the blend modes and see what works best.

Here are a few to try first:

- Screen mode and Lighten mode will lighten the wall beneath the graffiti.
- Darken mode and Multiply mode will darken the wall beneath the graffiti.

In this composition, Screen and Lighten modes looks positively horrible, while Darken and Multiply looks pretty good (see Figure 25-6). The texture of the wall shows through and the graffiti looks like a believable, if dark, part of the wall.

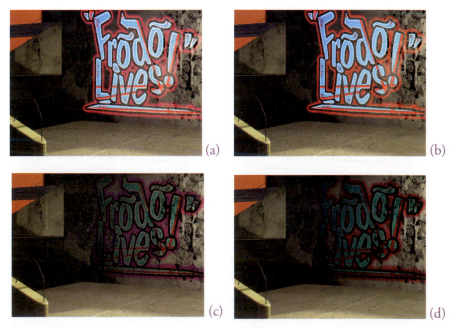

Figure 25-6: (a) Screen mode, (b) Lighten mode, (c) Darken mode, and (d) Multiply mode

Put In a Window

Our night scene needs a window to cast light and sport some nifty reflections to further tie things together. I used a snapshot of the front of an upscale storefront, shown in Figure 25-7.

Open the photo store-front.jpg, or your own storefront photo, in Elements. From the menu choose Select | All, and then choose Edit | Copy to copy the photo to the clipboard.

Return to your working document and choose Edit | Paste to paste the photo into a new layer above the graffiti. In the Layers palette, rename the new layer Shop Window.

From the menu choose Image | Transform | Free Transform, and position and size the new photo as you did the graffiti. Again, remember to alter the perspective of the photo to match your final scene. Look for floor lines and other lines to help you match the perspective. I wanted to replace the left side of the original photo with the new window; perspective dictates that the window appears to grow smaller from left to right, as shown in Figure 25-8.

Figure 25-7: A shop window

Figure 25-8: Adjust the size and perspective of the shop window to fit the scene.

> ### Tip
>
> If you have trouble seeing what you're doing to position the window photo, try reducing that layer's opacity in the Layers palette. This will allow you to see through it to the layers below. When it's in position, turn the opacity back up to 100%.

Cut Off the Extras

You'll want to trim off extra bits of foreground that go in front of your window. I needed to trim off extra wall beneath the window and also erase the areas that obscured the stairs in the foreground.

With all that erasing comes the risk of messing something up, so it's best to duplicate the window layer. In the Layers palette, select the Shop Window layer. From

Figure 25-9: Hide the original Shop Window layer.

Figure 25-10: Extra floor selected with the Polygon Lasso tool

the menu choose Layer | New | Layer via Copy. Hide the original Shop Window layer by clicking on the eye icon; it's just there in case you need to start over with a new copy, as shown in Figure 25-9.

In the Layers palette, select the Shop Window Copy layer again. Use the Polygon Lasso tool to select the extra area beneath the window, as shown in Figure 25-10, and press DELETE to delete it. Use the Eraser tool with small, hard brushes to carefully erase around the stairs in the foreground.

Add Reflections

For the window to be tied firmly into the scene, it should feature reflections of its new environs, including the graffiti-decorated wall beside it. Let's create some reflections.

From the menu choose Select | All to select the entire canvas. Now, choose Edit | Copy Merged. This copies everything—wall, graffiti, and window—to the clipboard. Choose Edit | Paste to create a new, merged layer. In the Layers palette, rename the new layer to Reflection. Lastly, let's flip it, as shown in Figure 25-11; reflections should be reversed, after all. From the menu choose Image | Rotate | Flip Layer Horizontal (not Flip *Image* Horizontal).

Figure 25-11: Merged layers flipped, right-for-left

Use the Polygonal Lasso tool to select the portion at far right—the portion of the image containing the window—and delete it. The window shouldn't reflect itself. Turn off the selection and that leaves you with something like Figure 25-12.

This looks nothing at all like a reflection. But, if you'll recall, the graffiti didn't look too good at first either. We'll fix the reflection in the same way: by using a different blend mode.

The default blend mode is Normal, which, we've established, isn't cutting it. In the Layers palette, try some of the other blend modes by selecting them from the Blend Mode drop-down list. See what suits you. Screen and Soft Light are good ones to try. Soft Light looked best for my composition, as shown in Figure 25-13.

Fine-Tune Position, Orientation, and Perspective

From the menu choose Image | Transform | Free Transform. In Free Transform mode, use the same techniques previously described to resize, rotate, and adjust the perspective of your reflection to better fit in your window, as shown in Figure 25-14.

Figure 25-12: This doesn't look like a reflection … yet.

Figure 25-13: Soft Light blend mode allows the window to show through.

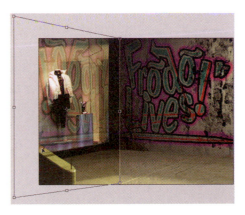

Figure 25-14: Positioning the reflection within the window

Figure 25-15: Select the Shop Window layer.

Figure 25-16: Reduce the opacity of the Reflection layer.

We want the reflection to exactly cover the window. In Elements, it's easy to trim one layer to match another. In the Layers palette, CTRL-click or CMD-click on the thumbnail of the Shop Window layer. This selects the filled pixels on that layer, as shown in Figure 25-15. From the menu choose Select | Inverse. Make sure that the Reflection layer is actually selected in the Layers palette, and then press DELETE to delete all parts of the reflection that don't cover the window. Turn off the selection (Select | Deselect).

Finally, adjust the opacity of your Reflection layer, if necessary. I set mine to about 50%. The results are shown in Figure 25-16.

Throw Some Color on It

One way to tie together a lot of disparate elements is to add a little of the same color to all of them. For example, if I add a little blue to every color in my composition, the reds become bluish reds, the greens become bluish greens, the whites become bluish whites, and so forth. This really ties the colors together.

Let's use that technique to tie the elements of this composition together and also to add a bit of mood. From the menu choose Layer | New Fill Layer | Solid Color. In the New Layer dialog, set the Mode to Color and click OK. When the Color Picker dialog appears, choose a nice orange. I went with 255,155,0, but it really doesn't matter too much at this point. Don't click OK yet. In Color mode, the new fill layer leaves all your work on lower layers visible, but colors them all the same shade of orange, as shown in Figure 25-17.

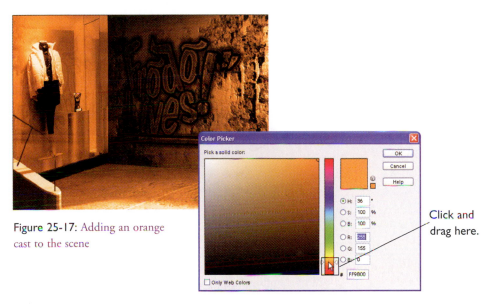

Figure 25-17: Adding an orange cast to the scene

Click and drag here.

Drag up and down within the tall, rainbow-shaded control at the middle of the Color Picker dialog to try out different hues, as shown in Figure 25-18. Does your image look better in warm orange or icy blue? You decide.

When you find the combination you like best, click OK to accept it. You can change the color at any time by double-clicking on the color layer's thumbnail in the Layers palette.

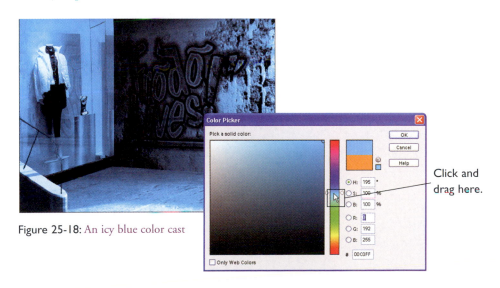

Figure 25-18: An icy blue color cast

Click and drag here.

Adjust the opacity on the new color layer. Opacity of 100% probably creates too strong an effect. I set my color layer to 60%, which colors the underlying layers, but still leaves a hint of red and green and purple showing through, as shown in Figure 25-19.

Figure 25-19: With the color cast reduced, the image is complete.

That's it; you're done. Save your work.

Day and Night: Transform a Daytime Photo into Night

In This Project You Will:

☐ Use Levels and Hue/ Saturation to simulate darkness

☐ Create lens flares

☐ Use the Magic Wand tool to select areas

☐ Use blending modes to combine layers

☐ Turn on lights in windows

There's a little trick that's used in the movie industry to shoot night scenes: they shoot them during the day, and then process the footage to make it look darker and more like nighttime. The process is called "day for night," and you can do the same thing in Photoshop Elements.

Grab Some Sky

Figure 26-1: Our daytime photo

Start by opening the file museum-day.jpg (Figure 26-1), or your own photo, in Elements. Save your document as day-for-night.psd. It's obvious that, whatever else we do to turn this into a nighttime photo, that blue sky has got to go. Let's create a new one.

Select the Magic Wand tool from the Toolbox. In the Options bar, set the Tolerance to 64 and check Anti-aliased. Leave the other boxes unchecked. Click somewhere on the sky to select it (see Figure 26-2).

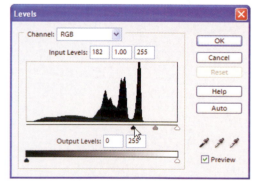

Figure 26-2: Sky selected

From the menu, choose Layer | New | Layer via Copy to copy the selected sky to a new layer. In the Layers palette, rename the new layer Sky.

That sky needs to be much, much darker. From the menu choose Enhance | Adjust Lighting | Levels. When the Levels dialog appears, click and drag the left black slider to the right until the first Input Levels box reads about 180, as shown in Figure 26-3. (Or just type 180 in the box.) Click OK. The sky is now a very, very, very dark blue—it'll probably look black to you, as shown in Figure 26-4.

Figure 26-3: Sky Levels

Figure 26-4: A much darker sky

Lose the Colors

Colors are much less vibrant at night. In the movies, day for night shots are usually tinted blue. Let's do that now.

In the Layers palette, select the Background layer. From the menu choose Enhance | Adjust Color | Adjust Hue/Saturation. When the Hue/Saturation dialog appears, check the Colorize box at the bottom right, as shown in Figure 26-5. This colors the entire image with a single color or hue. Drag the Hue slider to about 235, a slightly purplish blue. Drag the Saturation slider left, to about 25, to reduce the intensity of the colors in the scene. Click OK. That's looking much more night-timey, doncha think? (See Figure 26-6.)

> **Note**
>
> We selected the sky earlier, rather than now, because then it was the only light blue area in the photo. Now all the colors are more or less the same, making the task of selecting the sky much more difficult.

Burn It

There's some funkiness where the trees at top left meet the sky, seen in Figure 26-7. These areas weren't light enough to be selected as part of the sky, but they are light enough to look odd when silhouetted against it.

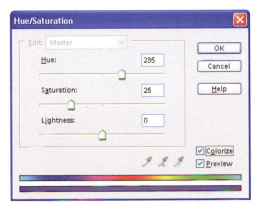

Figure 26-5: Hue/Saturation adjustments

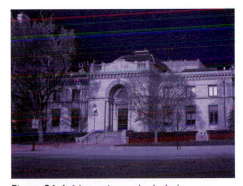

Figure 26-6: It's starting to look dark.

Figure 26-7: Burn this area.

Figure 26-8: The trees blend better with some judicious burning.

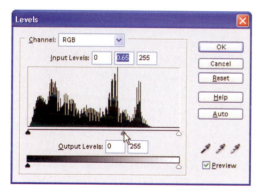

Figure 26-9: Darkening via Levels

In the Layers palette, select the Background layer. Select the Burn tool from the Toolbox. In the Options bar, select a soft, round, 65-pixel brush. Set the Range to Highlights and the Exposure to 25%. Use multiple strokes with the Burn tool to darken the light fringe around the trees and to darken the extra building and other details on the left side of the image, as shown in Figure 26-8.

Leveling Off

Not bad. The building still looks a little too bright for my tastes, but that is easily fixed. From the menu, choose Enhance | Adjust Lighting | Levels. When the Levels dialog appears, drag the center (gray point) slider to the right to about 0.65 or 0.70, as shown in Figure 26-9. This stretches the shadows, making the dark parts of the image darker. Click OK.

A Light in the Window(s)

If it's nighttime, perhaps there should be some lights on, no? Let's add some. Select the Magic Wand tool from the Toolbox. In the Options bar, set the tool to a Tolerance of 32 and check Anti-aliased and Contiguous. Find the top-right window in the building and click on one of the two panes to select it. Hold down the SHIFT key and click on the other pane to select it, as shown in Figure 26-10.

Figure 26-10: Select the first window.

From the menu choose Layer | New | Layer via Copy to copy the windows to a new layer. In the Layers palette, rename the new layer Window 1. With the Window 1 layer still selected, choose Enhance | Adjust Color | Adjust Hue/ Saturation. When the Hue/Saturation dialog appears, check Colorize. Move the Hue slider to the left to about 60. Leave the other sliders where they are. This selects a warm yellow color for the light in this window; choose another color if you want. Click OK.

From the menu choose Filter | Blur | Gaussian Blur. Set the blur radius to 1.5 pixels and click OK. This blurs the edges of the light a bit, making it look less sharp-edged and pasted in. The results should look something like Figure 26-11.

Figure 26-11: New window

In the Layers palette, select the Background layer. Use the Magic Wand tool again, with the same settings as before, to select the two panes in the lower-right window, as shown in Figure 26-12. From the menu choose Layer | New | Layer via Copy to copy these windows to a new layer. In the Layers palette, rename the new layer Window 2. Change the layer's blending mode to Screen. This will cause it to lighten the layer beneath it. We skipped this step with the first window, because that window was already very light. This window, however, is curtained and dark in the original photo. It will have to be lightened up somewhat if it is to appear that the curtains are being illuminated from within.

Figure 26-12: Select a second window.

From the menu choose Enhance | Adjust Color | Adjust Hue/Saturation. Check the Colorize box. Drag the Hue slider to 60. Drag the Saturation slider left to 40, and drag the Lightness slider right to 20.

As before, blur the layer slightly by choosing Filter | Blur | Gaussian Blur from the menu. Set the blur radius to 1.5 pixels and click OK.

If either window seems *too* bright, use the opacity slider in the Layers palette to reduce that layer's opacity.

You can repeat the process with more windows, if you want. When you're happy
with your work so far, save your document.

Stars

If you'd like to add some stars to the sky, use the method described in the Starry
Night section of Project 16. Don't create a new document; instead create a new
layer in the current document (Layer | New | Layer), name it Stars, and create your
stars on that.

When you have your star field finished, set the Stars layer to Screen blending
mode. The stars show through the building and trees and so forth, but we'll be fix-
ing that in a moment. Right now, check the overall brightness of the stars. If they
are too bright, reduce the opacity of the Stars layer. If they are too dim, choose
Enhance | Adjust Lighting | Levels. Drag the middle (gray point) slider to the left
until the stars are bright enough to suit you and click OK.

When you're happy, CTRL-click (CMD-click on a Macintosh) on the Sky layer
thumbnail in the Layers palette to select the sky. From the menu, choose Select |
Invert to select everything except the sky. In the Layers palette, make sure the Stars
layer is still selected and, with the selection still active, press
DELETE to eliminate all the stars that don't fit in the sky.

Lighting the Lamps

Flatten the image (Layer | Flatten Image). Fit the image on
the screen (View | Fit on Screen).

If it were night, the lamps on either side of the main entrance
would be lit. Let's light them. Create a new layer (Layer |
New | Layer). Name the layer Lamp Glow and set its Mode
to Screen. Click OK. Fill the Layer with black by choosing
Edit | Fill Layer and setting the contents to Black. With the
layer in Screen mode, the black won't be visible at all. To
add the glow, choose Filter | Render | Lens Flare from the
menu. Set the brightness to 25% and select 105mm Prime
as the Lens Type, as shown in Figure 26-13. Click within the
Preview window to place the flare as close to the very center
as you can and click OK.

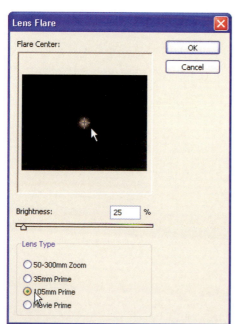

Figure 26-13: Lamp lens flare

To give the flare a warmer, yellow tint, choose Enhance | Adjust Color | Adjust Hue/Saturation. Check Colorize and drag the hue slider right to 50 to color the flare yellow. Leave Saturation at 25, Lightness at 0, and then click OK.

Use the Move tool to drag the flare into position over one of the lamps by the building's entrance, as shown in Figure 26-14.

Figure 26-14: One lamp placed

Figure 26-15: All lamps in position

Note

If the Move tool keeps selecting the wrong layer when you try to move your lens flares, turn off Auto Select Layer in the tool's Options bar.

From the menu choose Layer | New | Layer via Copy to copy the Lamp Glow layer. Repeat this step four times, to give you a total of six flares, as shown in Figure 26-15. Move them all into position over each of the six lamp globes by the entrance. Zoom in so you can see exactly what you're doing.

When all the glows are in place, select the topmost Lamp Glow layer in the Layers palette. Now, in each of the other Lamp Glow layers, click on the blank square next to the eye icon to turn on the chain link icon there, as shown in Figure 26-16. This links all the Lamp Glow layers together. With all the Lamp Glow layers, *and only the Lamp Glow layers,* linked, choose Layer | Merge Linked from the menu to merge them into a single layer. The picture turns black with only the glow visible. Set the new layer blending mode to Screen to reveal the building below.

The glows are a little spread out and not quite intense enough in the center: you can still see the glass globes through them. To fix that, choose Enhance | Adjust Lighting | Levels. In the Levels dialog, enter the values 0, 0.65, and 235 in the input levels boxes. This makes the brightest part of the flares even brighter, while darkening

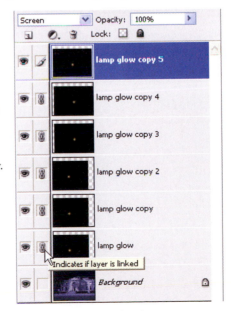

Figure 26-16: Lamp Glow layers

Figure 26-17: Before and after tweaking the Lamp Glow levels

Figure 26-18: Paint in some tree limbs.

the rest of the flare. The whole effect makes the light more intense at its center, where we want it, as shown in Figure 26-17.

The lamps on the right side of the door ought to be obscured by the trees that they're behind. To simulate the effect, create a new layer (Layer | New | Layer) and name it Branches. Set the Foreground Color to black (type D). Then select the Brush tool and use a soft, round, 3-pixel brush in Normal mode to paint in some tree limbs as shown in Figure 26-18. From the menu, choose Filter | Blur | Gaussian Blur. Set the Radius to 1.5 pixels and click OK. In the Layers palette, set the new layer to Multiply mode and reduce its opacity to about 15%. The results should resemble Figure 26-19.

Figure 26-19: Branches in place

Mooning

If you'd like a nice, gibbous moon in your image—and who wouldn't?—now's the
time to put one there. Fit the picture on the screen (View | Fit on Screen). Open
the file moon.jpg, or your own favorite moon photo. From the menu choose Select
| All and then Edit | Copy to copy the photo to the clipboard. Return to your day-
for-night.psd document and choose Edit | Paste to paste the moon to a new layer.
In the Layers palette, name the new layer Moon and set the layer's blending mode
to Screen. From the menu, choose Image | Transform | Free Transform. Resize and
reposition the moon to suit, as shown in Figure 26-20.

Use the Eraser tool to get rid of any stars that show through the moon.

Save your work; you're done.

Figure 26-20: Add a moon.

Chez Dracula: Turn a Mild-Mannered Museum into a Spooky Castle

27

In This Project You Will:

- ☐ **Create** lightning from scratch

- ☐ Adjust levels and hues to simulate nighttime lighting

- ☐ Create a hill with filters and simple brushwork

Everybody loves a spooky castle. You won't often find them lying about, but fortunately, you can create one from nearly any imposing stone building.

First We Need a Building

Open the photo museum.jpg (Figure 27-1). This is a photo of the Sedgwick County Historical Museum, taken from across the street on a sunny spring day. It isn't very spooky … yet.

From the menu, choose Layer | New | Layer via Copy to copy the original photo to a new layer. In the Layers palette, hide the Background layer by clicking its eye icon, as shown in Figure 27-2. Rename the new layer Castle. Save the document as castle-work.psd.

Remove the Background

That blue sky's the first thing to go. Select the Magic Eraser tool from the Toolbox. In the Options bar, set the tool's Tolerance to 32 and deselect Anti-aliased and Contiguous, as shown in Figure 27-3. Click a few times in the sky to delete it, as shown in Figure 27-4. Don't worry too much about the area around the limbs of the tree.

Figure 27-1: A friendly museum

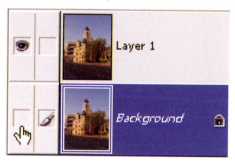

Figure 27-2: Hide the Background layer.

Figure 27-3: Magic Eraser options

Figure 27-4: Erase the sky.

Select the Eraser tool and, in the Options bar, select a hard, round, 9-pixel brush. Carefully trace around the left side of our castle to be, as shown in Figure 27-5. Make sure that the building is completely isolated from the buildings on the left. Increase the size of the Eraser brush to 19 pixels and erase a little farther out than before, as shown in Figure 27-6.

Increase the size again to 100 pixels and erase the remaining area, as shown in Figure 27-7. Don't worry about the bottom part of the image (the street) as we'll be covering that up later.

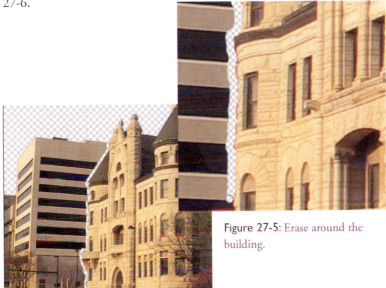

Figure 27-5: Erase around the building.

Figure 27-6: Widen the erasure.

Figure 27-7: The main building, isolated

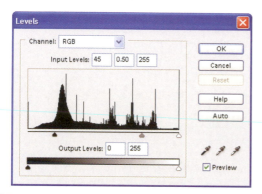

Figure 27-8: Adjust Levels to darken the scene.

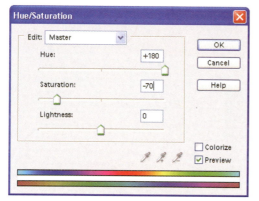

Figure 27-9: Adjust Hue/Saturation to blue the scene.

Darken It Up

Our building is a little too brightly lit to be spooky; let's darken it up. From the menu, choose Enhance | Adjust Lighting | Levels. In the Levels dialog, set the Input Levels to 45, 0.50, 255, as shown in Figure 27-8. This stretches the shadows and makes them darker. Click OK.

Next, let's change the hue of the scene; blue seems more evocative of night. Choose Enhance | Adjust Color | Adjust Hue/Saturation. Set Hue to 180, Saturation to –70, and Lightness to 0, as shown in Figure 27-9, and click OK. This pulls most of the color out of the walls and gives what's left a bluish tone, as shown in Figure 27-10. Save your efforts to this point.

Next, let's get rid of that big tree obscuring the front of our castle. Select the Rectangular Marquee tool from the Toolbox and use it to select the left wall of the castle to halfway through the front-most round tower as shown in Figure 27-11.

Figure 27-10: Our work so far

Select to halfway through the tower.

Figure 27-11: Select the left wall.

Copy the selection to a new layer (Layer | New | Layer via Copy). Now flip the new layer by choosing Image | Rotate | Flip Layer Horizontal. Don't choose Flip Horizontal; that flips the entire canvas.

Select the Move tool from the Toolbox. Drag the new layer to the right until its left edge is in the center of the tower, as shown in Figure 27-12. Grab the right handle and drag to the right, stretching the wall to about 150% of its original size, as shown. Press ENTER (RETURN on a Macintosh) to accept the transformation.

Go in with the Erase tool and a small brush and erase any extra bits where the new wall joins with the old to improve the quality of the join.

In the Layers palette, select the original Castle layer. Use the Rectangular Marquee tool to select everything to the right of the chimney as shown in Figure 27-13, and then press DELETE to eliminate it. The results should look like Figure 27-14.

Figure 27-12: Resize the right wall.

This chimney

Figure 27-13: Select everything to the right of the chimney.

Figure 27-14: It's beginning to look like a castle.

Figure 27-15: Darken the wall.

Figure 27-16: Paste on cloud background.

Remove the selection (Select | Deselect).

In the Layers palette, make sure the Background layer is still hidden, and then select Layer | Merge Visible to merge the two castle layers into one.

The front of the castle is now too bright; it should be in shadow. In the Layers palette, select the Castle layer and CTRL-click (CMD-click on a Macintosh) on the thumbnail to select the filled pixels. With that selection still active, create a new layer (Layer | New | Layer). Set the Foreground Color to black (0,0,0). Select the Brush tool from the Toolbox. In the Options bar, select a soft, round, 100-pixel brush, and reduce the tool's opacity to 25%. Use multiple strokes and go over some areas more than others to make some shadows deeper, as shown in Figure 27-15.

If the results seem *too* dark, you can lower the layer's opacity. When you're happy, merge the shadows with the castle (Layer | Merge Down). Save your work.

Clouds

Open the photo, clouds.jpg, or your own favorite stormy sky photo. (If you use your own, crop or resize it to 500 pixels by 768 pixels.) Now, return to your castle-work document (Window | castle-work.psd). From the menu, choose Select | All, and then choose Edit | Copy. Switch back to the stormy sky photo (Window | clouds.jpg) and paste the castle into a new layer (Edit | Paste). Save the new document as castle.psd. Save and close the castle-work.psd document.

In the Layers palette, rename the new layer Castle. It will be bigger than the canvas, but that's okay. Use the Move tool to position the castle in the middle of the frame, as shown in Figure 27-16.

Perspective Distort

Our castle still isn't very imposing. Here's why: I took the photo standing on the sidewalk, near the bottom of the museum. But, in the final image, we want to create the impression of a castle on a hill, seen from below. For the castle to look really imposing, you need to alter its perspective.

Begin by zooming out to 50% so you can see the area around your image. In the Layers palette, select the Castle layer. From the menu, choose Image | Transform | Perspective. Click and drag on either of the top corner handles, pulling them inward as shown in Figure 27-17. This makes the building seem to tower up into the distance. When you're happy with the perspective, press ENTER to accept it.

Figure 27-17: Distort the perspective.

Making a Hill

There's something still wrong with the castle—it doesn't seem to be towering over us. In fact, the perspective makes it clear that the bottom part of the building is actually *beneath* our vantage point. We're going to chop off the parts of the building nearer to the ground and hide them behind a hill.

Create a new layer (Layer | New | Layer). Name the layer Hill and click OK.

Figure 27-18: Sketch in a rough hill.

Set the Foreground Color to white (255,255,200), and select the Brush tool from the Toolbox. In the Options bar, select a hard, round, 9-pixel brush and make the opacity 100%. Draw a line more or less running between the second and third floors of the building, and then increase the size of the brush to 100 pixels and paint in everything beneath that line, as shown in Figure 27-18.

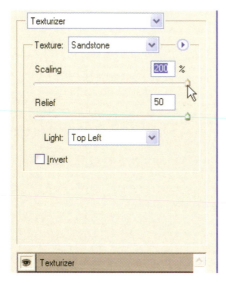

Figure 27-19: Fill the hill with a sandstone texture.

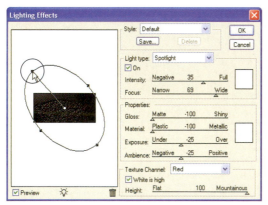

Figure 27-20: Apply lighting effects.

Run the Texturizer filter (Filter | Texture | Texturizer). Select Sandstone from the Texture drop-down list, and then slide both the Scaling and the Relief sliders all the way to the right, as shown in Figure 27-19. Click OK.

Looks pretty bad; let's darken it up and give it some texture. From the menu, choose Filter | Render | Lighting Effects. In the Lighting Effects dialog, choose Default from the Style drop-down list, and then set both Gloss and Material to –100, and Exposure and Ambience both to –25, as shown in Figure 27-20. Choose Red from the Texture Channel drop-down list and drag the Height slider all the way to the right, to Mountainous. This generates a faux 3-D texture. Finally, grab the handle indicated in Figure 27-20 and rotate the source of the light to the top left, as shown. Click OK.

Darken the hill further by choosing Enhance | Adjust Lighting | Brightness and Contrast from the menu. Set Brightness down to –40 and click OK.

The texture is still too regular. To give the hill a bit more definition, let's add some shadows. Select the Hill layer in the Layers palette, select the Brush tool, and then select a soft, round, 100-pixel brush from the Options bar. Set the tool's opacity down to 50%. Paint darkness over the hill texture, in the areas shown in Figure 27-21. Save the work you did to create the hill.

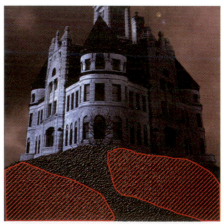

Figure 27-21: Paint these areas black.

Lightning

Time to add a bolt or two of lightning. Begin by creating a new document (File | New | Blank File). Make it 400 by 400 pixels, and set Color Mode to RGB Color. Click OK.

Restore the default black and white foreground and background colors, and choose the Gradient tool from the Toolbox. In the Options bar, select the Foreground to Background gradient, and the Linear style as shown in Figure 27-22.

Click and drag across the canvas from left to right. From the menu choose Filter | Render | Difference Clouds. The results won't look much like lightning yet.

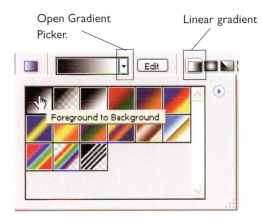

Open Gradient Picker.

Linear gradient

Foreground to Background

Figure 27-22: Choose the Foreground to Background gradient.

From the menu, choose Enhance | Adjust Lighting | Levels. In the Levels dialog, set the Input Levels to 0,1.00,5, and click OK. The results look a bit like lightning, but the colors are reversed. Invert the colors by choosing Filter | Adjustment | Invert.

Add a little blue tint to the lighting by choosing Enhance | Adjust Color | Adjust Hue/ Saturation. Check Colorize, and then set Hue to 230, Saturation to 50, and Lightness to 0. Click OK. The results should resemble Figure 27-23.

Select the entire image (Select | Select All), and copy your lightning to the clipboard (Edit | Copy). Return to the castle document (Window | castle.psd) and paste the

Original   Levels   Final

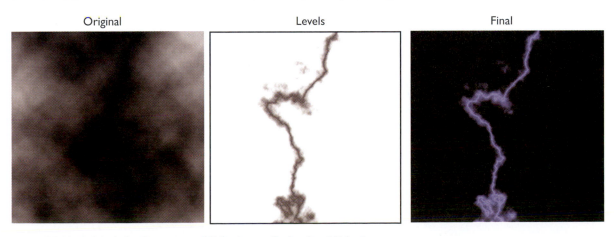

Figure 27-23: Original clouds … reversed lightning … final, colored lightning

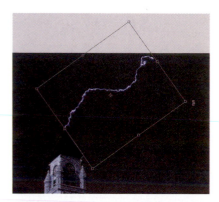

Figure 27-24: Position the lightning.

Figure 27-25: Position the lens flare.

lightning into a new layer (Edit | Paste). In the Layers palette, name the new layer Lightning, and set it to Screen mode.

Select the Move tool and resize and reposition the lightning bolt to fit, as shown in Figure 27-24. Then save your work.

You can repeat this process multiple times to create multiple lightning bolts. Difference Clouds is random, so every bolt is unique.

Flash

To add a flash at the point where the lightning strikes, create a new layer (Layer | New | Layer). Name the layer Flash and set it to Screen mode. Fill the new layer with black (Edit | Fill Layer). From the menu, choose Filter | Render | Lens Flare. In the Lens Flare dialog, select the 105mm Prime, and set the Brightness to 50%. Click in the preview window to position the flare as close as possible to the center, and then click OK. Use the Move tool to reposition the flare, as shown in Figure 27-25.

Save your work.

Spooky Tree

To add a spooky tree, open the photo spooky-tree.jpg. Copy and paste the tree to a new layer in the castle document (Select | All, then Edit | Copy, then Window | castle. psd, and finally Edit | Paste). Use the Magic Eraser tool to remove the sky as you did with the original museum photo, as shown in Figure 27-26, and then resize and reposition to suit. Adjust the tree's levels (Enhance | Adjust Lighting | Levels) to make it dark enough to fit into the scene. Save your finished work.

Figure 27-26: Remove the sky before dropping the spooky tree into the scene.

Rhythm Ramblers: Create an Old-Style Vinyl Record Album

28

In This Project You Will:

☐ Create a custom gradient

☐ Flip text upside down and bend it in circles

☐ Use the Polar Coordinates filter … in both directions!

Vinyl record albums are an icon that spans everything from the sock hop to hip-hop. In this project, you'll learn how to create one of your own.

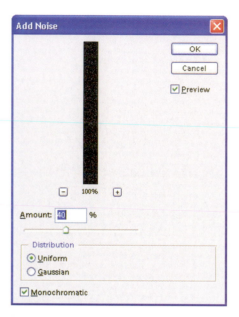

Figure 28-1: Add noise.

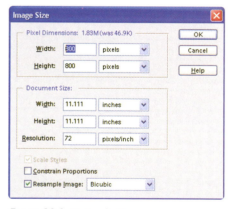

Figure 28-2: Resize the image.

Get into the Groove

Start by creating a new document (File | New | Blank File). Make it 20 pixels wide by 800 pixels tall. Make sure the Color mode is set to RGB color and click OK. From the menu, choose Edit | Fill Layer. Under contents, choose Black and click OK to fill the image with black. That's a little skinny, but we're going to stretch it out in a moment. Save your work as record.psd.

Duplicate the background on a new layer by choosing Layer | New | Layer via Copy from the menu. In the Layers palette, rename the new layer Grooves.

From the menu, choose Filter | Noise | Add Noise. In the Add Noise dialog, set the Amount to 40%, and Distribution to Uniform. Make sure Monochromatic is selected, as shown in Figure 28-1, and click OK.

From the menu, choose Image | Resize | Image Size. In the Image Size dialog, uncheck Constrain Proportions. This allows you to alter one dimension—in this case the width—without altering the other. Be sure Resample Image is checked. In the Pixel Dimensions section, enter a new Width of 800 pixels, leave the Height at 800 pixels, as shown in Figure 28-2. Click OK to stretch the canvas out square, as shown in Figure 28-3.

Figure 28-3: Some sideways grooves

Grooves, of course, should run *around* the record. From the menu, choose Filter | Distort | Polar Coordinates. In the Polar Coordinates dialog, select Rectangular to Polar, and click OK. The results are shown in Figure 28-4.

In the Layers palette, reduce the Grooves layer's opacity to about 30%. This nearly makes the grooves invisible, but the upcoming step will bring them back out.

Highlight

From the menu, choose Layer | New | Layer. Name the new layer Gradient, and click OK.

Select the Gradient tool from the Toolbar. In the Options bar, select Angle gradient and click the Edit button, as shown in Figure 28-5.

Figure 28-4: The grooves bent in a circle

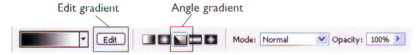

Edit gradient   Angle gradient

Figure 28-5: Gradient options

Select the Black to White gradient from the Presets, and then click on the first color stop, as shown in Figure 28-6. Make sure the stop's color is set to black (0,0,0). Next, click the second color stop and set its color to black as well. Finally, click between the two existing stops to create a new color stop. Set the new stop's color to white (255,255,255), as shown in Figure 28-7.

Black to White gradient

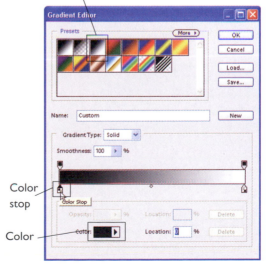

Color stop

Color

Figure 28-6: Editing the gradient

Figure 28-7: Add a white color stop.

Figure 28-8: The edited gradient

Click and drag the white middle color stop to the left until its Location reads 10%. Click and drag the right black color stop until its Location reads 70%, as shown in Figure 28-8. Then click OK.

Figure 28-9: Click and drag from left to right.

Make sure the new Gradient layer is selected in the Layers palette, and then SHIFT-click and drag from the center of the left edge of the canvas to the center of the right edge, as shown in Figure 28-9, to fill the layer with the gradient.

Run the Polar Coordinates filter again (Filter | Distort | Polar Coordinates), but this time, select Polar to Rectangular. Set the Gradient layer to Color Dodge; this puts a nice highlight across the grooves of the record, as shown in Figure 28-10. However, it also generates some ugly blotches where the highlight meets the grooves. Select the Grooves layer in the Layers palette, and choose Image | Rotate | Free Rotate Layer from the menu. Click and

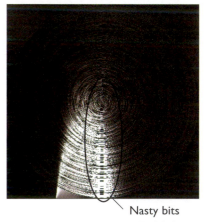

Nasty bits

Figure 28-10: Some noise is highlighted.

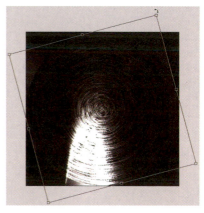

Figure 28-11: Rotate the noise out of sight.

drag on one of the corner handles and rotate until the uglies are out of the light, as shown in Figure 28-11. If you can't see the handles, choose View | Zoom Out from the menu. When you like the result, press ENTER (RETURN on a Macintosh).

Flatten the image by choosing Layer | Flatten Image from the menu. If the Rulers aren't visible, turn them on now (View | Rulers). Right-click (CONTROL-click on a Macintosh) on one of the Rulers and select Percent from the pop-up list, as shown in Figure 28-12.

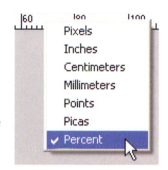

Figure 28-12: Set your rulers to percent.

Select the Ellipse tool from the Toolbox. In the Options bar, set the color to black (0,0,0) and open the Ellipse options, as shown in Figure 28-13. Select Fixed Size and From Center, and set the width (W) and height (H) both to 320 px. Move the cursor to the center of your image (50% on both rulers as shown in Figure 28-14), and then click to create your circle.

Flatten the image again (Layer | Flatten Image), and save your work.

Label

We'll create the label in a new file. Choose File | New | Blank File. Name the document *Label*. Make it 800 pixels by 800 pixels. Set the Color mode to RGB Color, the Background Contents to White, and click OK.

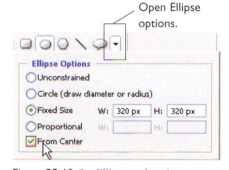

Figure 28-13: Set Ellipse tool options.

Select the Line tool from the Toolbox. In the Options bar, set its weight to 14 pixels, and its color to black (0,0,0).

Right-click or CONTROL-click on one of the ruler bars and select Pixels from the pop-up list. Using the rulers, click and drag left to right from a point about 50 pixels down the left side, as shown in Figure 28-15. Hold down the SHIFT key as you drag to constrain the line to horizontal. Repeat the process to draw a second line at 170 pixels.

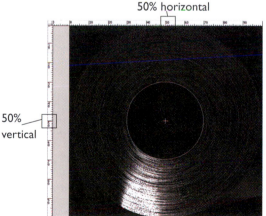

Figure 28-14: Create a dark circle in the center.

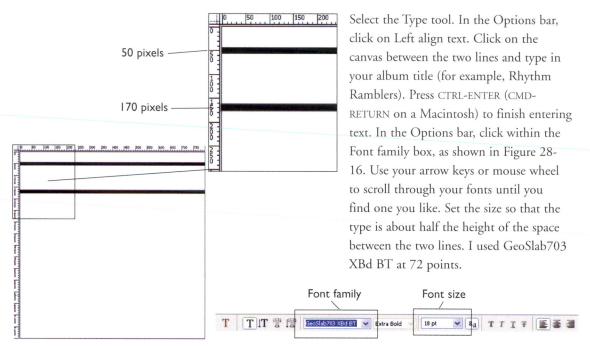

50 pixels

170 pixels

Select the Type tool. In the Options bar, click on Left align text. Click on the canvas between the two lines and type in your album title (for example, Rhythm Ramblers). Press CTRL-ENTER (CMD-RETURN on a Macintosh) to finish entering text. In the Options bar, click within the Font family box, as shown in Figure 28-16. Use your arrow keys or mouse wheel to scroll through your fonts until you find one you like. Set the size so that the type is about half the height of the space between the two lines. I used GeoSlab703 XBd BT at 72 points.

Font family   Font size

Figure 28-15: Draw two horizontal lines.   **Figure 28-16:** Choose a font.

To create some smaller copyright text, SHIFT-click to start a new type layer and type in your copyright or other info (such as Copyright 1958, Jayhawk Records, Wichita, Kansas). Reduce the font size by about three-quarters: I used 72 point text for the title, and 18 point for the copyright notice. Press CTRL-ENTER or CMD-RETURN to finish entering text.

Select the Move tool and position the smaller text directly below the title, and more or less centered. In the Layers palette, link the two text layers, as shown in Figure 28-17.

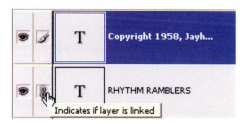

Figure 28-17: Link text layers.

From the menu, choose Image | Transform | Free Transform. Click and drag outside of the handles which appear to rotate the text. (If you can't see the handles, choose View | Zoom out.) Hold down the SHIFT key and rotate the text 180 degrees, to stand it on its head. Next, grab the right side handle and drag to the left to squeeze the text horizontally to about 50% of its original width, as shown in Figure 28-18. Press ENTER to accept the change.

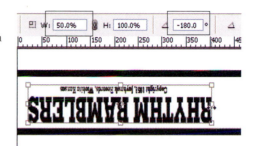

Figure 28-18: Shrink the text.

Position the text between the two black lines, at the left edge of the canvas, as shown in Figure 28-19.

Flatten the image (Layer | Flatten Image) and choose Filter | Distort | Polar Coordinates. Select Rectangular to Polar and click OK.

Figure 28-19: Label text upside down

This wraps your label around the center, but it's pointing to 9 o'clock. To fix that, choose Image | Transform | Free Transform. Elements will ask you if you want to convert the background into a layer. Assure it that you do. Name the new layer Label and click OK. When the handles appear around the image, rotate it until the title is centered at the top, as shown in Figure 28-20. (If you can't see the handles, choose View | Zoom out.) Then click OK to accept the change.

Now's the time to add any additional text on the label. I added the names of ten tracks, in a 6 point font. Remember to SHIFT-click with the Type tool to force Elements to create a new type layer every time.

Figure 28-20: Rotate the label.

When you're done typing, select the Elliptical Marquee tool. In the Options bar, select Anti-aliased, set the mode to Fixed Size, and set the Width and Height both to 225 pixels, as shown in Figure 28-21. Click to center the selection marquee around the label, as shown in Figure 28-22. If necessary, use the arrow keys to nudge the selection into position. From the menu, choose Edit | Copy Merged to copy everything visible, not just the current layer, to the clipboard.

Figure 28-21: Set the Elliptical Marquee options.

Figure 28-22: Select the label.

Return to your record.psd document (Window | record.psd) and paste the label onto a new layer (Edit | Paste). Elements automatically centers the label on the new layer. If you'd like to tilt it at a jaunty angle, choose Image | Transform | Free Transform, rotate it to taste, and then press ENTER when finished.

Close the Label document without saving. We're done with it.

To create the hole in the center of the record, select the Ellipse tool. In the Options bar, set the tool's color to black, and then open the Ellipse options and enter a width and height of 12 pixels. Keep Fixed Size and From Center turned on, as shown in Figure 28-23. Zoom way in on the center of the album and click to create the dark center hole, as shown in Figure 28-24. If you need to, use the Move tool to fine-tune the position. Your results should resemble Figure 28-25.

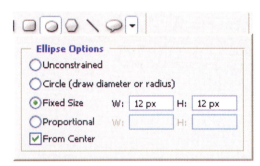

Figure 28-23: Set Ellipse options.

Figure 28-24: Create a center hole.

Cut It Out

Flatten the image (Layer | Flatten Image).

Select the Elliptical Marquee tool and in the Options bar, set the mode to Fixed Size and set the Width and Height both to 795 pixels. Click near the upper-left corner of the canvas to create a circular selection containing the record album, as shown in Figure 28-26. Use the arrow keys to nudge it into place so that it doesn't go outside the canvas at any point.

Copy the selected album to a new layer (Layer | New | Layer via Copy). In the Layers palette, rename the new layer Album. Select the Background layer and fill it with white (Edit | Fill Layer).

Save your work.

To give the album some context, I took this project a little further and created an 800×800 pixel album cover using the same techniques used in Project 14 (Figure 28-27). The cover features the hand-tinted photo of my dad, from Project 4.

Figure 28-25: Almost finished …

Figure 28-26: Select the album.

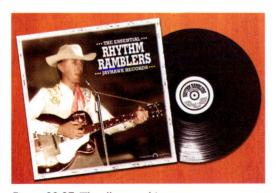

Figure 28-27: The album and its cover

Night Sight: Create a Night Vision Look

29

In This Project You Will:

☐ Add static and noise to an image

☐ Use Levels to brighten an image

☐ Fill selections with color

☐ Create vector shapes

☐ Use Blur to blend layers

Night vision is a nifty, novelty effect you can add to any photo. It turns a boring snapshot into the seeming product of high-tech gadgetry, and something worthy of a James Bond movie.

Figure 29-1: A gorilla in the daylight.

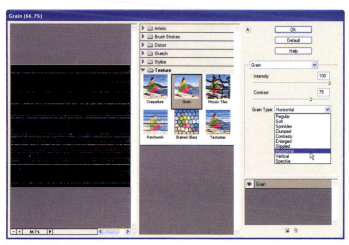

Figure 29-2: Add some grain.

Figure 29-3: Noise in place

Video Noise

Open a photo, such as gorilla.jpg, shown in Figure 29-1. This will form the basis of the night vision project. Save your document as night-vision.psd.

This photo is way too clean; convincing night vision goggles need lots of video noise. Let's create some. Create a new layer by choosing Layer | New | Layer from the menu. Name the layer Video Noise, set the Mode to Screen and click OK.

From the menu, choose Edit | Fill Layer. Use Black for the Contents, and click OK to fill the layer with black. The new layer's invisible, but only for a moment.

Restore the default foreground and background colors (black and white). From the menu choose Filter | Texture | Grain. When the Grain dialog appears, set the Intensity to 100 and the Contrast to 75. Set the Grain Type to Horizontal, as shown in Figure 29-2. Click OK.

This should result in white streaks of video noise over your background photo, as shown in Figure 29-3.

Night Vision Green

It's not enough for night vision goggles to look a little noisy; they've got to look green as well. That's the next step. From the menu choose Layer | New | Layer. Name the new layer Green Gradient and set the Mode to Multiply. Click OK.

Set the foreground color to a light green (125,255,125). Set the background color to a much darker green, about 0,80,0.

Select the Gradient Tool from the Toolbox. In the Options bar, choose Foreground to Background from the Gradient Picker drop-down, as shown in Figure 29-4. Make sure Radial Gradient is selected, and Mode is set to Normal, as shown in Figure 29-5.

If the rulers aren't visible, turn them on now by choosing View | Rulers. Right-click (CONTROL-click on a Macintosh) on one of the ruler bars and check Percent from the pop-up list.

Use the rulers to position your mouse as near to the center of the photo (50 on both rulers) as you can. Now SHIFT-click and drag from the center to the top edge of the photo. This fills the layer with a gradient of greens—the lightest in the center and the darkest around the edges. You should see something like Figure 29-6. If not, use the Gradient tool to try again.

That's not bad for starters. This is a good time to save your work.

Figure 29-4: Choose the Foreground to Background gradient.

Figure 29-5: Radial Gradient selected

Figure 29-6: Night vision green

Static Interference

To add a bit more video feel, let's throw in some static. From the menu choose Filter | Noise | Add Noise. Select Gaussian Distribution and make sure Monochrome is *not* selected, as shown in Figure 29-7. Some photos will look better with a little more or less noise added to the mix. Try different amounts and watch the results in the preview window. I went with 16%. When you're happy, click OK. The effect is subtle, but it adds significantly to the overall realism, as shown in Figure 29-8.

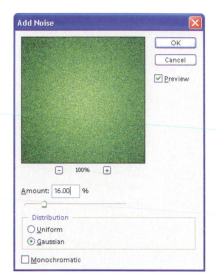

Figure 29-7: Add noise.

Figure 29-8: Subtle noise in place

Binoculars

Let's give the image that cool, binocular effect. Select the Ellipse tool from the Custom Shapes fly-out menu in the Toolbox. In the Options bar, set the Color to black and bring up the Ellipse Options as shown in Figure 29-9. Select Fixed Size and enter 350 px for both width and height. Make sure to type px (for pixel), or Elements defaults to inches. Select From Center.

Position the cursor over the canvas as shown in Figure 29-10, to the left of center. Click to create a new circle shape, as shown in Figure 29-11. If necessary, select the Move tool and reposition the shape. It should be more or less centered from top to bottom.

Open Ellipse Options

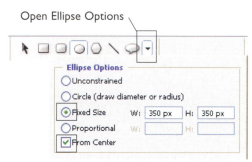

Figure 29-9: Set the Ellipse Options.

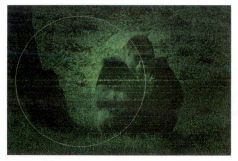

Figure 29-10: Position the circle on the left side.

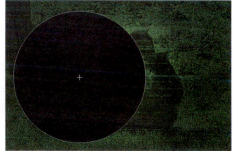

Figure 29-11: The black circle in place

The Ellipse tool creates a vector shape layer. That's great for some things, but for later on, we require that it be simplified. From the menu, choose Layer | Simplify Layer.

From the menu choose Layer | New | Layer via Copy. From the menu choose Select | All, and then choose Image | Rotate | Flip Selection Horizontal. This swaps the second circle over to the right side of the canvas, as shown in Figure 29-12. If you hadn't selected the entire canvas first, though, the command would have just flipped the circle in place, with no visible result.

Choose Select | Deselect to remove the selection, and then choose Layer | Merge Down to combine the two halves of the binoculars onto the same layer. In the Layers palette, name this layer Binoculars.

All right. That looks more or less like binoculars, except … the black shadow is on the inside, not the outside. No worries, mate. In the Layers palette, CTRL-click (CMD-click on a Macintosh) on the Binoculars layer thumbnail to select the filled pixels. Press DELETE to erase the selected pixels, leaving the layer empty for the moment. With the selection still active, choose Select | Inverse to select everything that wasn't selected before. From the menu, choose Edit | Fill Selection. Choose Black for the Contents and click OK to fill the selection as shown in Figure 29-13.

The binocular shape is too crisp; let's blur it. First, remove the selection (Select | Deselect). Now, from the Filter menu choose Blur | Gaussian Blur. Set the Radius to 10 pixels, and click OK. This blurs the edges, as shown in Figure 29-14.

Figure 29-12: The binocular shape emerges.

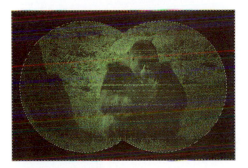

Figure 29-13: Fill the selection.

Figure 29-14: Blurred edges

If the effect is too strong, reduce the opacity of the Binoculars layer in the Layers palette. When you're happy, flatten the image (Layer | Flatten Image).

If your image has gotten a bit dark, as this one has, use Levels to pump up the gain. From the menu, choose Enhance | Adjust Lighting | Levels. Drag the white point to the left to brighten the image, as shown in Figure 29-15. Click OK.

Save your work. Again, you can stop here, or …

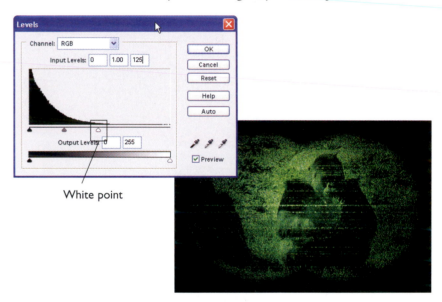

White point

Figure 29-15: Tweak the Levels to brighten the image.

Doodads and Geegaws

Elements comes with a wide selection of shapes, everything from simple boxes to trees. You can add some of these to your night vision shot if you'd like to give it more of a high-tech look. Let's do at least one.

Select the Custom Shape tool from the Toolbox. In the Options bar, set the color to 30,255,0 (a bright green). Click on the Custom Shape Picker, and then click the small arrow at the top right to open the Shape libraries pop-up, as shown in Figure 29-16. Choose Symbols, and then choose the Compass shape from the Shape Picker palette. SHIFT-click and drag in the top-left corner of the canvas to create the compass shape, as shown in Figure 29-17.

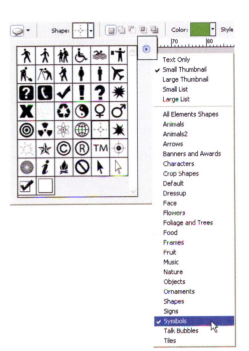

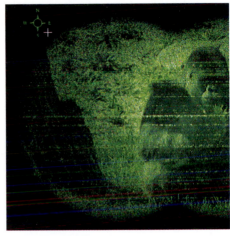

Figure 29-17: Create the compass.

Figure 29-16: Choose Shapes.

In the Options bar, open the Custom Shape Picker and click the small arrow at the top right. Choose Shapes from the pop-up list, and then choose the filled Triangle shape from the palette. Click and drag near the compass to create a small triangle, as shown in Figure 29-18. Do not hold down the SHIFT key, or the triangle will be added to the same layer as the compass. Use the Move tool to rotate and reposition the triangle until it forms the compass's pointer, as shown in Figure 29-19.

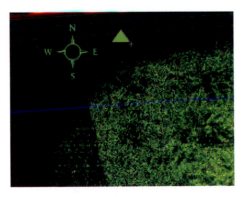

Figure 29-18: Add a triangle.

Figure 29-19: Move the pointer into position.

Explore Elements' other shapes. Don't forget simple boxes, circles, and lines. You can use the Type tool as well to create some abstruse numerical displays.

When you're happy, flatten the image (Layer | Flatten Image) and save your work. If so inspired, you can keep working and add even more doodads and geegaws, as shown in Figure 29-20.

Figure 29-20: An alternate final image

He Said, She Said: Swapping Heads in a Photo

30

If there's one simple photo trick that's sure to get a laugh, it's the headswap: putting Mom's head on Dad's body, or Grandpa's head on the baby. This project will teach you how to perform the ol' switcheroo yourself.

In This Project You Will:

☐ Use blending modes to alter flesh tones

☐ Use the Clone Stamp tool to remove unwanted details

☐ Use the Move tool to resize clothing and body parts

Figure 30-1: Select the girl's head.

Figure 30-2: Move the copy into position.

Figure 30-3: Resize the head by 105%.

Getting Started

Open the file prom.jpg. Save the document as headswap .psd. This photo has an empty background, all more or less the same color. That makes the job easier.

Select the Elliptical Marquee tool from the Toolbox. Click and drag to select the girl's head, as shown in Figure 30-1. Make sure you get all the head, hair, and neck. Don't worry about getting too much, but don't get too little. With the selection in place, copy its contents to a new layer by choosing Layer | New | Layer via Copy from the menu. In the Layers palette, name the new layer Girl's Head.

Select the Move tool from the Toolbox and move the girl's head into position over the boy's, as shown in Figure 30-2.

The boy is larger than the girl in this photo, so her head looks too small on his shoulders. To fix that, click with the Move tool on one of the corner handles surrounding her head. Hold down the SHIFT key and drag outwards to enlarge the head a bit. As you drag, the Options bar displays the amount you've enlarged the head, as shown in Figure 30-3. I scaled it up to about 105%. When you're happy, press ENTER (RETURN on a Macintosh) to accept the transformation.

Now, hide the Girl's Head layer by clicking its eye icon in the Layers palette, as shown in Figure 30-4. Select the Background layer.

Figure 30-4: Hide the layer.

Use the Elliptical Marquee tool again to select the boy's head (see Figure 30-5). Again, make sure you get the entire head selected. Copy the contents of the selection to a new layer (Layer | New | Layer via Copy). In the Layers palette, rename the new layer Boy's Head.

Select the Move tool and use it to slide his head into position on the girl's shoulders, as shown in Figure 30-6. His head, of course, looks too large on her shoulders. Shrink it by SHIFT-clicking on one of the corner handles and dragging inward until the Options bar reads 85–90%, as shown in Figure 30-7. Some of the girl's head will probably show through from underneath, but don't worry about that just now. You should have something like Figure 30-8.

In the Layers palette, reveal all the layers.

Figure 30-5: Select the boy's head.

Figure 30-6: Move the head into position.

Figure 30-8: New heads in place

Figure 30-7: Resize the head.

Cleaning Up

Zoom in on the boy's head where it sits on the girl's shoulders. Time to erase those bits of hair and shadow showing through from the original photograph.

In the Layers palette, select the Background layer, and then select the Clone Stamp tool from the Toolbox. In the Options bar, choose a soft, round, 17-pixel brush. ALT-click (OPTION-click on a Macintosh) to sample from the area to the left of the boy's head and then paint over the protruding hair, as shown in Figure 30-9. Since you are painting on the Background layer, rather than the Boy's Head layer, there's no danger of accidentally painting over his face with the background. Still, don't get carried away and paint over parts of the photograph that we still want to use: her neck and dress.

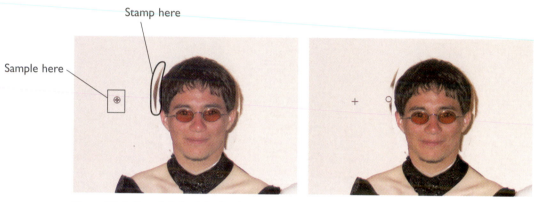

Stamp here

Sample here

Figure 30-9: Sample left of the head.

Repeat the process on the right side of the boy's head, as shown in Figure 30-10.

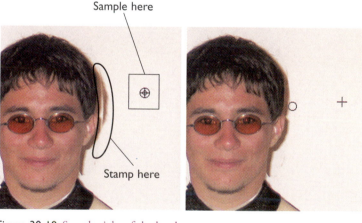

Sample here

Stamp here

Figure 30-10: Sample right of the head.

In the Layers palette, select the Boy's Head layer again. Select the Eraser tool from the Toolbox and, in the Options bar, choose a soft, round, 5-pixel brush. Zoom in on the bottom of the boy's neck and carefully erase any of his collar that was selected along with the head, as shown in Figure 30-11.

In the Layers palette, select the Girl's Head layer. Zoom in on the bottom of the girl's neck and carefully erase any of the black neck of her dress, as shown in Figure 30-12.

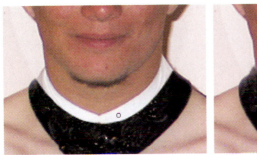

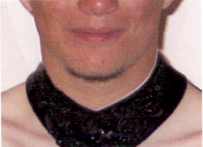

Figure 30-11: Erase the extra collar.

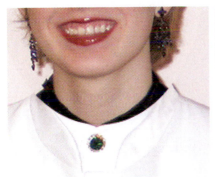

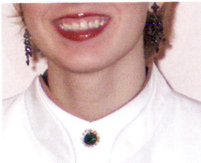

Figure 30-12: Erase remaining bits of the dress.

Narrow the Neck

The girl's neck is far narrower than the boy's, even after up-scaling her head. It's never going to fit properly within his collar. But we can fix that by making the collar narrower.

In the Layers palette, select the Background layer. Select the Rectangular Marquee tool from the Toolbox and click and drag to select the area around the collar, as shown in Figure 30-13. Copy this selection to a new layer by choosing Layer | New | Layer via Copy from the menu. In the Layers palette, name the new layer Collar.

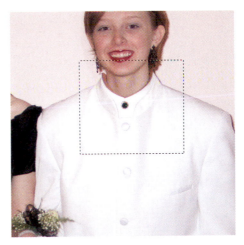

Figure 30-13: Select an area around the neck and collar.

Figure 30-14: Distort the perspective to fit the neck.

Select the Move tool. Click on one of the top corner handles, hold down the CTRL-ALT-SHIFT keys all at once (CMD-OPTION-SHIFT on a Macintosh), and drag the handle toward the center as shown in Figure 30-14. Drag until the size of the collar better matches the girl's neck, and press ENTER to accept the transformation. The CTRL or CMD key allows you to move one handle without affecting others; the ALT or OPTION key tells Elements to resize both sides from the center; and the SHIFT key constrains your movements to a straight line.

If necessary, tap the up or down arrow keys to nudge the new layer into a better position, and eliminate any obvious breaks in the shoulder line, as shown in Figure 30-15. The results should be a big improvement, as shown in Figure 30-16.

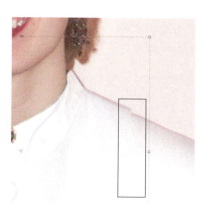

Figure 30-15: Nudge the new layer down to match the line of the shoulders.

Figure 30-16: Before and after

Cloning Up

Make sure your heads are where you want them, then flatten the document (Layer | Flatten Image) and save your work.

If you look closely at either head, you'll see a halo of slightly off-color background surrounding them, as shown in Figure 30-17. Let's use the Clone Stamp tool to get rid of that. Select the Clone Stamp tool and, in the Options bar, choose a soft, round, 17-pixel brush. ALT-click or OPTION-click to select the background outside of the halo, and then carefully paint along the edges of the halo to blend it into the background, as shown in the figure. Repeat the process around both heads.

Halo of color ————

Figure 30-17: Stamp to erase the halo around the head.

Skin Tones

The two skin tones, the boy's and the girl's, don't really
match. For a last little touch, let's address that. Zoom
way in on the boy's face. Select the Elliptical Marquee
tool from the Toolbox. Click and drag to select a small
area of his skin. Then hold down the SHIFT key and
click and drag in several more places on his face to select
more skin, as shown in Figure 30-18. The SHIFT key tells
Elements to add to your existing selection, rather than
starting a new selection each time. Do not sample hair,
beard, glasses, or other non-flesh-tone bits.

Figure 30-18: Select some areas of flesh tone.

Figure 30-19: The average flesh tone sampled

Copy the samples to a new layer (Layer | New |
Layer via Copy). Creating the new layer removes
our selection and we need it back. In the Layers
palette, CTRL-click or CMD-click on the new layer's
thumbnail to select its contents. Now, from the
menu, choose Filter | Blur | Average. This fills the
selection with the *average* of all the colors you sampled from the boy's face, as shown in Figure 30-19.
Use the Eyedropper tool to sample this color, making it the new Foreground Color.

Figure 30-20: Paint the new flesh tone onto the girl.

Select the entire image (Select | All) and press DELETE to erase the blurred ellipses from the new layer. Remove the selection (Select | Deselect).

In the Layers palette, name the now empty layer Flesh Tone, and set its blending mode to Color.

Select the Brush tool and choose a soft, round, 17-pixel brush in the Options bar. Use the Brush tool to paint over the girl's exposed skin, her arms, hand, and shoulders, as shown in Figure 30-20. If you make a mistake, switch to the Eraser tool and paint it away. That effect is way too strong, so when you're done, reduce the Flesh Tone layer's opacity to about 30%.

You can fine-tune the effect by bringing up the Hue/Saturation dialog (Enhance | Adjust Color | Adjust Hue/Saturation) and sliding the Hue slider slightly in one direction or the other.

If the skin seems too dark or, as is the case here, too light, duplicate the Flesh Tone layer (Layer | New | Layer via Copy). Set the new Flesh Tone Copy layer's blending mode to Multiply to darken the underlying flesh, or set it to Screen mode to lighten. Adjust the layer's opacity to tweak the effect. I used the same 30% as for the Color mode (Flesh Tone) layer.

Flatten the image (Layer | Flatten Image) and save your work.

Your Logo Here: Add an Insignia to Your Image

31

It's a common task in Photoshop Elements to replace a sign or logo in a photograph with one of your own choosing. The difference between an obvious fake, and an image that will fool the eye, is attention to detail. Let's see how it's done.

In This Project You Will:

- ☐ Use the Spot Healing tool to remove elements from a photo

- ☐ Use the Clone Stamp tool to remove elements from a photo

- ☐ Skew elements to match a photo's perspective

- ☐ Add noise to blend new elements into an existing photo

Out with the Old

Out with the Old

Begin by opening the file candy-shop.jpg from Project 8 and save it as diner.psd. Zoom in on the sign that reads Mark's Candies.

Let's start by removing the old text. Choose Layer | New | Layer via Copy from the menu to make a copy of the Background layer. In the Layers palette, rename the new layer to Photo.

Select the Spot Healing Brush tool from the Toolbox. In the Options bar, choose a hard, round, 19-pixel brush, and make sure that Type is set to Proximity Match, as shown in Figure 31-1.

Figure 31-1: Healing brush tool options

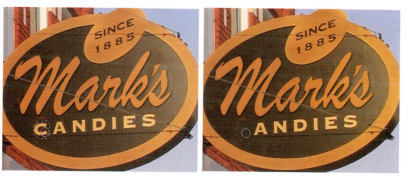

Figure 31-2: Spot Healing

Click and drag over the C in "Candies" to select the entire letter, as shown in Figure 31-2. Release the mouse button to remove that unsightly letter. Repeat this process with the remaining letters in "Candies." Do not continue on to the letters in "Mark's."

Figure 31-3: Stamp out the M from above.

Select the Clone Stamp tool from the Toolbox. In the Options bar, select a soft, round, 35-pixel brush. Make sure Mode is to Normal, Opacity is 100%, Aligned is selected, and Use All Layers is unchecked. Hold down the ALT key (OPTION on a Macintosh) and click in the background gray color, as shown in Figure 31-3. Release the key. Then click and drag on the top of the letter M to begin erasing it, as shown in Figure 31-4. Click and drag multiple times. If part of a letter reappears, ALT-click or OPTION-click to start a new sample. When the top of the letter is more or less gone, repeat the process to erase the bottom of the M.

Figure 31-4: Continue removing the M.

Clone over the rest of the letters in "Mark's." ALT-click or OPTION-click often to reset your sample. Sample from the same general area of background as the letter you are erasing: clone from the left side to erase the M, and clone from the right side to erase the S. The results will look a bit sloppy (see Figure 31-5). To smooth it out a bit, select the Blur tool with a soft, round, 100-pixel brush. Set its Strength to 100% and paint over the sign's background to smooth out any jagged bits.

Figure 31-5: All text removed.

Return to the Spot Healing Brush tool. Use a hard, round, 25-pixel brush to paint over the words at the very top of the sign, as shown in Figure 31-6. Again, use the Blur tool if necessary to smooth things out a bit.

This process will erase the cables holding the sign up, and their shadows, but we'll replace those later. Save your work.

Figure 31-6: Use Spot Heal to remove this text.

Figure 31-7: Introducing Joes

New Text

Time for some new text. Select the Eyedropper tool, and click within the orange ring surrounding the sign to sample its color.

Select the Type tool and in the Options bar, set the font size to 200 point. (Don't worry about the font family yet.) Click on the sign and type "Joes" (without an apostrophe) as shown in Figure 31-7. Press CTRL-ENTER (CMD-RETURN on a Macintosh) to finish your text.

In the Options bar, click within the font family box, as shown in Figure 31-8. Use your arrow keys or mouse wheel to scroll through your installed fonts and find the font you like best. If your chosen font is too big or too small, adjust the font size in the Options bar. Use the Move tool to reposition the word, if necessary. I went with a 220 point MisterEarl BT.

Font family

Figure 31-8: Choose your font from the font family.

Figure 31-9: An apostrophe typed as part of the word

With the Type tool still selected, SHIFT-click on the canvas to start a new Type layer, and type in the apostrophe. (Holding the SHIFT key forces Elements to create a new layer.) Press CTRL-ENTER or CMD-RETURN to finish typing.

Select the Move tool and position the apostrophe between the E and the S. You can make the apostrophe smaller or larger by clicking and dragging on the corner. The apostrophe is on its own layer so you can resize and reposition it independently of the rest of the text. If we had put the apostrophe in the original text, we'd have Figure 31-9, instead of Figure 31-10.

In the Layers palette, select the Joes layer, and then link the two text layers, as shown in Figure 31-11. From the menu, choose Layer | Merge Linked.

Note

If you didn't create a second text layer, select your single text layer in the Layers palette and choose Layer | Simplify Layer from the menu.

Figure 31-10: An apostrophe created on a separate layer

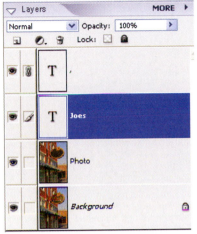

Figure 31-11: Link the layers.

Position Believably

For the text to fit the scene, its perspective must match the real-world elements. Let's look again at that scene. In the Layers palette, hide every layer except the Background layer by clicking on each layer's eye icon, as shown in Figure 31-12.

The small word "Candies" will be our reference. Select the Line tool from the Shapes tool fly-out menu in the Toolbox. In the Options bar, set the tool's Weight to 4 pixels and its Color to bright green. Click and drag the line so that it lines up with the word "Candies" as shown in Figure 31-13. Undo and redo this step if you need to.

If necessary, click and drag the new Shape layer to a position above the Photo layer in the Layers palette, as shown in Figure 31-14. Turn visibility back on in the hidden layers.

Figure 31-12: Hide the top layers.

Figure 31-13: Draw a reference line.

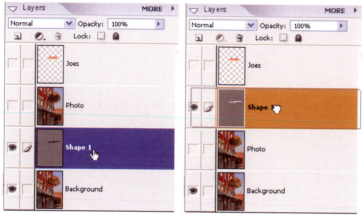

Figure 31-14: Drag the text layer between the other two layers.

Select the Joes layer in the Layers palette, and then select the Move tool from the Toolbox. CTRL-click (CMD-click on a Macintosh) on the handle on the right side of the text and drag up, as shown in Figure 31-15, skewing the text to match the sign's perspective and aligning the bottom edge of the bounding box with the green line. Click and drag the corner handles to resize the text overall. When you're happy, press ENTER (RETURN on a Macintosh).

New Text, Part II

Select the Type tool again. SHIFT-click on the image to start a new type layer. Type "Diner" and press CTRL-ENTER or CMD-RETURN to accept. Once again, experiment with different fonts and sizes; I used a 48 point Aachen BT. In the Options bar, set the text's color to 255,200,130. (I sampled this color for you from the original sign. You're welcome.)

Figure 31-15: Adjust the text to fit.

From the menu, choose Layer | Simplify Layer, and then choose Image | Transform | Free Transform. As before, click and drag on the handles to skew, resize, and reposition the text into position, as shown in Figure 31-16.

SHIFT-click again with the Type tool. In the Options bar, select a small, simple font (such as 36 point Arial Black). Set the font color to 115,35,0 (a dark red). Then type "Eat At" and press CTRL-ENTER or CMD-RETURN. Simplify the new text layer (Layer | Simplify Layer), and use Free Transform (Image | Transform | Free Transform) to position it as shown in Figure 31-17.

Figure 31-16: Skew the Diner text.

In the Layers palette, select the Shape layer with the green line and delete it (Layer | Delete Layer). Save your work.

3-D Definition

A drop shadow will add some 3-D definition. In the Layers palette, select the Joes layer. In the Styles and Effects palette, choose Layer Styles and Drop Shadows from the drop-down lists, and then select the Hard Edge shadow, as shown in Figure 31-18. In the Layers palette, double-click on the small "f" icon in the Joes layer to edit the layer's style settings. In the Style Settings dialog, make sure Use Global Light is selected, change the Lighting Angle to 135°, and reduce the Shadow Distance to 3 pixels, as shown in Figure 31-19. Click OK. This better matches the natural shadows under the orange rim of the sign, as shown in Figure 31-20.

Repeat this process for the Diner layer: apply the Hard Edge shadow, and then reduce the Shadow Distance to 3 pixels to match the first shadow. Do not add a shadow to the Eat At layer.

Save your work.

Figure 31-17: Position the Eat At text.

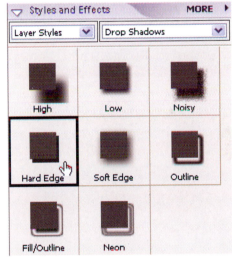

Figure 31-18: Select a Hard Edge shadow.

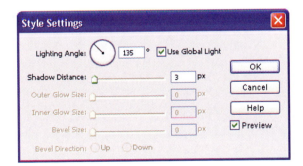

Figure 31-19: Adjust the Shadow settings.

Figure 31-20: Shadows tie the text into the sign.

Gradient Colors

The color on our sign text is too uniform. The colors in the original sign aren't a single color but rather a range of similar colors. A gradient helps simulate this effect.

Sample here — — Sample here

Figure 31-21: Sample the colors for your gradient.

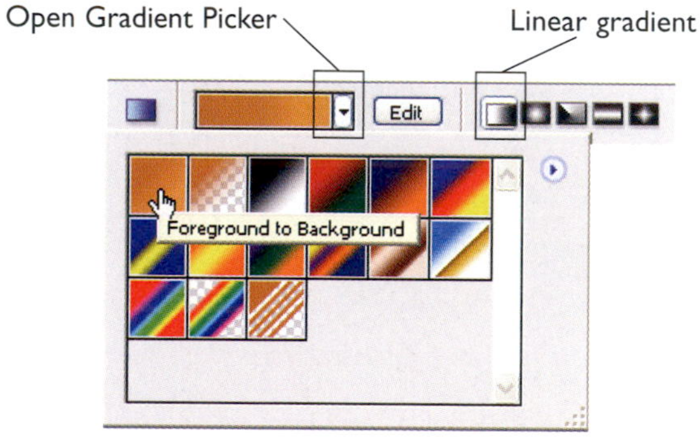

Open Gradient Picker — — Linear gradient

Figure 31-22: Choose the Foreground to Background gradient.

Figure 31-23: Draw the gradient.

Select the Eyedropper tool and sample a new foreground color from the left side of the sign's orange rim, as shown in Figure 31-21. Now ALT-click or OPTION-click on the right side to sample a new background color.

Select the Gradient tool from the Toolbox, and in the Options bar, select Linear Gradient. Open the Gradient Picker, as shown in Figure 31-22, and select the Foreground to Background gradient.

In the Layers palette, CTRL-click or CMD-click on the Joes layer thumbnail to select the filled pixels in that layer. Now, drag the Gradient tool from left to right across the selected text to fill it with the new gradient, as shown in Figure 31-23. Deselect the text (Select | Deselect).

The Diner text is smaller and less prominent, but if you want you can return to the original photo layer (Background) and repeat the process: sampling new foreground and background colors from the original Candies text, and then filling the Diner text with the resulting gradient.

Noise

Our new text is still too clean. As the close-up in Figure 31-24 shows, the original photo has small amounts of noise, but our new text doesn't.

In the Layers palette, select the Eat At layer, and link the other text layers to it, as shown in Figure 31-25. From the menu, choose Layer | Merge Linked to combine all our new elements on a single layer. With that layer selected, choose Filter | Noise | Add Noise. Reduce the Amount to 1%, select Gaussian Distribution and deselect Monochrome. Click OK to add the noise. You might need to increase the setting when working with noisier or grainier photos but, for this one, 1% is about right.

Lines and Shadows

It's finally time to address those cables and shadows which we erased early on. Select the Brush tool and, in the Options bar, select a hard, round, 3-pixel brush. Zoom way in on the bottom of the sign. Hold down the ALT or OPTION key and sample the color of the partially erased shadow, as shown in Figure 31-26. Click once on one remaining end of the shadow, and then hold down the SHIFT key and click once on the other end, to paint a straight line between the two points.

Figure 31-24: The new elements lack the natural noise of the original photo.

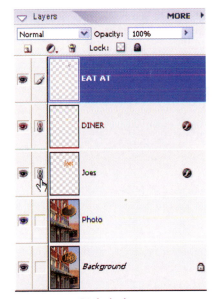

Figure 31-25: Link the layers.

Figure 31-26: Sample the existing shadow color, and then paint in the replacement shadow.

Repeat the process for the cables and the other cable shadow, as shown in Figure 31-27.

Cables

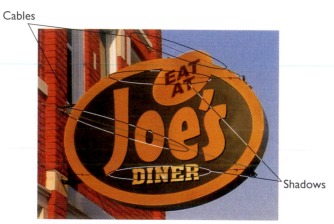

Shadows

Figure 31-27: Shadows complete

That's it! Flatten your image (Layer | Flatten Image) and save your work. I chose to crop the finished image to better emphasize the sign, but that's entirely optional.

INDEX

Note: See the Introduction, "Tips, Techniques, and Conventions Used in This Book," on pages xvi-xxvi for helpful information about using various features of Photoshop Elements.

Type tool
    using, 272
    using with digital graffiti, 204
    using with magazine cover, 108, 110
    using with record.psd, 248

U

Unconstrained Custom Shape, creating box
        with, 146
undoing cloning steps, 40

V

vector text, converting to pixels, 109
vector shape layer, creating with Ellipse
        tool, 257
vertical lines, straightening out in Golden
        Buddha, 6–8
video noise, creating, 254

W

warehouse photo, selecting for nighttime
        scene, 214
watercolor effect, creating, 63–64
windows
    adding lights in, 226–228
    adding to nighttime scene, 217
wine bottle, creating, 180
words. See also text
    drawing reference lines for, 273
    replacing and repositioning, 272

Z

zits. See blemishes
Zoom tool, using with lilac bush, 74

INTERNATIONAL CONTACT INFORMATION

AUSTRALIA
McGraw-Hill Book Company
Australia Pty. Ltd.
TEL +61-2-9900-1800
FAX +61-2-9878-8881
http://www.mcgraw-hill.com.au
books-it_sydney@mcgraw-hill.com

CANADA
McGraw-Hill Ryerson Ltd.
TEL +905-430-5000
FAX +905-430-5020
http://www.mcgraw-hill.ca

GREECE, MIDDLE EAST, & AFRICA
(Excluding South Africa)
McGraw-Hill Hellas
TEL +30-210-6560-990
TEL +30-210-6560-993
TEL +30-210-6560-994
FAX +30-210-6545-525

MEXICO (Also serving Latin America)
McGraw-Hill Interamericana Editores
S.A. de C.V.
TEL +525-1500-5108
FAX +525-117-1589
http://www.mcgraw-hill.com.mx
carlos_ruiz@mcgraw-hill.com

SINGAPORE (Serving Asia)
McGraw-Hill Book Company
TEL +65-6863-1580
FAX +65-6862-3354
http://www.mcgraw-hill.com.sg
mghasia@mcgraw-hill.com

SOUTH AFRICA
McGraw-Hill South Africa
TEL +27-11-622-7512
FAX +27-11-622-9045
robyn_swanepoel@mcgraw-hill.com

SPAIN
McGraw-Hill/
Interamericana de España, S.A.U.
TEL +34-91-180-3000
FAX +34-91-372-8513
http://www.mcgraw-hill.es
professional@mcgraw-hill.es

UNITED KINGDOM, NORTHERN, EASTERN, & CENTRAL EUROPE
McGraw-Hill Education Europe
TEL +44-1-628-502500
FAX +44-1-628-770224
http://www.mcgraw-hill.co.uk
emea_queries@mcgraw-hill.com

ALL OTHER INQUIRIES Contact:
McGraw-Hill/Osborne
TEL +1-510-420-7700
FAX +1-510-420-7703
http://www.osborne.com
omg_international@mcgraw-hill.com

Sound Off!

Visit us at **www.osborne.com/bookregistration** and let us know what you thought of this book. While you're online you'll have the opportunity to register for newsletters and special offers from McGraw-Hill/Osborne.

We want to hear from you!

Sneak Peek

Visit us today at **www.betabooks.com** and see what's coming from McGraw-Hill/Osborne tomorrow!

Based on the successful software paradigm, Bet@Books™ allows computing professionals to view partial and sometimes complete text versions of selected titles online. Bet@Books™ viewing is free, invites comments and feedback, and allows you to "test drive" books in progress on the subjects that interest you the most.